NEW COSMIC CRYSTALS

NEW COSMIC CRYSTALS

THE ULTIMATE COURSE IN CRYSTAL CONSCIOUSNESS

✦

R. A. BONEWITZ WITH
LILIAN VERNER-BONDS

Thorsons
Directions for Life

Thorsons
An imprint of HarperCollins*Publishers*
77–85 Fulham Palace Road,
Hammersmith, London W6 8JB

The Thorsons website address is: www.thorsons.com

First published 2000

1 3 5 7 9 10 8 6 4 2

A catalogue record for this book
is available from the British Library

ISBN 0 7225 3973 8

Set in 10.5/15 pt Linotype Postscript Stempel Schneidler
Typeset by Rowland Phototypesetting Ltd, Bury St Edmunds, Suffolk
Printed and bound in Great Britain by The Bath Press, Bath, Avon

CONTENTS

To Abraham Maslow
The mentor I never met

People say that what we're all seeking is a meaning for life.
I don't think that's what we're really seeking. I think what
we're seeking is an experience of being alive, so that our
life experiences on the purely physical plane will have
resonances with our innermost being and reality, so we
can feel the rapture of being alive.

Joseph Campbell

INTRODUCTION

RONALD BONEWITZ

I have been involved with crystals since I was six years old, when I began my first crystal collection. I was a self-taught lapidary by the age of 16, and went on to university to take a degree in geology.

My professional work has included gem-mining, studies of crystal chemistry (I did some early studies on the properties of ruby for lasers), and advanced studies in geochemistry, specializing in crystal chemistry. On a more esoteric level, I have been involved with crystals since 1977, when I found and cut a set of crystals for the Findhorn Community in Scotland. In the early 1980s I wrote several books under the name suggested by my first initials: Ra Bonewitz. Through the intervening years, I have been very involved in the New Age movement, and have expanded my studies to include cosmology, and a Ph.D. in psychology.

I have seen the crystal movement develop throughout the world over these past few years, and I have become increasingly uncomfortable with what I have been seeing. Crystals have begun to take on their own mythology, and I have watched thousands of people lead themselves into quite an extraordinary set of illusions about them. From a varying set of motivations, I see people being led further and further from their own purpose in being on the earth: to discover themselves, and to bring that discovery into full manifestation as a fully realized human being. To this end, much of what is taught about crystals is worse than useless – it is a false path and a distraction from the crystal user's true quest in life. Not that anyone's immortal soul is being swallowed up by them; no real harm is being done, but a great deal of time is being wasted.

This is a time of major change on the Earth. Forces are working to bring the Earth and its inhabitants back into alignment with the Universe's own purpose. We are part of the essential Being of the Universe, and it is our own inner connection to this Beingness that is personally and individually moving us toward greater alignment. What I am presenting to you in this book is a very direct line to your own personal realization. If you are through playing games with your life, then this book is for you. I have designed this book to help you avoid many of the pitfalls in the self-realization process – I could do this because I have fallen into a great many of them myself! Through this book I hope to demystify the entire process and help you get directly to your goal without a great deal of energy-wasting mumbo jumbo in the process. Everything in this book works. I do not pretend that this book is the final answer to your own self-discovery process, but you will find much in it that will supplement other inner processes, or stimulate them.

If you were not already well down the path of your journey, you would not have been drawn to this book. It is a well-trodden path, and the way is clearly marked. Crystals, if used to their best advantage, can be important beacons along the way. They have been so for me, and can be so for you.

LILIAN VERNER-BONDS

My introduction to colour came from the unlikeliest of sources – the bleak greyness of post-war Britain. As a small child hiding in a bomb-shelter during the war, I had already discovered that I could just hold someone's hand and learn about them without words – words that couldn't be heard anyway because of the noise of the bombing. It was the beginning of my palmistry work, and the first step on my path of discovery. I already knew I could see future happenings, but what I didn't know at the time – I was just four – was that my great-grandmother was a famous clairvoyant who read for royalty, or that my father was a remarkable healer who healed where conventional methods failed. My mother didn't want me to develop similar talents, but it happened anyway.

We had been forced by the government to leave central London to live in the East End, to be near my father's work with radar. In the dank rubble of the bombsites, there were inevitably pools of water into which leaked oil from a thousand ruptured pipes – and the most marvellous rainbows in the oily film! It was virtually the only colour around, and I soon realized that I could understand its language, not so much in words, but as a guide for knowledge. Learning to get the sense of things was important for me, because as soon as I started school, my dyslexia became apparent. As the language of written words became an impossible barrier, so my other senses expanded, especially that of colour. Pink became the colour that changed my life. Its message – the development of one's potential – was a pair of pink ballet slippers, which I couldn't wait to dance in. When I managed to get into theatre school, I began to win national dance competitions, and by my early teens I was appearing on stage, on radio, in films, and on television. But the language of colour always spoke to me. All through my career I also kept up with my psychic gift, and spent 15 years sitting in a developing psychic circle. Later studies included counselling, marriage guidance, the Chinese Five Elements, and Shiatsu. I took further training with colour, and when I gave up acting it wasn't long before I became a full-time colour therapist.

I now have a private practice using colour, counselling and palmistry, and I use specialized body-work developed from long practice of yoga and Shiatsu too. Referrals come frequently from the medical profession, and phobics and schizophrenics are regularly treated. I am also an interior colour scheme consultant, advising on colour use in homes, clinics and in commerce. Over the last two years I have completed over 80 television appearances for colour healing, divination, and phone-ins for counselling.

Further work includes numerous appearances and courses world-wide, the House of Commons Committee on Alternative Practice, a local authority project working with the elderly and senior citizens, and the Spirit of Peace Millennium Coach, resulting in a private audience with the Pope. I am also the colour consultant to a national newspaper group, and other clients vary from computer firms to health professionals, and students in all walks of life.

In the mid-1980s I met Dr Ron Bonewitz, who introduced me to the world of crystals. We taught many courses together, with colour playing an increasingly important role in the understanding of the message of crystals. We were looking at one of the crystal 'cookbooks', which suggests specific uses for crystals, and I noticed that many of the 'uses' were, in fact, due to the *colour* vibrations. It was from this realization that the coloured-crystal material in this book was born. It comes from my own well-proven colour practice, but here it is specifically related to crystals for the first time.

Ronald Arthur Louis (RA) Bonewitz
Lilian Verner-Bonds
England, 2000

PART ONE

THE TOOLS

CHAPTER 1

THE STORY SO FAR . . .

Nothing is meaningful as long as we perceive only separate fragments. But as soon as the fragments come together in a synthesis, a new entity emerges, whose nature we could not have foreseen by considering the fragments alone.

Piero Ferrucci, *What We May Be* (1982)

Crystals are all around us. Crystals or crystalline matter are part of our living body; we eat crystals; we use them a hundred times a day in various forms. Despite appearances, all that we see on the surface of the Earth makes up very little of its total mass. If the Plant and Animal Kingdoms are removed, that which is left – the Mineral Kingdom – makes up over 99.9999 per cent of the Earth. Indeed, of the Plant and Animal Kingdoms, over 75 per cent of the bodies of plants and animals is made of the molten form of the mineral ice. That which is not water? More minerals. It is *all* minerals.

The Mineral Kingdom is the foundation for all life, on the Earth and beyond. A special state of mineral matter – crystals – have properties that make them unusually powerful tools for the Kingdom of Man. But there is a much larger picture here, and without the larger picture we are both limited within ourselves, and limited in the results we can obtain with the tools we use.

In the past decades, we have experienced the growth of 'crystal consciousness' – an awareness of the life of the Mineral Kingdom. But without the larger picture, we have misunderstood much of what we have learned. Many properties are attributed to crystals that they simply don't have; or, for that matter, *can't* have. The misunderstood nature of minerals, and of the nature of nature itself, comes as a direct result of our highly limited Western understanding of the world around us. It is not just our comprehension of the mineral world that is flawed; it is our entire world-view.

There have been many books and courses about crystals proposing many uses and properties for them. Yet crystals have, for the most part, been a disappointment to their users. The problem is not with the crystals. Because they have been used within the limited world-view of our culture, they have failed to achieve the results promised for them. They never will achieve those results, until we shift our paradigm: the whole framework of belief through which we interact with the world. The clarity of crystals has its place in this process.

This book has two aims: to guide the reader through the learning necessary to undertake the necessary inner shifts, and, through practical exercises using the genuine properties of crystals, to bring that learning into personal, inner experience. One is not much use without the other – undirected experience wastes time and energy and often leads to more confusion and lack of clarity; and learning ungrounded in experience is just empty words.

There is a real and powerful place for crystals in the unfolding of the human spirit, but they are not magic pills for enlightenment as crystals have sometimes been portrayed. The answers found herein are not easy-fix, no-effort-required-except-buy-the-right-crystal ones. What is in this book is real, and proven. It is for those who are ready to step beyond pop spirituality and make the effort needed for genuine spiritual growth.

The tendency in crystal teaching in the past decades has been to treat crystals either as medicines or gadgets; that is, as something external that is applied in some manner to achieve an inner result – be that healing, enlightenment, increase of intuition, or whatever. At a superficial level, some of these things appear to happen. But this is just scratching the surface; an inkling of what is really possible. Seeing them as nothing more than this not only limits their usefulness, it also limits *us*.

SCIENCE

It may be tempting for some readers to skip over some of the material in this book, as it is 'science'. We need to understand that there is no difference at all between science and mysticism within the realms properly covered by science. Science has a limited ability to describe the whole of reality but, within its limitations, it is a useful tool of understanding. My personal definition of science is that it is *'the branch of mysticism that deals with the measurable'*.

The basic idea of science was revolutionary when it was developed: an objective way of looking at reality that did not depend on your beliefs or nationality. The Medieval world of religious dogma and hateful superstition, teetering on the brink of collapse as an outmoded system anyway, fell before science.

But . . .

One of the greatest dangers of science is the deliberate exclusion of humanity from the scientific equation, creating a confusing lack of real values in a science-centred society. If human consciousness, and thus human values, are kept out of scientific observation, then in science all things are equal. But all things are *not* equal. They either sustain and expand life or they do not. They are, in the most profound sense, either good or bad.

This is underlined in the tendency of science to totally ignore questions of our own humanity, of the human beingness that is the domain of human instinctual life. These are the types of questions science deems not worth asking because it does not have any answers for them. It cannot find any answers, because the answers are not in the realm of science. They are in the realm of human instinct – within the natural part of ourselves we will work toward returning to here. It is the inner part of each and every one of us that responds most clearly to the real properties of crystals.

Herein lies the great missed opportunity of science – to use its tools through the guidance of natural human instinct. There is a golden opportunity to see life and our place in the universe not in bleak, humanless terms, but instead to see the richness of life which abounds in all things – a richness that is invisible to the science that selectively sees only what it can measure, and only asks itself the questions it can answer.

Psychiatrist and social theorist Abraham Maslow, listed four criteria that help to put the reality of science and its possibilities into perspective:

> (1) Creativity has its roots in the non-rational, (2) language is, and must always be, inadequate to describe total reality, (3) any abstract concept leaves out much of reality, and (4) what we call 'knowledge' (which is usually highly abstract and verbal and sharply defined) often serves to blind us to those portions of reality not covered by the abstraction.[1]

What Maslow shows us is a science that is not the be-all and end-all of everything. Rather, we see a science that is highly limited by its own tools – abstraction and language – which, if it is not careful, may be mistaken for reality. Reality is not found in the mind. It is an inner sense, that inner 'ring of truth' when we just *know*. It is one of the facets of the real you that will be strengthened through the exercises contained here.

Albert Einstein once said that knowledge is what you have left over when you have forgotten everything you learned in school. *Knowledge is an essence,* and the rational side of the brain is not equipped to deal with essence – only information. To be sure, one side of the brain feeds the other. But it is the balance between the two, their right relationship, that we seek. Much of what we are remembering and being told about crystals falls into the category of information. What we really seek is knowledge. To a Western mind, the distinction between the two can be difficult.

HISTORY OF CRYSTAL CONSCIOUSNESS

Let's look back for a moment at the history of the use of crystals and other stones, for in that history we find the roots of many of today's misunderstandings about them.

The ancient Egyptians, Babylonians and Assyrians were the first to use stones for healing. The stones originally used were of the colours that the disease caused in the body: yellow jaundice, blue lips, fever-red skin. Particularly prized were transparent stones in intense colours – the first gemstones, in effect. However, they were valued not for themselves, but for their colours: yellow beryls were used for jaundice, bloodstones for bleeding, and lapis lazuli for the blue of restricted circulation. Diamond was a cure-all, prized for its transparent brilliance.

[1] Abraham Maslow, *Toward a Psychology of Being* (New York: Van Nostrand Reinhold, 1968), p.208.

Other coloured materials were also used: flowers and plants, white oil, red lead, red ochre, black lizards and indigo. Verdigris, a green copper carbonate, was mixed with wax for the treatment of cataracts.

The earliest known uses of stones for esoteric purposes occurred around 3000 BC in Egypt and Mesopotamia. Amulets were cut from agate, carnelian, turquoise and lapis lazuli, and seals and other important objects were carved from quartz and other crystals. The later Babylonians and Assyrians attributed magical properties to cylinder seals made from various materials. A surviving text states that Ka-Gi-Ma stone will help a man destroy his enemies; a seal made of lapis lazuli contains a god, and 'His god will rejoice in him'. A seal made of rock crystal was believed to extend a man's possessions, and one of green serpentine to draw many blessings to its owner. The possessor of a seal made from red jasper or carnelian would, it was believed, never be separated from his god. So, even at that time, a mythology was growing around the use of particular stones.

Also within this same time period there occurs probably the best-known ancient example of the use of stones for magical purposes, on an object known to history as the Breastplate of Aaron. On this breastplate were set twelve carved stones, each with the name of one of the Twelve Tribes engraved upon it. The stones said to have been in the breastplate emphasize one of the greatest single problems that the modern scholar has in dealing with old texts and descriptions, which is that certain mineral names have been applied through history to a variety of different substances, most of which are entirely unrelated to the present substance called by that name. For example, in ancient times the term 'sapphire' was frequently applied to any blue stone, and in the breastplate it may have referred to lapis lazuli. In many translations 'diamond' is listed as one of the principal stones of the breastplate; however, the name of one of the Twelve Tribes of Israel was engraved on this stone. With the technology available at that time it is utterly impossible to have ground a flat face on a diamond, much less to have engraved on it. Another stone listed as being on the breastplate is carbuncle. A number of different writers guess at what this stone might have been but, although the evidence points to almandine garnet, there is no great certainty on this point. Thus we see the problem of old texts and legends, in that we are never certain that the stone referred to is one that is known today by that name.

The first serious writing regarding stones does not appear until about 300 BC, when Theophrastus, a student of Aristotle, wrote a thesis entitled *On Stones*. The work comprises 120 short paragraphs and in them he describes what a modern mineralogist would recognize as about 16 mineral species. Most of the rest of the treatise is involved in the description of the then known metals and certain 'earths' (ochre, marls, clay, etc.).

The next ancient author of note to write on stones was the Roman Pliny the Elder, who lived between AD 23 and 79. He was killed while observing the eruption of Mount Vesuvius that buried Pompeii. His writings, entitled *Historia Naturalis*, comprised 37 books. Only portions of the last four books relate to stones, however. This is the most voluminous of ancient works on the subject. To give some idea of the small quantity of ancient writings available, the whole of Pliny's writings on minerals and crystals would comprise no more than perhaps 15 pages of this text.

It must be remembered that both Theophrastus and Pliny were simply compilers of information: they neither worked with, nor, in all probability, could they even identify most of the stones that they describe.

Most of what is written from the time of Pliny until the rediscovery of classical learning in the fifteenth and early sixteenth centuries was more related to alchemy than directly to the study of mineralogy. Alchemy, at least in the purely scientific sense of the term, relates more to metallurgy than to mineralogy, but there are, nonetheless, occasional references to minerals in the writings of several authors.

We owe much of the preservation of early writings such as those of Aristotle and Pliny to the Arabs, who preserved scientific knowledge at a time when Europe had sunk into the Dark Ages, when much of the work of earlier writers disappeared into the chaos. One of the Arabs to whom we owe a great deal is Avicenna (980–1073), who was a physician of great note, and translated many of the Greek and Roman classics into Arabic.

The next important writer on the subject during this period was Albertus Magnus, a Dominican monk, who was writing around 1270. Once again, though, it must be remembered that he was a compiler of other people's work. His writing on mineralogy, except for a few books on gems, is the only writing of any consequence on that subject between the time of Pliny and that of Georgius Agricola in the mid-sixteenth century. It was during this period that much of the lore associated with the use of crystals and gems was accumulated. But it must be re-emphasized that the names applied to minerals in those days were not necessarily the same as those used today: many modern writers still fail to sort out modern from ancient terminology. Thus, in a book published as late as 1973, a writer can still list six different types of 'rubies', only one of which is actually ruby

– the other five refer to different minerals altogether. What is even more extraordinary, is that in a book published in 1977 (which has already gone through 17 printings) is a list of names of 115 stones and their properties. Of these, 97 are names totally unknown to modern mineralogy. It would be interesting to have the author of this book produce samples of the various minerals he lists.

Most early references to the various powers of stones seem to be related more to their colour than to anything else. The use of colour for healing is certainly a well-proven technique, and the application of coloured crystals is explored later in chapters 7 and 8.

We have examined some of the historical background of the science of mineralogy, in which the writers have done little more than accumulate bits and pieces of information from numerous sources. The modern science of mineralogy had to wait until 1546 for its real roots.

In that year, Georgius Agricola published his *De Natura Fossilium*, in which he classified minerals on the basis of physical properties; he actually studied and described minerals himself, and added new mineral descriptions to those already published by earlier writers. In 1556 Agricola published an even more remarkable book concerning mining, mineralogy and metallurgy, called *De Re Metallica*. This was the standard reference book for the mining industry for over 200 years, and even today it is one of the most highly respected classics of scientific literature.

Following the lead of Agricola others, such as Carolus Linnaeus and Jöns Jakob Berzelius, began to study and classify minerals, following the separate routes of classification by external characteristics and by chemical composition. However, the true nature of minerals and crystals was waiting for another science – chemistry – in order to provide a basis and an explanation for many of the characteristics of minerals.

The concept of the atom had been around since before Aristotle's day, but it was John Dalton, an eighteenth-century English chemist, who took the next step. Using the newly invented burning glass, he heated the mineral cinnabar (an oxide of mercury) in a closed container. He discovered that a very pure gas was given off, which another chemist, A.L. Lavoisier, named oxygen. Although the concept of chemical elements had been stated as early as 1661, this was the first 'new' element to be discovered.

With the growth of modern atomic theory, the science of mineralogy gained a firm grounding for growth. By 1800, reliable chemical analysis of minerals began, and by 1809 the rapid and precise measurement of crystal angles became possible. By that time it was becoming apparent that chemical composition and crystallographic characteristics were the fundamental properties of minerals. As more and more data became available, it fell to an American, James White Dana in 1837, to propose a system of mineralogy based both on chemical constituents and crystal structure, as discussed in Chapter 4. By the turn of the twentieth century the first experiments with growing crystals synthetically were begun, and as our understanding of how crystals grow in the laboratory grows, our understanding of natural processes has increased.

This is just one of several threads that now draw together to complete our understanding of the world in which we live.

SELF-AWARENESS/MINERAL AWARENESS

On the Earth we live the paradox of people who must stand with one foot in dense matter and one foot in the freedom of their inner infinity. They must be masters of this dimension, but such mastery can only come through the application of the higher love and understanding born in the deepest inner levels of the heart. Discovery of truth does not come about through haphazard events left to chance and whimsy. The steps are carefully planned, and those who are involved with one another are placed within their life patterns to meet and exchange energy with those who will be most likely to provide the mutual learning experiences.

The ultimate goal is the discovery of the Christ within. Christo-Genesis depends on one very important factor: the individual's ability to believe in himself. Without this quality Christ cannot be born. For Christhood is ultimately the pinnacle of self-acceptance, self-trust, and belief and one-ness with the indwelling source of our own being. It is within every person upon Earth and is given many names: Buddhahood, Enlightenment, Self-Actualization, and so on.

As the Inner Self awakens, other aspects of the surrounding world come into awareness. There is a pattern to this which most human beings seem to be following at the moment: first a higher degree of self-awareness – an awareness of one's own thoughts, emotions and the physical body. Secondly, an awareness of the physical world around us, especially the other Kingdoms of nature – animals, plants and, finally, minerals.

Because the Mineral Kingdom exists at the lowest level of consciousness, it is necessary for the re-awakening of the Self to have progressed to some extent before the mineral level of energy comes into awareness.

A large number of souls on the Earth began to develop to this stage of awareness around the years 1979–1981, and a second resurgence began to take place in 1984. During the courses I was giving at that time, my question to each group was, 'How many of you have just become aware of crystals within the last two years?' In 1980 usually two-thirds to three-quarters of each group had become aware within a two-year period, while the remainder had become aware just within the previous few months. That pattern began to change in 1983, with as many as 90 per cent of each group indicating the awakening of their interest and awareness within the previous six months. This accelerating awareness continues up to the time of writing. But why is this re-awakening happening, and what, ultimately, does it mean? It can be seen as a symptom of a large-scale awakening of other levels of consciousness as well, for (as I have said) awareness of the levels of energy of the Mineral Kingdom only occurs when other levels have already been re-awakened.

The very first stage of this re-awakening is (and must be) to evolve a new view of the world around us; or perhaps more accurately, to go back to our ancient, but in many ways accurate view of how the world really is. We have finally started to get away from the belief that the Earth is our personal property, to be punched and pummelled and plundered at our leisure. The Earth is just like your own body: made up of millions of interacting and mutually dependent components. Most of the components are individuals, even as the cells of your body are individual cells, but each interacting in a way that provides the greatest opportunity for mutual survival. *You* are part of the cellular structure of the Earth Being. Human beings might even be the brains of the Earth, although we could find reasonable cause to doubt it. However, when a cell of your own body begins to be self-centred, taking only in regard to its own needs and ignoring those of others around it, we call it *cancer*.

This doesn't mean that one's needs should not be fulfilled, or that the other Kingdoms of the Earth should not provide for those needs. You *are* those Kingdoms – the Mineral Kingdom provides the chemical building blocks; the Plant Kingdom provides the oxygen to energize those building blocks, as well as the stored energy of sunlight as fuel for the oxygen; and the Animal Kingdom, especially at the microscopic level, provides the physical building blocks that create your own body and its systems – those few trillion cells that decided to be *you* for a while. When you take from the environment you are only taking from yourself – and that is not a bad thing, as long as you do so in harmony with that environment. The mineral–biological world we live in is a system of energy exchange and movement, and *energy moving throughout structure is called life.*

THE MINERAL BODY

We are not only one with the same life-force as the Mineral Kingdom; we *are* the Mineral Kingdom. Your body is half a bathtub of water (molten ice), and a few cups of powder – minerals.

You are an evolved mineral.

The biological Kingdoms are just another way of embodying minerals at higher and higher states of consciousness. The Universe, and the Earth within it, is a place that is alive at many different levels. It has created many minerals in the Mineral Kingdom, and many species in the Plant and Animal Kingdoms. All are different ways of embodying *Life.*

CHAPTER 2

THE MINERAL KINGDOM

✧

Fishing baskets are employed to catch fish; but when the fish are got, the men forget the baskets; snares are employed to catch hares; but when the hares are got, men forget the snares. Words are employed to convey ideas; but when the ideas are grasped, men forget the words.

Chuang-tzu *c.* 300 BC

To this ancient Taoist quote, we might also add: Chaos is the raw material employed to create order; when the order is perceived, men forget the chaos.

CHAOS AND ORDER

In the creation of the Mineral Kingdom, we see the 'first thought' of the Creator in the descent (or ascent, depending on one's viewpoint) of energy into matter. We often think of the universe as being made of *things*: stars, planets, light, carrots, doorknobs, etc. But there is another way of seeing the universe: it is made of only two 'things': *energy*, and *relationships*. These relationships have an outward expression as 'things': as matter, as light, as thought, as feeling. But if there were no energy relationships, none of these would or could exist. All would remain energy, chaos. Relationship, then, becomes the fundamental means of bringing order from chaos. It is true for universes, and it is true for humans. Whether it is the chaos of disordered energy bursting forth from the Cosmic Egg into impending order and form as a soup of energy and basic particles, or the disorder of our own lives seeking meaning and a higher state of being, increasingly higher states of relationship bring that chaos into greater order. The fundamental characteristic of these relationships is that they move in cycles and rhythms and patterns. As we observe the unfolding of the universe and of the Earth and of our own lives in the following chapters, we will see how this is so – and the role that the Mineral Kingdom plays at all levels.

Chaos must always precede order; whether it is the chaos of unformed energy to create a universe or the chaos of unformed energy we personally experience as 'confusion' – the period between the breaking down of old ideas and beliefs and the reforming of new, clearer ones. Hindu mythology recognizes this in the person of Shiva the Destroyer. The old must die, must be destroyed, must return to chaos, before the new can be reborn. It is the Phoenix rising from its own ashes.

The ultimate source of all of the cycles, rhythms and patterns, chaos manifesting form, is the universe itself. Fifteen thousand million years ago, the entire universe was confined in a sphere about the size of a *pea.* Every light beam from every star, every moon, every planet, what you ate for breakfast, every atom in your body, every thought you will ever think, every feeling you will ever feel – *everything* in that little ball of *energy.* All One. What is energy? In purely scientific terms, we don't know, but we do know that everything in the universe is made from it, and every bit of it was there in that little cosmic egg, awaiting birth.[1] But it was energy without form, energy without order. Energy in a pure state of Chaos.

And yet within that little seed of chaos was all that the universe has become and will yet be. In this state it was not unlike the human ovum: within it is the entire human being in an unformed state, waiting to unfold. And like the human ovum, at the moment of conception a new pulse of life infuses the imminent being and a great expansion takes place. For the universe, it was an event called the Big Bang: the universe beginning its leap from energy into matter, from chaos to order, from the unmanifest into the manifest. Energy moving into new *relationships* with itself, to form the four basic building blocks that would themselves later form other new relationships: atoms, stars, minerals, planets and, finally, you.

[1] Here is a thought for you: perhaps 'energy' is love. Love unformed, but love seeking manifestation in the myriad of forms that make a universe. Every time you read the word 'energy' in the text, try substituting the word 'love', and see how it reads then.

The four basic particles, the four basic building blocks created in the first moments of the universe's new life, born in approximately equal amounts, are *photons,* light; *neutrinos,* particles so small they pass right through the Earth without hitting anything; *electrons,* negatively charged particles; and *positrons,* positively charged electrons.

In many esoteric writings we read that the universe and all within it are made from 'light'. If 'light' is to be taken literally, we know now that it is not so. Light (photons) makes up only a quarter of the basic particles from which the universe is built. Photons have been discovered to be what are called 'gauge' particles, or carriers of electromagnetism. But if we substitute the word 'enlightenment' for 'light', a new meaning emerges. If we take 'enlightenment' to mean 'right relationship' (isn't an 'enlightened' person one who is in right relationship both with his inner Being and the world around him?), then we could say that the universe is made of energy and right relationship – of enlightenment.

What are those right relationships? In the beginning, there was only primal matter – the four basic particles, energy in its new right relationship with itself – and the mass of energy from which they were emerging. An exploding, expanding ball of energy at a temperature near the infinite. The Big Bang.

After about one-hundredth of a second, the temperature of the embryonic universe cooled to about 100 thousand million degrees centigrade, and basic particles continued to condense in large amounts from energy. Yet the universe was still only a broth of particles, energy and radiation, still without form. The universe was so compact at this stage that neutrinos, millions of times smaller than an atom, were colliding with themselves and other particles. The density of the universal broth at this point was about 3.8 thousand million times the density of water. A thimbleful would have been as heavy as a mountain range on today's Earth.

By the end of the first second a new relationship appeared. Other emergent particles began to bind themselves into even larger, denser particles as yet other new particles emerged to 'glue' them together. As further cooling took place over the next 10 seconds, all of these new particles began to bind together to form simple atomic nuclei. By now the universe had 'cooled' to three thousand million degrees centigrade.

After a few minutes had passed, the universe cooled further to a thousand million degrees centigrade – 'only' about 70 times hotter than the heart of the Sun. By then all of the fundamental relationships which shape the universe and all within it (including you) were set in motion. But these relationships needed to persevere for another 70,000 years, and the universe to cool considerably, before the nuclei could begin to capture electrons to form the next relationship phase of universe-creation: the birth of atoms.

To the time-frame of these events can be added the concept of *relative time*. Relative time is literally that: time relative to the observer or to the experiencer. A few minutes with a lover is a very different expanse of time to those same few clock minutes when we are late for an important appointment and stuck in a traffic jam. Thus in the experience of the universe in the first few seconds and minutes, a second may have been a very long time.

Your own birth repeated the pattern of the birth of the universe: an explosion of cells from the moment of conception that are at first undifferentiated – any cell can become anything, like the first particles. As growth continues, particles specialize to become atoms, and atoms grow to become more specialized atoms. Just as, eventually, your cells began to specialize to become brain cells, heart cells, and so on.

Although order had begun to emerge at one level – energy condensing into particles and particles re-arranging themselves into atoms – these particles and atoms still constituted a fairly small portion of universal energy. And those particles and atoms were widely scattered and in a state of disorder. 'Specialization' in the aborning universe required a new set of relationships, new rhythms, and new patterns.

THE FUNDAMENTAL PATTERNS OF CREATION

The very largest scale patterns are the rhythms and cycles set by the creation of the universe itself. These permeate all creation and are *the* fundamental rhythms and patterns of creation. They are as much a part of your daily life and the unfoldment of your own personal growth as they are that of the universe itself.

Expansion and Contraction is the most basic process of creation. We see it reflected in all levels of life: in prosperity and recession; in the flowering and decline of civilizations; in the turning inward of a 'dark night of the soul' followed by an expansive re-emergence into the world with a renewed sense of self.

In the ultimate act of expansion, the Big Bang, the universe has explosively expanded. The evidence is that it will get a great deal larger before it contracts back into itself, to be reborn again in yet another 'Big Bang' through rebound. As, indeed, it may have already done before.

The first contraction following the expansion of the Big Bang was the contraction of energy into the elementary particles, which contracted even further to create atoms. This key movement of *Energy into Matter* is the second basic universal pattern. We follow this same creative pattern when we take a thought – a pattern of energy – and create something around that thought: a garden, a building, a piece of music, a meal. It is also a perfect example of the old esoteric truism, 'as above so below'.

The third universal pattern is the *Birth–Life–Death–Rebirth* cycle. Particles re-create themselves into atoms. Atoms re-create themselves into molecules. Molecules re-create themselves into minerals. And finally, minerals re-create themselves into planets, where the cycle begins again as minerals are remelted into new molecules that, in turn, re-create new minerals. In addition, on the surface of some planets, minerals are chemically broken down to re-create themselves into organic life, which in turn dies to become mineral matter once again.

The Birth–Life–Death–Rebirth cycle begins with the Big Bang – the birth of the universe. At its birth, after the first contraction of Energy into Matter, the first atoms that formed were mostly hydrogen gas, the lightest and simplest element. The first 'physical body' of the universe was an expanding cloud of hydrogen gas, gauge particles, and yet unformed energy. While the universe was experiencing a contraction of energy into matter at one level, it was still physically expanding. We experience this ourselves: we continue to grow physically and psychologically and to develop even as we contract into the 'dark night of the soul' developmental phase.

At this early birth stage the universe was still several thousand times hotter than the Sun, but as it continued to expand it also cooled. Probably due to uneven cooling the hydrogen began to separate and concentrate in smaller, more compact clouds. Gravity began to draw more hydrogen to each condensing cloud, and in the centres of the clouds, an even more compacted area began to form. This increased the gravity in turn, further drawing in yet more gas. As the flow toward the middle increased the clouds started to rotate, setting up whirls and eddies. It was the beginning of the next basic pattern of the universe – the movement of *Matter into Density*.

Hot spots began to develop in the centres of eddies as more and more gas was gathered in. As yet more was drawn in by the still increasing gravity, more compaction and heating occurred. This contraction cycle continued until the gas at the centre became so hot that the atoms of hydrogen began to fuse together, to create helium. This fusion triggered another stage of expansion – the release of light particles bound up in the fusing atoms. The first stars were birthing. The concentrated light from these first stars began to fill the universe – light that is an expansion outward even as its sources moved into greater contraction; contraction that started the last of the five universal patterns: *Movement into Complexity*.

As hydrogen fuses to form helium and release light, more heat is released, causing the centres of stars to become even hotter and raising the pressures higher. At higher temperatures and pressures helium begins to fuse to itself to form even more complex atoms. This fusion releases yet more heat and light, causing yet more fusion to form ever more complex atoms: carbon, oxygen, iron, silicon and other heavy elements. The stellar expansion and contraction cycle reaches an equilibrium where the gravity of the contracting centre holds its expansion into heat and light exactly in balance. And so it stays for the life of the star. When enough of the hydrogen supply is used up to upset the equilibrium, the star either collapses inward on itself or explodes into a supernova – the two forms of star death.

Like all things in the Universe, stars die, going through their own Birth–Life–Death–Rebirth cycle. Hydrogen-rich stars explode: they expand as they die, scattering their core of heavy elements and their remaining hydrogen back into the broth of the universe. It is at this stage of explosive star-death that the very heaviest elements are created: uranium, platinum, gold, and so on. Hydrogen-poor stars contract. They collapse inward to become a more compact star – a white dwarf. Eventually they collapse again to become neutron stars, and finally again to become black holes: matter so dense that it begins to approximate the original density before the Big Bang.

In the beginning, and even now since the universe is a relatively young place, the majority of stars are hydrogen-rich. Such stars tend to 'live fast and die young'. In the autumn and winter skies in the northern hemisphere you can see stars being born: the Pleiades. They are seven stars surrounded by a dimly-lit gas cloud – the cloud from which they are contracting. If you had walked the earth 70,000 years ago, as our ancestors did, there would have been nothing to see. They are that new. Stars younger than Man.

THE BIRTH OF THE SUN

The rebirth from which all that lives on the Earth was ultimately born began about five thousand million years ago, from the remains of perhaps dozens of dead stars and planets. Drawn together by gravity, heating and fusion began as the local density of dust and gas increased. The very first photons were released and started their journey to the surface of the cloud, a journey taking perhaps a million years. At last they burst free, to become the first light: the birth-cry of a new-born star. Our Sun had come into life, expansively spreading its light through the dustcloud from which other new life would also be born. As its birthing continued, more gas and dust was drawn together, and as the density increased the whole local mass of gas and dust began to rotate – just as was happening around other points of density in the same cloud. Within the great cloud, other points of light appeared as the other stars of our Sun's family were born.

Our own star is a 'collapser', and it will go through a predictable pattern of star death. Before the final collapse it will expand to become a red giant – a star that will fill most of the inner solar system and engulf Mercury, Venus and the Earth as it expands. It will stay in this expanded state for a while, until more hydrogen is used up and the new equilibrium with gravity is upset. Then it will implode inward in a matter of seconds, taking the rest of the Solar System with it as it dies.

The Sun is itself a third-generation star; a star made up of the remnants of two earlier phases of star death. Two other generations of stars have lived and died to supply the material for our Sun, its brothers and sisters and their moons and planets (not to mention for your physical body too). Stars are born in batches. Somewhere in this part of the galaxy are the brothers and sisters of our Sun. Family relationships exist even among the stars.

THE BIRTH OF THE EARTH

Around our Sun, as undoubtedly around many other suns, the heavier dust particles were drawn into a flat disc, where they began to collide with themselves to form larger particles. Scattered dust was reborn as sand grains; sand grains entered new relationships to become pebbles; pebbles merged to become boulders; boulders integrated to become planets and moons. Thus were the Earth and moon born, and the other planets and moons of our Solar System created: matter in contraction, matter becoming denser, matter becoming more complex as melting took place and new minerals began to crystallize from cosmic dust. Somewhere in all of this was the mineral matter of your own body; star dust starting its long journey to become minerals, crystals, plants, animals and, above all, you.

All of the planets and moons of our Solar System appear to have formed at about the same time from this primal dust cloud. Evidence comes both from moon rocks and meteorites. Meteorites come from two sources: the break-up of earlier-formed planetary bodies, and fragments of the original accretion that were never incorporated into larger bodies. Of the first type there are both 'irons' (composed of various alloys of iron and thought to be similar in composition to the core of the Earth), and 'stones' (material resembling the mineral composition of the Earth's mantle).

The second, unincorporated type of meteorite is also a stony one – one which gives us an insight into the origins of the Mineral Kingdom as it condensed from star dust. These are the *carbonaceous chondrites*, meteorites rich in carbon and more loosely consolidated than the 'stones'. Their chemical and mineral compositions are close to that of the non-gaseous make-up of the Sun, suggesting their origin in the primal gas and dust cloud. It is possible that they are older than the Sun, and that they are planetary debris from the older stars that died to provide new material for our Sun and its siblings. There is even some evidence that the earliest organic life-forms may have a connection to the chondrites.

Age determinations of Moon rocks show the Moon to have formed just over four-and-a-half thousand million years ago, making it exactly the same age as the Earth. Moon rocks are similar to certain lavas that have erupted from Earth volcanoes; there have been few surprises in the mineral make-up of the Moon. What has been a surprise to scientists is that the Earth and the Moon were almost certainly once one body. The Moon is made from material blasted off the primal Earth by a collision with another huge body during the formation of the Solar System.

MINERALS AND CRYSTALS

There will be much more about minerals and crystals in later chapters, but for now, in order to see them in their larger, universal context, we need a brief definition. A *mineral* is nothing more than a naturally occurring, inorganic, chemical substance. There are about 2,500 individual chemicals that are found in inorganic nature. Each of these is a mineral, and each has its own unique name. Astonishingly each of these 2,500 minerals is made from one of just *14* basic atomic patterns: 14 patterns to build the entire Mineral Kingdom; 14 patterns to build planets and moons and asteroids; 14 basic energy relationships to build most of the physical universe.

How do atoms get together in the first place? Where did the *first* minerals come from? The answer is from dead stars. The first minerals formed from the scattered remnants of the first stars to die in supernova explosions. They formed from the 'dust' that was the remains of their cores. Most of the dust was too small to be seen – literally a cloud of single atoms. Because of the varying atomic attractiveness of the atoms to each other (as the following chapters explain) they began to connect with each other, and with like patterns of identical chemical composition – the first chemical 'cells'. Therefore the truism of 'like attracts like' is at the very heart of the Mineral Kingdom. These chemical cells were the tiny bits of solid matter that accumulated around newly forming stars, building planets and moons.

We may regard the Mineral Kingdom as the 'backbone' of the universe. While the most prominent denizens of the universe are the stars which swirl in the galaxies, there is still an insubstantialness about them – they are, after all, just large balls of gas. Minerals, whether occurring as disparate dust particles or as planets, have rigid structures and long-term stability. While their structures may change as a result of geological conditions, they change only into other stable and fixed forms. Thus in a universe of emerging forms, they are the first fixed and stable forms upon which everything else is built.

IN SUMMARY

In the Mineral Kingdom we observe, in perfect form, the five universal patterns of creation: *energy into matter, matter into density, matter into complexity, contraction and expansion*, and the cycle of *birth–life–death–rebirth*. And yet there is more here than just the mechanical movement of atoms and particles and minerals.

The five universal patterns yield three basic principles:

1 Man is part of a larger set of patterns and rhythms which ultimately ends (and begins) with the universe itself.

2 The patterns of our own development parallel and are an intimate part of the developmental patterns of all creation.
3 Rhythm and pattern connect all levels of life to each other. It is the essential link between man and minerals.

Even physicists recognize this, or perhaps we should say that physicists, above all, recognize it. The Nobel Prize-winning physicist Werner Heisenberg states:

> . . . one has now divided the world not into different groups of objects but into different groups of connections [relationships] . . . The world thus appears as a complicated tissue of events, in which connections of different kinds alternate or overlap or combine and thereby determine the texture of the whole.[2]

In the next chapter, we examine those 'different groups of connections' as they apply to crystals, upon which the foundations of life itself are laid.

[2] W. Heisenberg, *Physics and Philosophy* (New York: Harper Torchbooks, 1958).

CHAPTER 3

THE LIVING EARTH

✧

The great extension of our experience [in physics] in recent years has brought to light the insufficiency of our simple mechanical conceptions . . .

Niels Bohr, discoverer of the electron

The movement of matter into density and complexity on its way to becoming you, began with the evolution of the Earth. As the Earth grew in size as more and more of the disc of stardust was swept up, heavier matter began to settle towards its centre and internal heating began, both from the forces of compression and the breakdown of radioactive elements created during the death of the Sun's and Earth's ancestors. As the intermixed minerals melted, denser matter like iron and nickel accumulated in the centre to become the *core* of the Earth. Also drawn towards the core were the heavy radioactive elements created in the supernova explosions that destroyed the Sun's ancestors. As these continued to decay the internal heat was maintained and even increased. Relatively lighter elements, such as silicon and oxygen, were probably already linked chemically (as in the chondrites) and now began to combine with other elements like iron to form minerals like olivine, which 'floated' out from the denser core to form a thick shell around the Earth – the *mantle*.

At the time the Earth formed, radioactive elements were present in much greater quantities than today and the consequent heating from their decay heated

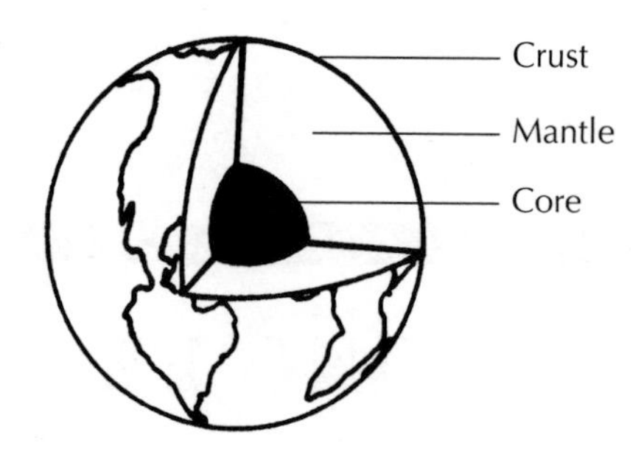

Figure 1: A section across the Earth

the earth to the point where even the mantle was in a molten or semi-molten state. The very lightest minerals, the 'froth', floated to the surface of the mantle to form a thin shell, called the *crust.* How thin the crust is, relatively, can be shown by making a model of the Earth the size of a soccer ball. The crust at its thickest point would be the thickness of a postage stamp. And, scaling the strength of the Earth to the same amount, our soccer ball-sized earth would have to be made of toothpaste! From this perspective the fragility of the Earth's physical body is apparent.

At this point then, new relationships had developed: the accumulation of heavy elements in the core of the Earth increased its density; new minerals formed to increase complexity; and contraction took place as heavier elements were drawn into the core while expansion occurred as lighter minerals moved to the surface. The Earth's own internal birth–life–death–rebirth cycles had begun.

Internal heating from radioactive decay causes the heated material to rise, and a corresponding sinking of cooler material. This sets up large-scale convection currents within the Earth that bring heat to the surface, remelt and recrystallize surface material, which is then pulled under through the movement of the continents, which in turn rises again. It is this process which propels the life forces of the Earth's mineral body.

The internal structure of the Earth is known through the study of earthquake waves as they pass through the Earth. Drill holes have only penetrated to a depth of eight km (five miles) or so, but there is rock that comes from a much greater depth available for study: that which rises from deep volcanoes. The Earth's crust appears still to be forming, with new material being brought to the surface all the time.

The existence of one of the Earth's major life processes was not confirmed until very recently. Although this process was first suggested in the late 1890s, even as

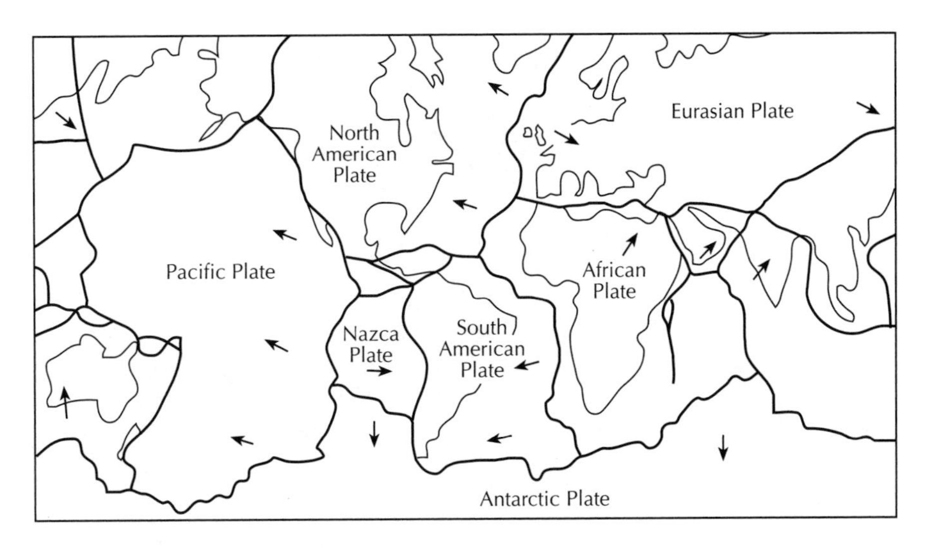

Figure 2: The major plates of the Earth and their direction of movement

late as the early 1960s it was still a theory widely dismissed by geologists. In those days it was called 'continental drift'; today it is called *plate tectonics*, and is the very foundation of geology. It has been discovered that the Earth's crust essentially 'floats' on the mantle, and large, continent-sized chunks of it drift about in different directions, sometimes away from each other, and sometimes bumping into each other. Where collisions between plates occur mountain ranges are pushed up, like the Himalayas and the Alps. Where plates are pushed apart, oceans form. Figure 2 shows the Earth's major plates and the direction of their movement.

The continents are propelled by the convection currents deep within the Earth mentioned earlier. Material is brought to the surface along rifts in the ocean floors that run parallel to the continental masses. This new material solidifies, and is pushed aside by newly rising material. This, in turn, gives the continents a shove sideways. This process is shown in Figure 3. Also illustrated is the means by which this was finally confirmed: the discovery of symmetrically alternating 'stripes' of rock running parallel to the ocean rifts in which the magnetic particles in the rock had oriented to the Earth's then magnetic field as they cooled.

This tells us that the magnetic field reverses from time to time (it *doesn't* mean that the Earth flips over), and that sea-floor spreading occurs from the rifts outwards –confirmed by the discovery that the sea-floor rocks furthest from the rifts are the oldest, and those nearest the rifts are the youngest.

The places where continental rock is being pulled under the crust to be remelted

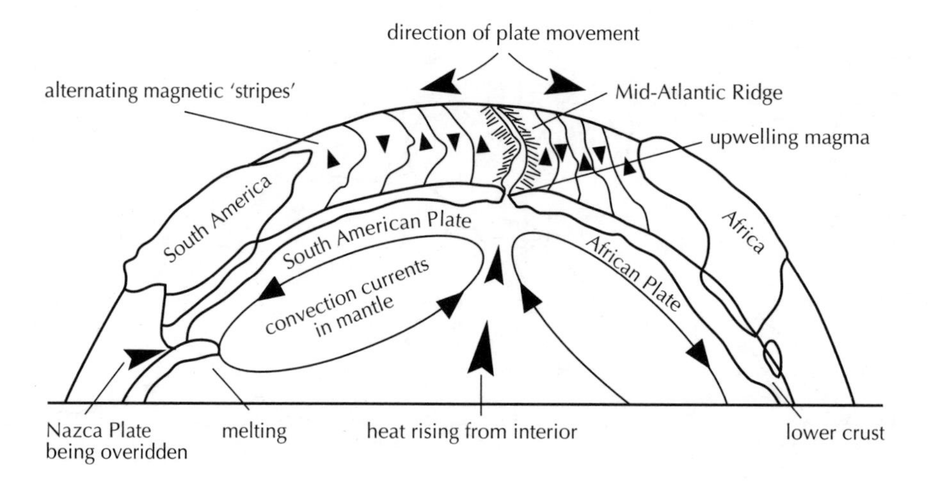

Figure 3: The sideways movement of continents

are called *trenches*. Some of the rock is drawn under to re-emerge in the ocean rifts, and some of it rises to create volcanoes. Almost all of the volcanic activity along the western Pacific Ocean lies along just such a trench. Along the west coast of the USA the North American Plate is over-riding the Pacific Plate. The Mt. St. Helens' eruption in the 1980s was a result of remelted continental rock reappearing as lava (Figure 4). A similar process creates the activity of Mt. Etna and Mt. Vesuvius in Europe, where the Eurasian Plate is overriding the African Plate.

(It was once proposed that these trenches would be a good place to dump our rubbish, until some wit pointed out that in a few years' time we would have volcanoes spitting out old refrigerators!)

Figure 4: Volcanoes along a plate margin

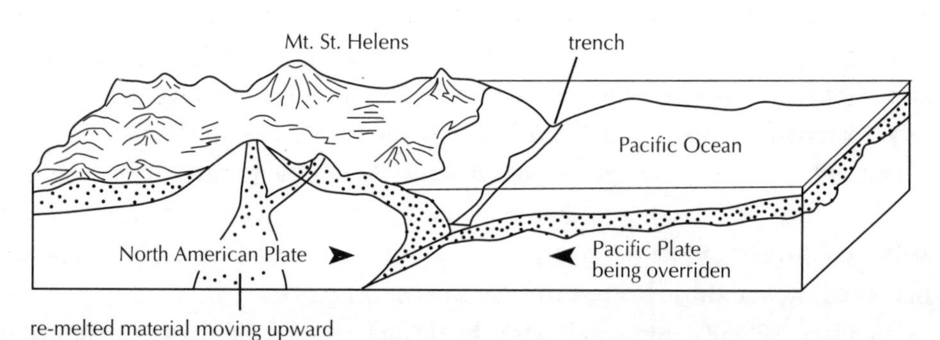

Other processes on the Earth's surface and immediately below it also transform minerals from one form into another. Lavas and other magmas weather when exposed at the surface, and become *sedimentary* rocks like sandstone and limestone. Many minerals in the lavas are broken down chemically to recrystallize as new minerals, when they combine with the weathering products of yet other minerals.

Because the surface of the earth is in constant motion, there is frequently flexing and bending of rock layers. Mountains can be thrust up, or other layers can be bent down and buried. Sometimes buried rocks are semi-melted and, while not totally melted to become new lavas, they become sufficiently hot to recrystallize, yielding minerals such as garnet (Plate 2), staurolite and mica. These rocks are called *metamorphic* rocks. Eventually sedimentary and metamorphic rocks are drawn back under the crust to be fully remelted. In this manner the physical body of the Earth continually renews itself: mineral matter constantly dying in the melting pot of the Earth's interior, to be reborn as new minerals in the womb of volcanoes, or intruded into other rock layers beneath the surface to become granite or other coarsely crystalline rocks, to weather to become the new minerals of sedimentary or metamorphic rocks – to eventually be remelted to start the cycle all over again.

Figure 5: The lifecycle of the Earth's surface

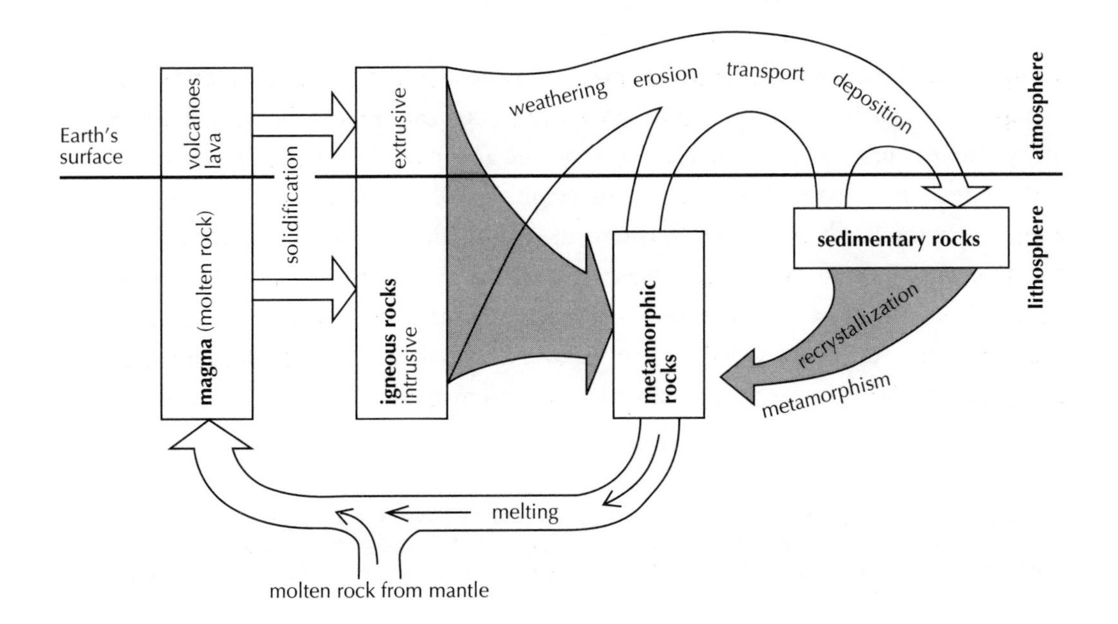

There is a parallel in your own body. If you are over 30, for the most part you do not have the same body you were born with. Your skin renews itself every seven years; other organs take greater or lesser amounts of time. But by the time you are 30, there are few cells left that are 'originals'.

The birth–life–death–rebirth cycle is recharged with new material on both the Earth and Moon (and presumably on other planets and moons too) as tons of cosmic dust in the form of micrometeorites are added each year. One estimate suggests that as much as a third of the Earth's diameter has been built up in this manner since it was formed. Although this process is not visually obvious on the Earth (with the exception of in a few places, like the meteor crater in Arizona), the recent cratering of the Moon shows that the process still continues.[1] Moon-quakes still occur too, indicating that while the surface is 'lifeless' in the conventional sense, the Moon is far from 'dead'.

Birth from the solar nebulae; life as rocks and minerals; death in remelting; birth in recrystallization: it is in this way that the life of the Mineral Kingdom express itself as part of the living body of the Earth. It is within this context that minerals and their crystals form.

CRYSTALS AND MINERALS

To recap what was said earlier in Chapter 2: a *mineral* is a chemical substance that is part of the Earth. It is not generated by any biological process. So, the name of any particular mineral is nothing more than the name of that particular chemical when it occurs as part of the Earth. For example, when aluminium and oxygen combine in the Earth as a mineral, the resulting mineral is called corundum (Plate 6). When silicon and oxygen are combined in the Earth, that chemical is called quartz (Plate 15). When sulphur and iron are combined in the Earth, that chemical is called pyrite (or 'Fool's Gold' – Plate 5). Every time there is a different chemical composition, the mineral that results has a different name. So, if we add a bit of

[1] You can collect micrometeorites yourself. Place a large plastic dish or bowl on a rooftop or other high place and put a brick in it to keep it from blowing away. After a couple of weeks, go through the detritus in the bowl with a magnetized needle. There are likely to be one or two small spheres clinging to it – micro-meteorites.

water to the silicon and oxygen above, the mineral is no longer quartz: it is now called opal. As previously said, there are approximately 2,500 different minerals, each of which is chemically distinct from all the others.

A *crystal* is a mineral whose atoms have arranged themselves in very precise patterns and, as a result of those precise patterns, occur in geometric forms, such as cubes, octahedrons, etc.

As we see, crystals are rather special conditions of minerals. What makes them useful to us we will discover in Chapter 4. Only a very small percentage of any particular mineral will actually manifest itself as crystals. For example, perhaps only a thousandth of 1 per cent of quartz will be found as crystals – the remainder will just be whitish lumps. Likewise, a similar percentage of pyrite might be found as distinct crystals – the remainder is just a brassy-looking mass.

There is another state in which minerals are found, *crystalline*. In this state, the patterns of atoms have formed as in crystals, but there has been no opportunity for the external geometric forms to develop.

All crystals are formed from solutions; i.e., something solid dissolved in something liquid. The liquid may be very fluid water carrying dissolved minerals coursing through cracks in other rocks, or it may be very thick and viscous magma, the consistency of putty. In either case, to varying degrees the atoms are free to move about and attach themselves in patterns that are consistent with their atomic attractiveness for one another.

At certain temperatures and pressures several atoms may be attracted to one another and yet other atoms will have no interest in them whatever. The other atoms, however, will be attracted to one another, and they will begin to form a different mineral at exactly the same time and place. This is why several minerals can form simultaneously, such as the minerals feldspar, quartz and mica, the three main constituents of the rock granite. They form more or less simultaneously, and because they form simultaneously they tend to grow into one another, forming interlocking grains. Each has formed its own inner pattern, but, because there was no space available for faces to develop, no crystals have formed. The mineral grains which make up granite, then, are crystalline.

In other instances, where liquid is flowing through some sort of hollow space (usually a fracture in pre-existing rocks), there is open space, and the geometric forms begin to develop. Unless the crack (called a 'vein') fills itself up entirely with mineral matter, there will be a hollow where crystals have formed. The majority of crystals that we will be using as tools have formed in this manner.

Let's now look in more detail at the rocks and rock-types that are the breeding ground for crystals – those exquisite products of the life-process of the planet itself.

THE ENVIRONMENTS OF CRYSTAL GROWTH

As part of our study of the environments in which crystals form, we shall also look at the accumulations of crystallized minerals that form major structural components of the Earth's crust. And therein we have the scientific definition of the word *rock*. By definition, a rock is composed of one or more minerals, and rocks are a major component of the crust. Although most rocks are mixtures of two or more minerals, if a single mineral exists on a large enough scale, it may also be considered a rock, in that it is an integral part of the structure of the Earth. A common example of a rock composed of only one mineral is limestone, made from the mineral calcite (Plate 5). A rock familiar to most readers, granite, is composed of at least three minerals: quartz, feldspar and mica. The actual name a rock is given in geology depends on both its mineral content and the size of its crystals.

Rocks form in three basic environments: *igneous, metamorphic* and *sedimentary*. The environments in which these three different types of rocks form provide us with different growing environments for crystals, with certain minerals and crystals associated with each environment. Briefly, igneous rock is formed from molten rock, sedimentary rock through the depositions of wind and water, and metamorphic rock is formed through changes in other types of rock through heat and pressure, and which does not involve full remelting.

Igneous Rock

The origin of igneous rock is deep within the Earth and it forms from a body of molten rock called a *magma*. Within the deep crust these magmas are probably not molten as we would think of the term, but exist in what is called a *plastic* state, having a consistency and strength similar to that of thick honey. Due to the shifting of the continents, zones of weakness and cracks occur in the overlying rocks, releasing the magma's pressure; it is this release of pressure that allows the temperature of the magma to rise, and for it to become sufficiently molten to flow upward through these cracks.

As the magma rises, it continues upwards through the cracks and out onto the

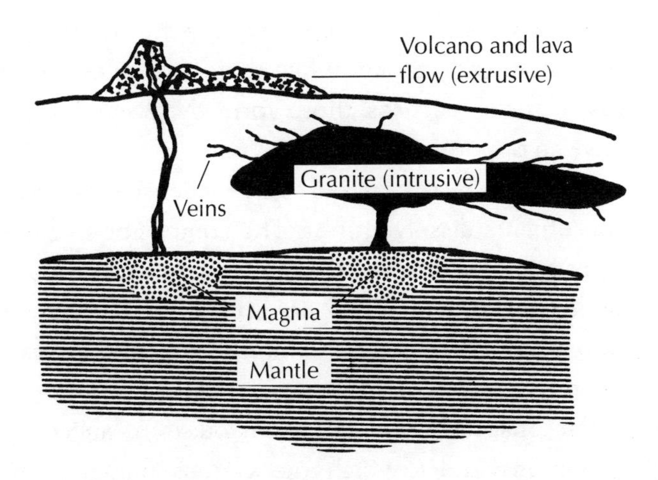

Figure 6: Extrusive and intrusive rocks

surface of the Earth as a volcanic eruption (if there is plenty of gas in the magma to propel it upward), or as a lava flow (if there is not). Such rocks are said to be extruded onto the surface and are therefore called *extrusive rocks*. Alternatively, before reaching the surface, the magma may reach a point within another, much cooler, rock layer where it solidifies without reaching the surface. These types of igneous rock are known as *intrusive rocks*, because they have intruded or forced their way into other existing rocks.

This process has been going on since the creation of the Earth and igneous rocks are being formed in the same way today as they have been during the long history of our planet. We know that there are numerous active volcanoes throughout the world – certainly the signs of the most obvious types of igneous activity – but the action of intrusion is much slower and, being below the surface of the Earth, is quite invisible to us. Few people may realize that as they are reading this book, they may be sitting on top of intrusive rocks that are forming crystals at this very instant.

Since intrusive rocks cool much more slowly than extrusive rocks (due to the insulating effects of the rocks surrounding them), there is a great deal more time for crystals to form, and intrusive rocks generally are made of large and well-formed crystals. Extrusive rocks, on the other hand, since they lose their heat to the atmosphere rather rapidly, tend to cool quickly, and form only small crystals (generally less than 1 mm in size).

Crystals making up intrusive rocks often do not take the forms illustrated in the later chapters, however, because as the intrusive rocks form, the crystals tend to inter-grow with one another. It is only when there are hollow spaces within the crystallizing intrusive rocks, such as those formed by gas bubbles, that well-formed crystals have an opportunity to form.

The igneous magma may be considered as a very dense solution, with all of the various atomic constituents dissolved in it. The composition of the magma will determine in large part the character of the minerals which compose the resulting rocks. The following constitute about 99 per cent of the elements present in the crust of the Earth: oxygen, silicon, aluminium, iron, magnesium, calcium, sodium and potassium, in that order. These elements occur in varying proportions in igneous rocks and the constituent minerals of igneous rocks are composed of these elements. The conditions under which the various minerals are formed are complex, but generally speaking, they crystallize from the cooling magma in the order of solubility. Although this order is fairly definite, the variations in chemical composition of the magma will affect the degree of solubility of the various mineral constituents, and thus the order of their crystallization can be altered. The presence of small amounts of substances such as water vapour, carbon dioxide, fluorine gas and sulphur will also greatly influence the temperatures at which various minerals crystallize. As all of these additional substances will be present in magma in varying amounts, the crystallizing temperatures can vary considerably.

It has been shown that unless substances such as water vapour or carbon dioxide are present, crystals will not form at all. It has been demonstrated that minerals like quartz and feldspar can rarely be formed from dry fusion, i.e., without the presence of some of these extra gases. When it is attempted, uncrystallized glasses result. But, in the presence of only a fraction of a percentage of water vapour, excellent crystals will form. These additional substances are called *mineralizers*.

A type of igneous activity that concerns us even more than the formation of large rock-bodies are those crystals that form from the high-temperature hot water solutions left over when magmas have crystallized. When the molten rock cools and solidifies, large quantities of liquid and gas charged with mineral matter are given off. Leaving the igneous rocks behind them, they make their way slowly towards the surface of the crust through cracks in the surrounding rock, forming mineral deposits wherever conditions are favourable. Thus, lower temperatures, reduced pressures, and the presence of limestone or other easily altered rocks, are conducive to the deposition of certain types of crystals.

As these mineral-laden solutions flow into natural cracks in other rocks, crystals form. The solutions filling these fissures often contain such metals as copper, lead, gold, silver and zinc, and it is from such filled-in fissures – called veins – that almost all of our precious metals originate, and many of the other economically important ones (see Figure 6).

There is one type of vein in particular that is of interest to us, as the crystals from such veins are usually well-formed and often quite large. This type of vein is called a *pegmatite* (Plate 12) and is characterized by its large crystals. Single crystals from such veins have been recorded up to 12 metres in length, and crystals of 30 cm or more are not all that uncommon. Pegmatites are normally associated with the formation of granites, and the basic crystals that form in them – now that there is open space – are the major minerals of granite: quartz, feldspar and mica. All three minerals are often present in pegmatites, but it is not unusual to find one made up entirely of quartz or feldspar.

In pegmatites, there is a flow of hot water solution (several hundred degrees centigrade and under great pressure) carrying the dissolved components of the various minerals; as the solution flows through the vein, the crystals form as linings, each crystal forming one layer of atoms at a time. In a typical pegmatite, the first crystals deposited will be feldspars, followed by a layer of quartz, and then by mica crystals.

The next stage of crystallization in a pegmatite depends on which metals are present in the solution. If the metal zirconium is present, then zircons form (Plate 16). If beryllium is present, the mineral beryl forms (the blue variety of which is aquamarine, the green variety emerald – Plates 7, 10). If fluorine is present, either the mineral fluorite (Plate 5) may form or, under certain conditions, topaz (Plates 3, 19); if boron is present, tourmaline may form (Plates 3, 12, 18); or, if various combinations of calcium, magnesium, manganese or iron are present, garnet may form. Quite clearly, such veins are of vital interest to the student of crystals. Figure 7 shows a hypothetical pegmatite.

In these veins, crystals always grow to fill the largest space available, even if they have to grow at a considerable angle to the vein wall. Some such crystals will grow almost sideways. If a crystal grows directly opposite another crystal where their points would meet if they grew towards each other, both will grow diagonally to miss each other.

Other igneous crystals grow from vapour, being mainly confined to volcanic regions, where mineralized gases are escaping through vents. Minerals deposited in this way are sulphur, realgar and hematite.

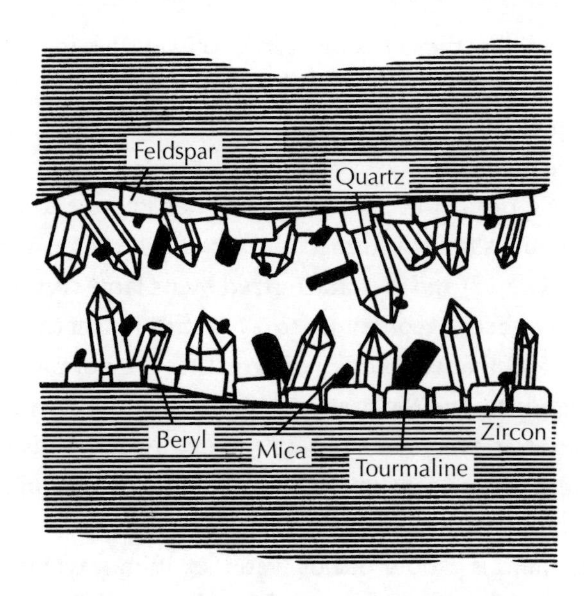

Figure 7: Diagram of a hypothetical pegmatite

Metamorphic Rocks

Metamorphic rocks are formed from either igneous, sedimentary or even other metamorphic rocks, and have undergone some sort of physical or chemical change after their original formation. This change is brought about by high temperatures and pressures, aided by the action of water vapour and other chemical agents. The temperatures and pressures are insufficient to melt the rocks, but there is enough movement of atoms to bring about the adding or subtracting of constituents to or from the existing minerals, and may involve the formation of entirely new minerals that are more stable under the new geologic conditions. Although many of the original minerals may continue to exist, there are others that characteristically are developed during the process of metamorphism, like kyanite, staurolite, talc and grossularite garnet (a green garnet).

Figure 8a shows how such a process can take place. In this instance, a layer of alumina- (aluminium oxide) rich clay is formed in a shallow inland sea. It has been covered over by a layer of sand, and eventually by layer upon layer of sand and gravel, as the area in which the lake existed gradually sank because of deformation of the Earth's crust. Eventually the pressure and temperature caused by the deep burial rose to the point where the alumina (Al_2O_3) began to recrystallize, to form hexagonal crystals of the mineral corundum (sapphire and ruby – Plate 6).

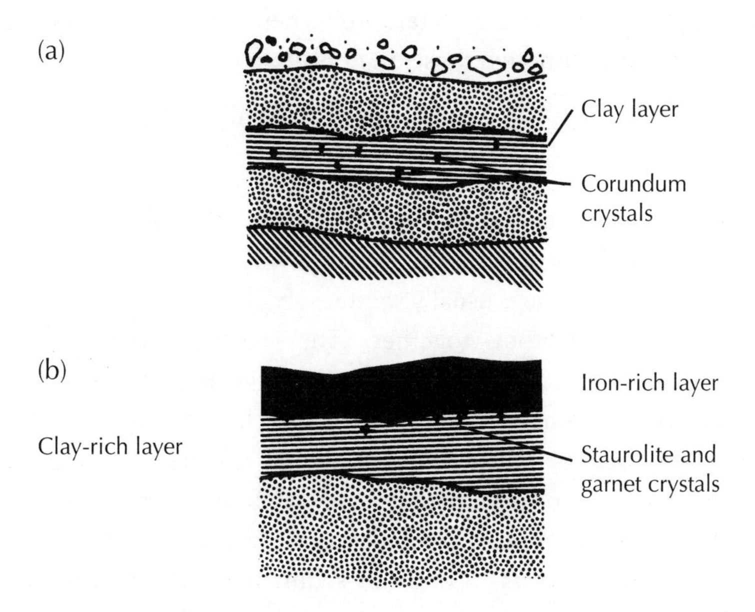

Figure 8: Crystals forming in metamorphic rocks

In Figure 8b this same alumina-rich layer has had another, clay layer deposited on top of it, but this time the overlying clay was rich in iron oxide. Here the temperatures and pressures were high enough to allow the atoms of iron to become highly mobile, as were the atoms of alumina in Figure 8a. As silicas are also available from the clay, all of these available atoms rearrange themselves to form the mineral staurolite ($FeAl_4Si_2O_{10}(OH)_2$ – Figure 23, page 57).

There are several minerals which occur in metamorphic rocks that also occur in igneous rocks, such as garnet, spinel (Plates 9, 17) and corundum. It can be seen that where igneous and metamorphic rocks are concerned, the basic chemical processes take place at a high temperature and pressure, and in many instances the dividing line between them is rather thin.

There is another type of metamorphic environment, called *contact metamorphism*. This occurs when an igneous body has been intruded into a surrounding rock, causing heating and remelting of the surrounding rock, and where gases of the igneous body have escaped into the surrounding rocks. If the metamorphosed rock happens to be limestone, there are a number of minerals which can form through the recrystallization of the limestone in combination with mineral constituents of the intruding materials. Again, garnets can form, along with spinel, corundum and pyroxene. Contact metamorphic deposits can also produce tourmaline, topaz and fluorite, although these do not often occur.

Sedimentary Rock

This type of rock is formed through the processes of wind and water. Crystals which form in these types of rocks are almost always formed from low temperature water solutions and are usually quite soft (because of the low energies involved in bonding the atoms together). These crystals appear to form quite rapidly, and in some places where crystals are regularly dug out of quicksand deposits, new crystals form within about a year. These are the so-called 'Desert Roses', which are multiple crystals of the mineral selenite (crystalline gypsum – Plate 10). Another common sedimentary mineral found in extensive deposits is halite (rock salt), which is often found in deposits hundreds of metres thick. But by far the most common mineral formed in sedimentary environments is calcite, which forms the rock limestone. Another commercially important sedimentary mineral is barite (or barytes – Plate 10), which forms beautiful blue crystals somewhat resembling aquamarine.

How long does it actually take for most crystals to form? For the most part, we simply do not know. In the laboratory, quartz crystals several centimetres in length can be grown in a matter of weeks, and it is possible that in nature such crystals may form almost as rapidly.

To grow a transparent crystal of several centimetres requires constant growing conditions – few changes in temperature or pressure. In a natural environment, stable conditions over a long period (say a year) are most unlikely, and so we would expect most crystals to form over a much shorter period – certainly not the millions of years previously thought. In Chapter 4 we take a closer look at crystal formation, and the forms crystals take.

MINERALS AND CRYSTALS

For a parallel to the lessons of atomic theory . . . [we must look to] those kinds of epistemological problems with which thinkers like the Buddha and Lao Tzu have been confronted, when trying to harmonize our position as spectators and actors in the great drama of existence.

Niels Bohr, discoverer of the electron

In this chapter we look at how a crystal forms and the forms crystals take, as well as the system for classifying the minerals which form crystals. It is divided into three sections, covering each one of these topics.

I – BUILDING A CRYSTAL

It is only within the last hundred years or so that man has begun to understand how and why crystals form. Much of the knowledge we now have about them has been dependent on other sciences, such as chemistry and physics, providing us with the method and means of study. Because crystals are naturally occurring chemical compounds, the ordinary laws of chemistry and physics apply – a fact which becomes very important when we try to discover what they really can and cannot do as tools of healing and enlightenment.

Crystal formation is based entirely on the atom and the behaviour of its electrons. Yet, the atom itself was not accepted as a reality until about 1803, the electron was not discovered until 1898, and the neutron was not discovered until the 1930s. Thus, we can see the monumental amount of work, supported by some extraordinarily intuitive insights about the nature of matter, that has led to the modern study of mineralogy. Until the turn of the 20th century the study of crystals was based almost entirely on their physical forms, which led to some remarkably correct guesses about their internal structure.

The Atom

The first thing to remember is that there is no such thing as *an* atom. There is no way to isolate one atom from the rest of the universe. Every single atom exists as a series of interactions at various levels with literally every other atom in the universe. Thus 'an atom' may have the same number of protons, neutrons and electrons as another atom, but because it is physically impossible for it to occupy exactly the same space as its 'identical' counterpart, it is in some subtle way acted upon differently than any other atom physically like itself. Like snowflakes, no two atoms are exactly the same. As we will discover, the atom is made of nothing but energy in a complex series of relationships.

It is only within the last decades that we have begun to understand the inner workings of atoms. There is a huge amount yet to learn about what an atom actually is, but at least as far as crystallography is concerned, we know how it works, even if we are still uncertain about why it works. In this section we will look at the mechanics of how atoms attach themselves to each other. This is an essential part of what makes a crystal a crystal, and how the crystal relates to energy. Virtually every response we experience when involved with crystals relates directly to its atomic arrangement, and hence its atomic bonding – the way in which the atoms are interconnected. Although the explanations herein are much simplified, the essentials are covered in sufficient detail to understand crystal energies, and to understand too the myths and realities about them discussed in the following chapters.

An atom is made up of dozens of building blocks, but the major components which concern us here are protons, neutrons and electrons. Protons and neutrons are about the same weight and form the central portion of the atom, called the nucleus. The proton has a positive electrical charge; the neutrons are electrically neutral. Electrons are tiny particles with a negative electrical charge. Electrons circle the nucleus at relatively great distances; they like to travel in pairs, and arrange themselves in specific layers (called 'shells') around the nucleus, rather like the layers of an onion. Each shell consists of a specific level of energy. Electrons do not move freely from shell to shell: only when their energy is increased or decreased by a specific amount, called a 'quantum' (which is always a multiple of the energy of a photon of light). Electrons can only move from one shell to another; they cannot be 'between', just as we cannot step up half a rung on a ladder.

The shells fill with electrons from the centre outwards, and each shell can only have a maximum of eight electrons in it. When it is filled, then the next shell fills, and so on until the positive charges of the nucleus are exactly balanced by the negative charges of the electrons. The outermost shell may not be completely filled – unless the protons in the nucleus are a multiple of eight – and because the energy shells become weaker the further from the nucleus they are, they can sometimes lose or gain electrons. Also, if the number of protons in the nucleus is an odd number, then one of the outermost electrons will be unpaired. It is the outermost shells of electrons that are of the most interest to us, because it is within these shells that the relationships form between atoms that connect them to one another, and which ultimately create crystals.

Although protons, neutrons and electrons are the building blocks of matter, they in turn are made up of even smaller particles, such as quarks, neutrinos and mesons – and lots more. The smaller the particles become, the more difficult it is to tell them from pure energy – whatever that is. These particles are incredibly small, and some of them pass through 'solid' matter as if it wasn't there at all. Neutrinos are amongst the smallest, and several million have passed through your body while you read this sentence. Then they continued on, right through the

Figure 9: The atom

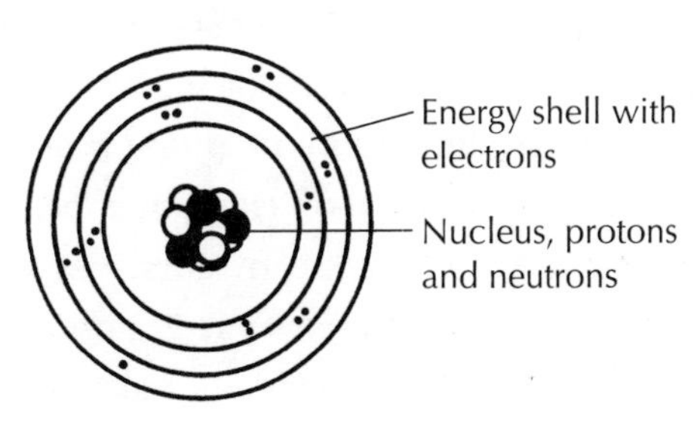

Earth and right out the other side – without hitting anything. Your body will be 'hit' by a neutrino only a few times in your entire lifetime.

The question that then arises is how solid is 'solid' matter? Let's take a closer look at the 'solidity' of the atom. Although atoms tend to behave as if they are solid little balls, they are anything but. If the nucleus of an average-sized atom was the size of a golf ball, then all the electrons combined would be smaller than a mote of dust, and the outer ones would be circling at a distance of three miles. Thus 'solid' matter is mostly empty space. In fact, if all the empty space was squeezed out of your body, you would occupy far less space than a grain of sand. So, what is 'matter'? Mostly empty space. Bits of energy held in place by more energy. Matter is another form of energy. Just like the mystics have been saying for thousands of years: it is all energy.

Matter can take three forms: solid, liquid or gas, depending upon the conditions it finds itself in. In a gas, the atoms are only weakly connected, move about at random, and are in no particular arrangement. In a liquid the connections are stronger, but not enough to lock the atoms into place. In certain liquids the atoms are relatively inactive, and although they are not arranged in a pattern, the liquid is thick enough to behave as a solid. Window glass is such a liquid, and very old glass that has been in place for a long period actually shows signs of flowing.

In a solid the atoms are strongly attached to each other, and are locked into place by their mutually interacting electrons. When the atoms form very precise and repeating patterns, the matter is said to be crystalline; when that inner pattern is repeated in the matter's external form, it is a crystal.

Bonding

Bonding is the term given to the manner in which atoms connect themselves to each other. The type of bond determines the pattern of the atoms, thus the structure and form of the crystal. This in turn determines, at some very subtle level, how the crystal mirrors – as later chapters reveal – and what the crystal can and cannot do with energy. With the exception of a very few liquids that take on crystalline properties under certain conditions (known as 'liquid crystals' – thin layers of liquid placed between sheets of glass that become crystalline when electrically stimulated), we need only concern ourselves with the solid state of matter in our discussion of crystals. However it is important to remember that both gasses and liquids also crystallize under the right conditions, and that they are in their gas or liquid state only because of the conditions on the Earth. Water, for example, when found on the outer planets such as Jupiter or Neptune, is a solid harder than steel on the Earth.

The force that attaches atoms to each other is referred to as the 'bond', and the process of connection is called bonding. There are three basic types of bonding: metallic, ionic and covalent. The *metallic* bond is the simplest and the weakest. The electrons of a metal move freely from atom to atom effectively forming a cloud, and hold the nuclei in place in a semi-rigid structure. This is why metal can be bent and formed without breaking. Under stress the electrons are 'herded' around the stress points, leaving the nuclei free to change positions. This is the type of bond found in the mineral group called the Native Metals: copper, gold, silver, and so on. These metals and the others of the group form crystals, but they are easily distorted.

The next type of bond is the *ionic* bond. An ion is an atom that has either an excess number of electrons or has missing electrons. This can come about because of the environmental conditions the atoms find themselves in: conditions that add or subtract energy from the atoms. In the Earth these are essentially heat and pressure. Figure 10 shows a crystal formed from ions – a crystal of the mineral halite (table salt). The sodium atoms are missing one electron (and so have a positive charge, $Na+$), and the chlorine atoms have one spare electron ($Cl–$). As the atoms of these two elements come into contact, the extra electron from the chlorine atoms pop over to the sodium atoms, and an attraction is created.

Ionic bonding is quite strong, but because the atoms are arranged in regular layers, the layers themselves are not necessarily well bonded to each other, and ionic crystals are often quite brittle. When they break, they break in flat surfaces in parallel with the atomic layers. The pattern of how a mineral breaks is referred to as its cleavage. How flat these surfaces can be is illustrated by the mineral fluorite

Figure 10: An ionic crystal

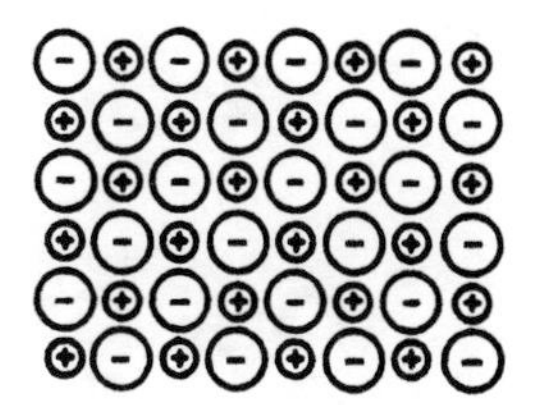

(Figure 23 shows a crystal of this), which is usually sold in octahedrons cleaved from the irregular cubic crystals in which it is usually found.

The third type of bonding is the *covalent* bond. The unpaired electrons or the electrons in the unfilled outer shells are referred to as the valence electrons, and the more electrons needed to fill the shell, the stronger the energy the atom exerts to try to fill its shells and balance itself perfectly. Thus the higher the valence, the more strongly a particular atom is attracted to others. We get a hint of this process of bonding by the name of the bond: co-valent. In this type of bond, the valence electrons are shared between adjoining atoms so that all of them get a chance to be in balance.

Looking at the atomic structure of quartz, made of silicon (Si) and oxygen (O), we can see how this works. In Figure 11a only the electrons in the outer shell are shown, and we see that in this shell the silicon atom has four electrons and the oxygen atom has six. If one oxygen atom moves to share electrons with one silicon atom (as in Figure 11b), one shell is filled. However, there are still two extra electrons because only eight are allowed in a shell at any one time. The problem is solved by the attraction of a second oxygen atom to use the surplus two silicon electrons, in Figure 11c.

It appears that the silicon is still a bit unbalanced, but this is remedied by attaching the whole structure to adjoining structures just like itself. In the end product the oxygen to silicon ratio is 2:1, giving us the chemical formula for quartz, SiO_2. We can also see from this exactly what causes crystals to have a precisely repeating structure. Crystals are built up, or 'form', or 'grow', by identical groups of atoms hooking themselves to each other in and endlessly repetitive pattern. Quartz is a relatively simple structure, but when a number of different

Figure 11: The formation of a quartz molecule

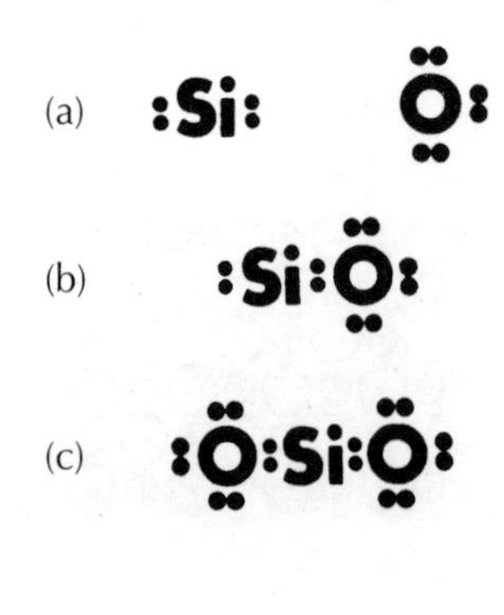

elements are present, there are some very complex ways of hooking together the structures they create. But what is it, precisely, that makes it a crystal?

The standard textbook definition from James White Dana's *Manual of Minerology* is that a crystal is a regular polyhedral form, bounded by smooth faces, and which is assumed by a chemical compound under the action of its interatomic forces, when passing, under suitable conditions, from the state of a liquid or gas to that of a solid.

Let's take this apart. First, it has to be in a 'regular geometric form'; that is, it has to come in a form or combination of forms that are, in some way, out of a geometry text – prisms, pyramids, etc. It is unstated, but these forms must obviously be three-dimensional. Next, it has to have 'smooth faces'. This really means 'flat', although irregularities are very common in crystal faces, But these irregularities are always repetitions of the flat, smooth faces that are attempting to form. Next, a crystal has to be a 'chemical compound'. This means that it has a definite chemical composition, and that for a crystal of the same mineral, the chemical composition is always the same.

Let's pause here and review the definition of a mineral. Simply, a mineral is a chemical substance found in nature. A chemist calls SiO_2 silicon dioxide. When it is found in nature, a mineralogist calls it quartz. To a chemist TiO_2 is titanium dioxide; to a mineralogist when found in nature it is the mineral rutile. If it is not SiO_2 then it is not quartz; if it is not TiO_2 then it is not rutile. It is some other mineral. Thus when its chemistry changes, it becomes a different mineral.

So, our crystal has a definite chemical composition and it is bounded by geometrically arranged, flat faces. If we take a lump of rose quartz and grind flat faces on it in the shape of a quartz crystal (as is often done), does it become a crystal? Absolutely not. The flat faces must result from the 'interatomic forces' within, not from the actions of a lapidary without. Dana's definition tells us more: that crystals occur under 'suitable' conditions, when passing from the state of a gas or a liquid into a solid. Thus we know that in some way crystals form from a gas or liquid solution of some kind, and that conditions must be 'suitable'; for example, a hollow space in a vein, or in a thick magma where the crystals are suspended until the whole magma solidifies. In fact, the majority of conditions that create minerals are decidedly unsuitable for creating crystals. Crystals are a relatively uncommon form of minerals.

From these definitions, it is clear that a crystal is always a mineral, but that not all minerals are crystals. If a mineral has no external crystal form and its atoms are not regularly arranged, it is said to be 'massive'. If it has a regular atomic structure but no flat faces, it is said to be 'crystalline'. If it has a more or less distinct crystalline structure that cannot be resolved into individual crystals, it is said to be 'crypto-crystalline'.

A look at the mineral quartz demonstrates all of these terms. Quartz is a mineral because it occurs in nature, is inorganic and has a definite chemical composition (one atom of silicon to two atoms of oxygen, SiO_2). The type of the mineral quartz known as rose quartz is massive in form, because it does not usually have flat faces; but it does have a regular atomic structure, making it crystalline.The type of the mineral quartz known as agate is also a massive form, composed of millions of microscopic crystalline bits, but which are not individual crystals. It is crypto-crystalline. It is only when we come to varieties of the mineral quartz such as rock crystal, amethyst, citrine, etc., that we find crystals; that is, although they are chemically identical to the massive forms (i.e., the chemical formula is still SiO_2), they take forms that have a regular atomic structure and flat faces arranged in geometric patterns.

II – FORMS

One of the earliest discoveries about crystals was that the angles between adjacent corresponding faces in a given crystal are the same for every crystal of that mineral and are characteristic of that mineral. This is called the Law of Constancy of Inter-facial Angles. To measure these angles instruments called goniometers were invented – little more than the simple plastic protractors schoolchildren use to measure angles in their geometry classes. Later, complex and highly accurate reflecting goniometers, resembling surveyors' instruments, were devised. Using data from instruments such as these, and the newly forming theories regarding atomic structure, by the turn of the 20th century certain predictions were being made regarding the spacing and arrangement of atoms in the crystal structures.

The exact internal arrangement of atoms in any given mineral in order to make it a crystal, depends on several things. As we saw, atomic balance is the first of these: whether as ionic, covalent, or metallic bonding. Second, how atoms are attached depends on their size. Size, in turn, relates to how many electron shells are filled. Thus 'heavy' atoms with lots of protons and hence lots of electrons, are larger than 'lighter' atoms with fewer of both. As a consequence, certain atoms just don't 'fit' together. When a large variety of atoms are present in melted rock or other liquid solutions, some atoms are simply not attracted to certain other atoms. But those atoms are in their own turn attracted to yet other atoms. As we saw with quartz, each chemical unit forms a definite arrangement with its atomic fellows; those arrangements are in turn connected to others like themselves. The old esoteric truism of 'like attracts like' begins even here. These fundamental arrangements, the smallest unit of which still retains the chemical and geometric properties of the mineral, is referred to as a 'unit cell'. The term, borrowed from biology, is not inappropriate: the cell is the basic building block of the living organism, just as it is the building block of the crystal. As we learned in Chapter 2, there are only 14 different cells in the whole of the Mineral Kingdom. As a comparison, in the organic kingdoms there are over half a million compounds of carbon alone.

The third parameter in forming a crystal is the unit cell from which it is created. Each mineral only has one type of unit cell; they do not mix. But, within the laws of electrical balance, there can be several ways to connect them to create different geometric forms. The simplest atomic arrangement is eight atoms whose centres occupy the corners of a cube (Figure 12a); it is called the simple cubic unit cell. There are two additional types of cubic unit cell, one with an additional atom in the centre of the cube (Figure 12b), and another with an additional atom in the

Figure 12: Three cubic unit cells

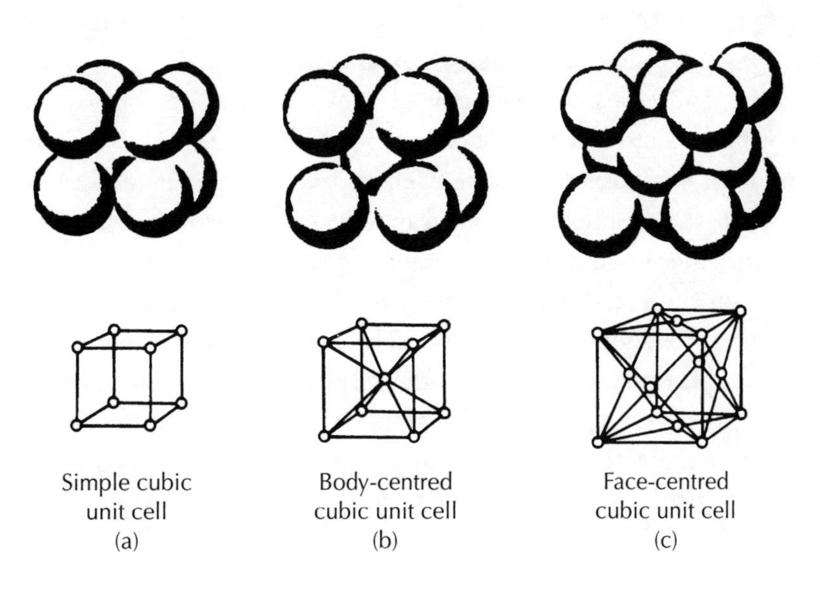

centre of each face (Figure 12c). Which of these cells forms for any particular mineral will be determined by the mineral's chemical makeup – the sizes and electrical potentials of the atoms involved. But in every case, the unit cell is nature's device for maintaining perfect electrical balance in three-dimensional space.

The three types of cubic unit cells are three of the fourteen possible unit cells that form minerals and crystals. As stated, each mineral or crystal of that mineral can only be made up from one type of cell. But, there are dozens of different crystal forms. How is this possible with only 14 cells? It is in how the cells are stacked up. However, in their stacking, the cells still have to maintain and repeat their basic structure and electrical balance; they cannot just be stacked any old way. Because the cubic cells give the largest number of possibilities, we will take a closer look at them.

In Figure 13a we see the simplest stacking of simple cubic unit cells – another cube. And, in nature, we find crystals that are perfect cubes! Pyrite ('Fool's Gold'), and halite (rock salt) are but two examples.

In Figure 13b simple cubic cells are stacked in the same way, but yield a different outer form – an octahedron. Whether simple cubic cells form a cube or an octahedron is dependent on the electrical balance of the atoms involved. Under slightly different geological conditions, which shift the balance slightly, pyrite can form octahedrons instead of cubes. There is even a third form which pyrite can take (again depending on conditions), called a pyritohedron by crystallographers, and a pentagonal dodecahedron in geometry (Figure 15). It is still made from simple cubic cells. Other minerals form both cubes and octahedrons depending on conditions: gold and fluorite are two examples.

The other two types of cubic unit cells can form more complex geometric forms. The body-centred cubic unit cell – the one with the extra atom in the centre – can link itself with other cells like itself in several ways: it can link corner-to-corner just like the simple cubes; or it can link centre-to-corner, where the centre atom becomes the corner atom of its adjoining cells, and its corner atoms become the centre atoms of those cells. In other words, the cells become interlinked. This interlinking can yield forms like the dodecahedrons commonly displayed in garnet crystals. The third type of cubic cell, the face-centred cell, can interlink in very complex ways to yield highly complex forms. Yet all of these forms will retain the basic geometric characteristics of the cubic cells from which they originate.

Crystals which form from unit cells with the same geometric properties are classed according to those properties. They are said to fall within the same Crystal

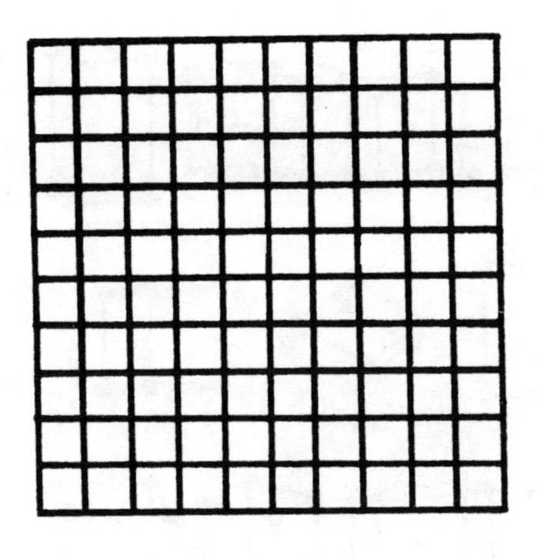

Figure 13a: Cubes stacked to form a cubic crystal
Figure 13b: Cubes stacked to form an octahedral crystal

System, of which there are only six. But before we look at the crystal systems, let's stay with atoms for a moment.

We have looked at three of the basic structures into which the constituents of a crystal arrange themselves – the cubic unit cells. The overall arrangement of multiples of a cell in three dimensions is called a *lattice*. In 1848 the French scientist Auguste Bravais demonstrated that there are only 14 different ways of forming regular arrangements of points in three-dimensional space. Although he was a mathematician, his arrangements proved prophetic: they are the exact arrangements atoms take when forming crystals. The crystal lattices are often referred to as Bravais lattices, and they are illustrated in Figure 14.

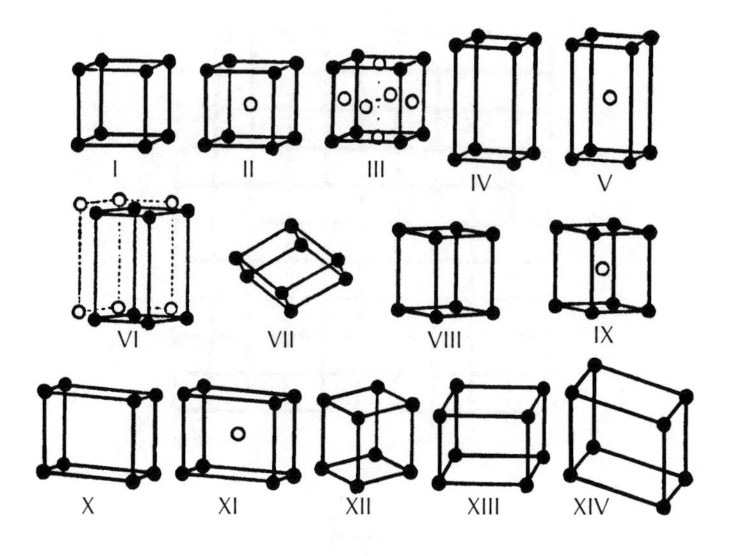

Figure 14: The 14 Bravais lattices

As we examine the Bravais lattices and the atoms that arrange themselves in those patterns to create crystals, we need to remember that the external form of the crystal is a perfect reflection of its inner form. Only when the newly discovered x-rays were directed at crystals in 1912 did the inner arrangement begin to reveal itself, and was, exactly as predicted, a perfect reflection of the outer form. It is, in many respects, a perfect example of the Law of Microcosm and Macrocosm: the universe reflects its basic patterns in all levels of itself. We just need the right tools to reveal it. As with the crystal, so it is with the inner Being of us all, of which crystals are a superb tool of revelation, as we shall see.

The Crystal Systems

It was mentioned earlier that the world-wide classification of crystals was the invention of James White Dana, in 1837. More data has been added since, but his original – and inspired – system is still the foundation of our understanding of the crystal processes.

Dana noticed that certain geometric properties of crystals – i.e., their symmetry, both by rotating the crystal and by putting imaginary planes through its centre – allowed him to sort crystals into six geometric categories. The first category is based on the cube. If you hold a cube in the thumb and forefinger in the

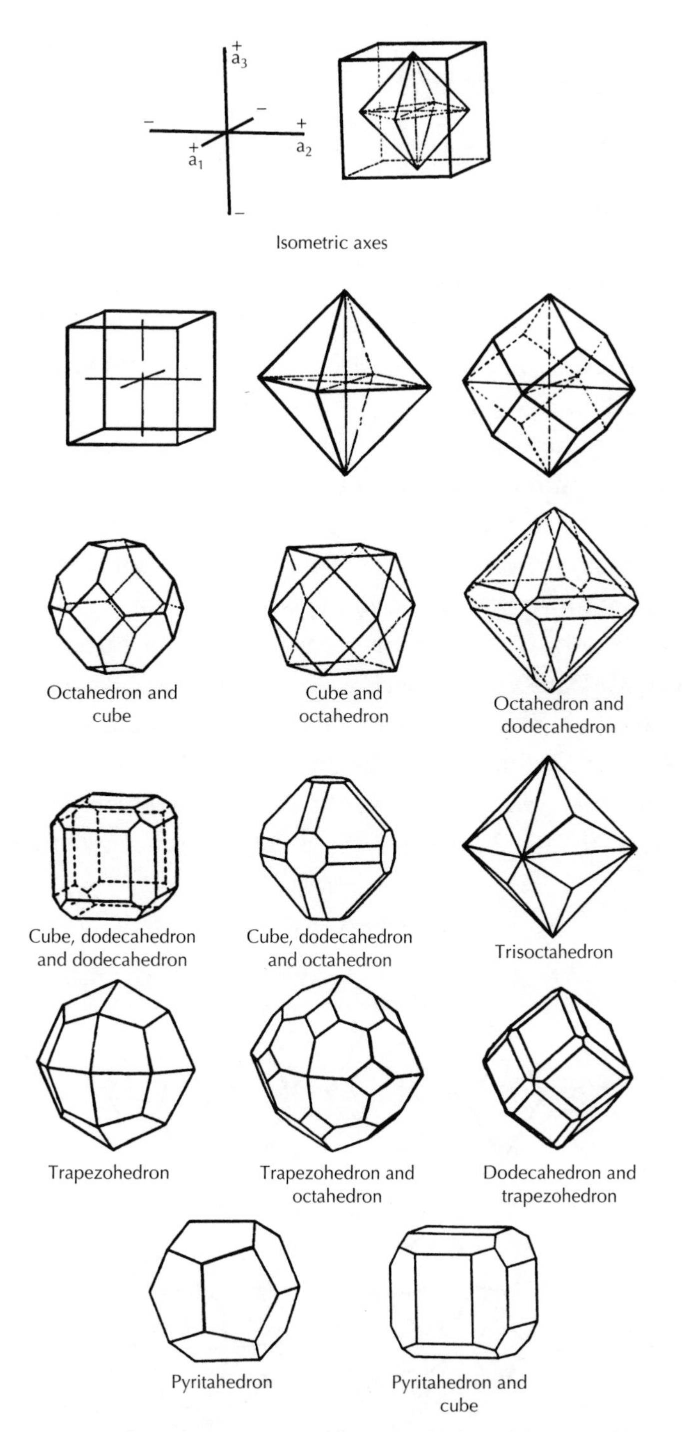

Figure 15: Isometric axes, basic isometric crystal forms, and a few of their possible combinations

centre of each of its three pairs of opposing faces, and rotate the cube through 90°, you see the same thing each time. Not only that but each of these axes of rotation are the same length.

In crystallography, this becomes the first crystal classification – the Isometric (a Latin word meaning equal-measure) system (which is also called the Regular or Cubic system). All crystals that have crystallographic axes of equal length at 90° to each other fall into the Isometric system. (The Isometric axes are shown in Figure 15, along with some of the Isometric crystals.) All crystals in the Isometric system also have a cubic unit cell (discovered long after Dana's system was devised) – cell numbers I, II or III in Figure 14.

Figure 15 shows how, in any individual mineral, any or all of the basic forms may be present, in various combinations. Sub-divisions in each system can also be made based on symmetry, although the unit cells are still the same and the crystallographic axes maintain their basic relationship to one another. Figure 16 shows the multiplicity of forms that can occur in just one mineral – garnet.

Having taken quite a few crystals from his box and placed them in the Isometric system, Mr Dana would then have turned to those crystals which remained and selected another group, discovering that, in this particular group, the crystallographic axes were still at 90° to one another, but that one axis was longer or shorter than the other two, which were still of equal length. In this system, the axes of equal length are labelled 'a–a' (as in the Isometric system), but the axis of

Figure 16: Garnet crystals

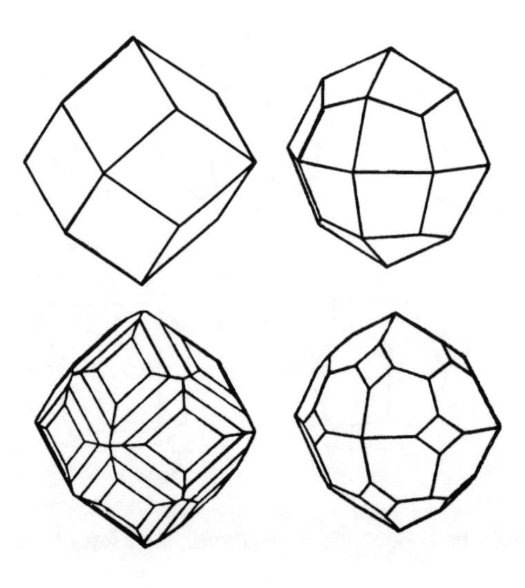

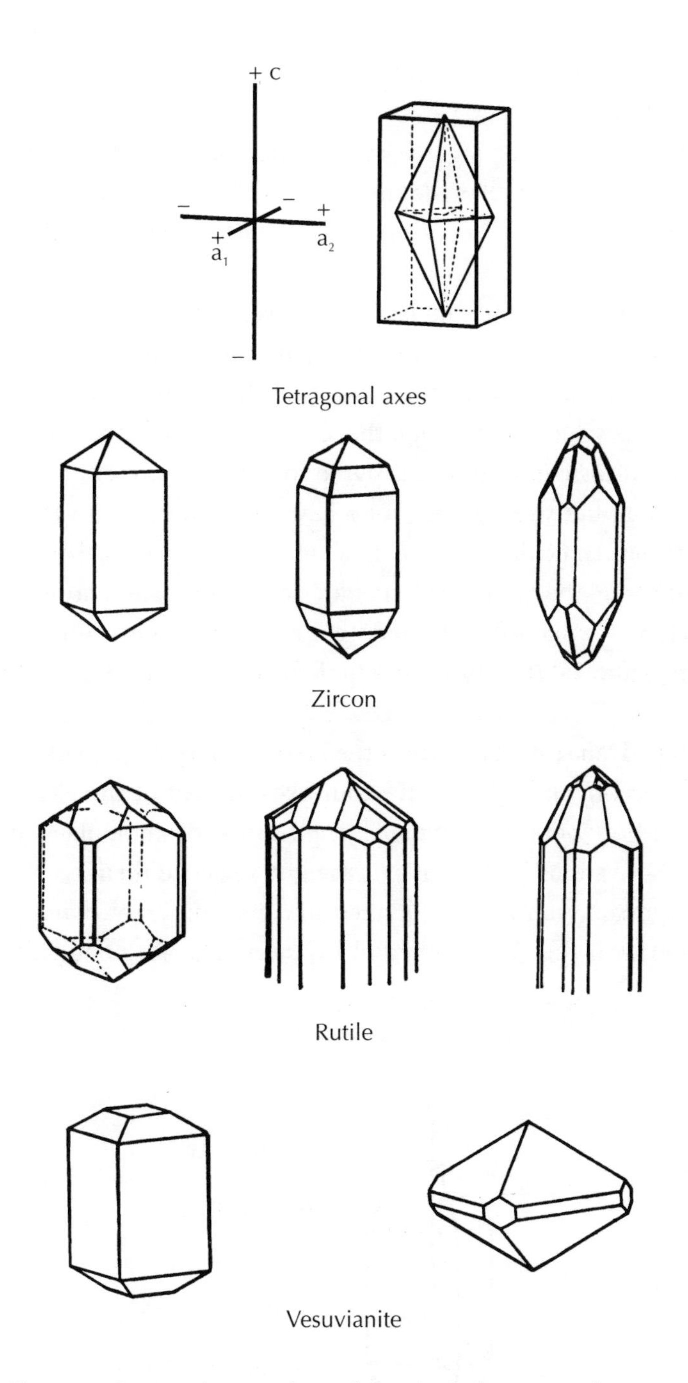

Figure 17: Tetragonal axes and crystals forming in the tetragonal system

differing length is called the 'c' axis (see Figure 17). This classification is called the Tetragonal system.

The unit cells of the Tetragonal system are Bravais lattice cells IV and V in Figure 14. It is easily seen that the unit cells of the Tetragonal system are square in section, and elongated. The Tetragonal crystals in Figure 17 all have a similar appearance.

All crystal systems beyond the Isometric system have a 'c' axis, and it is on the basis of this axis that crystal faces are given particular names. A crystal face parallel to the 'c' axis is called a prism face, and such faces are generally rectangular in appearance. Faces which cut through the 'c' axis are called pyramid faces, and they are often triangular in appearance. If pyramid faces are present at differing angles to the 'c' axis, all but the last face may have their points cut off, or 'truncated'. Faces that are perpendicular to the 'c' axis are called pinacoids. The combination of faces that makes up the 'point' of a crystal is called the termination.

Pinacoid faces are shown at the very 'point' of the termination of the beryl crystal shown in Figure 19. If a crystal has 'points' at both ends it is said to be double terminated.

James White Dana's next system is the Hexagonal system, made up of unit cells VI to IX (Figure 14), and which have four axes instead of three. In this instance, there are three horizontal axes of equal lengths in a common plane, intersecting at angles of 60°, and a fourth, vertical axis at right angles to them.

The Hexagonal system is sub-divided into two different divisions, the Hexagonal division, and the Rhombohedral division. The Rhombohedral division is

Figure 18: The names of crystal faces

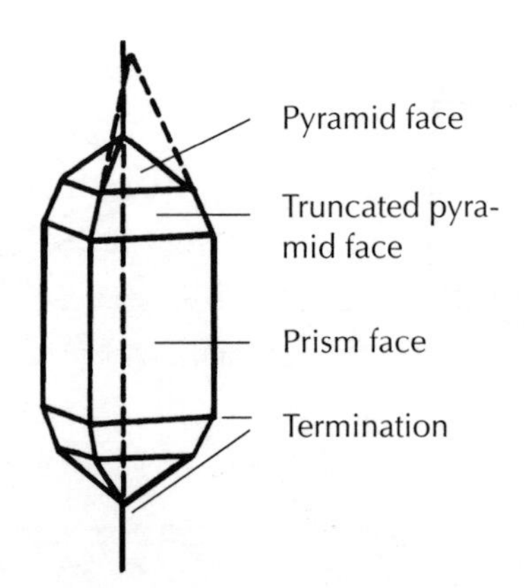

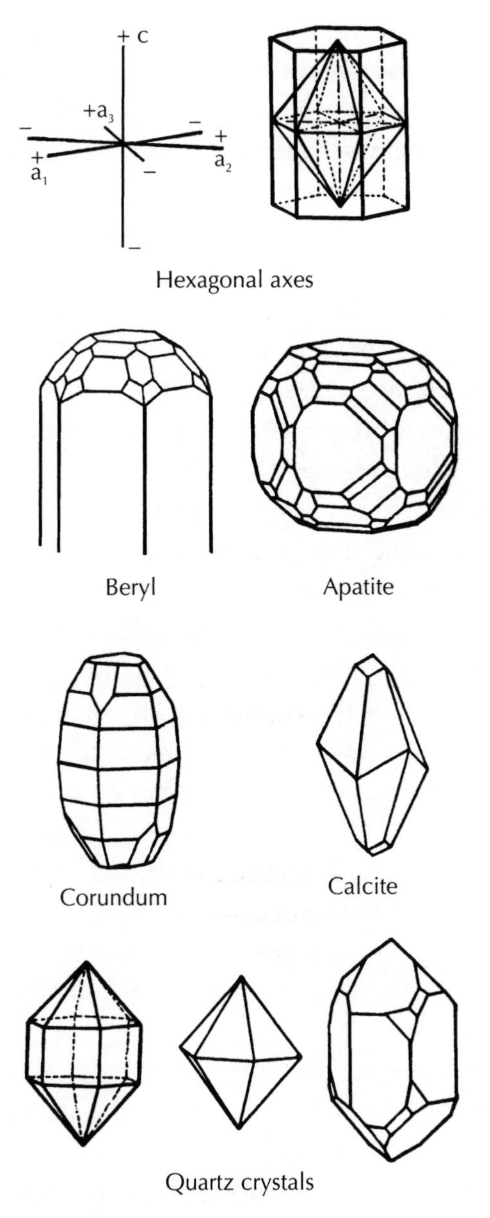

Figure 19: Hexagonal axes and crystals forming in the hexagonal division (beryl and apatite), and in the rhombohedral division (quartz, corundum and calcite)

also called the Trigonal system by some writers, and in some (mainly European) text books it is listed as a separate system from the Hexagonal system, giving a total of seven rather than six systems as described by Dana. Personally I believe that it is rightfully a part of the Hexagonal system, as the hexagonal axes still apply. In addition, many crystals, such as quartz crystals, which are clearly hexagonal in form, are included in this division. The temptation for some crystal writers is to use seven systems – based on the esoteric significance of the number seven, creates other problems. One writer of a 'New Age' book on quartz crystals made much of the 'seven crystal systems', while continually describing quartz as 'Hexagonal'. If seven systems are used, quartz is Trigonal.

As in the other systems, there are further divisions into classes, depending again on symmetry. Crystals of various minerals in the Hexagonal and Rhombohedral divisions of the Hexagonal system are shown in Figure 19. As can be seen from the drawings, most of the minerals traditionally considered as hexagonal occur in the Rhombohedral division.

Mr Dana's box of crystals was now well past half empty and, having disposed of the Hexagonal system, he then discovered another group of crystals, which were similar to the first two Isometric and Tetragonal systems (in that the crystallographic axes were once again at 90° to each other), but in this instance, the axes were all of different lengths. This system he called the Orthorhombic system (also referred to in some texts as the Rhombic or the Prismatic system). The axes of the Orthorhombic system are shown in Figure 20, along with crystals of various minerals which form in this system. These crystals are made from unit cells X and XI (Figure 14).

Mr Dana's box was now nearly empty, but still contained a significant number of crystals of one very large mineral group, the feldspars. Feldspars are the most numerous of all crystals on the Earth and are principally made either of potassium and silica, or of sodium and silica. Most of the feldspars crystallize in the fifth system, and a few in the sixth.

Crystals in the fifth system have the characteristic of three crystal axes of differing length, with the 'a' and 'b' axes lying in the same plane, but that plane being tilted in relation to the 'c' axis. This system is called the Monoclinic system. Minerals that crystallize in the Monoclinic system, and their forms, are shown in Figure 21. These crystals form from Bravais unit cells XII and XIII (see Figure 14).

The last crystal system is called the Triclinic system and is characterized by three axes of different lengths. None of the angles between any of the axes are right angles. The triclinic axes are shown in Figure 22, with examples of typical triclinic crystals. The triclinic unit cell is cell XIV (see Figure 14).

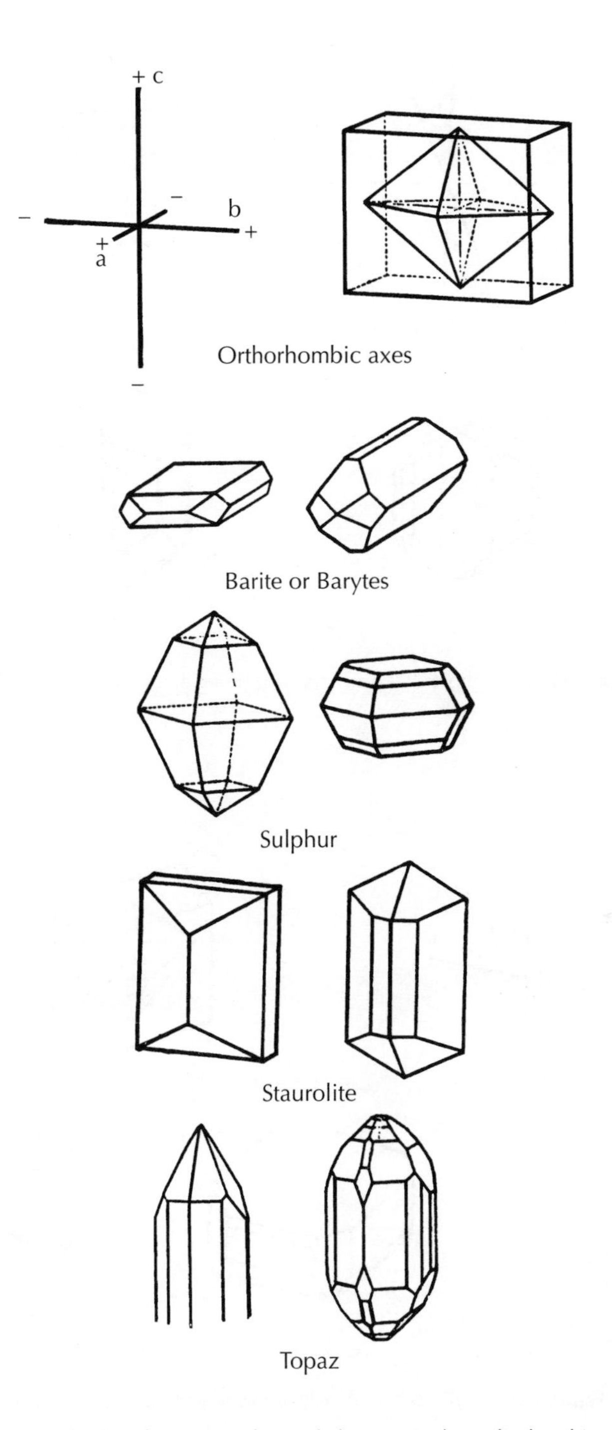

Figure 20: Orthorhombic axes and crystals forming in the orthorhombic system

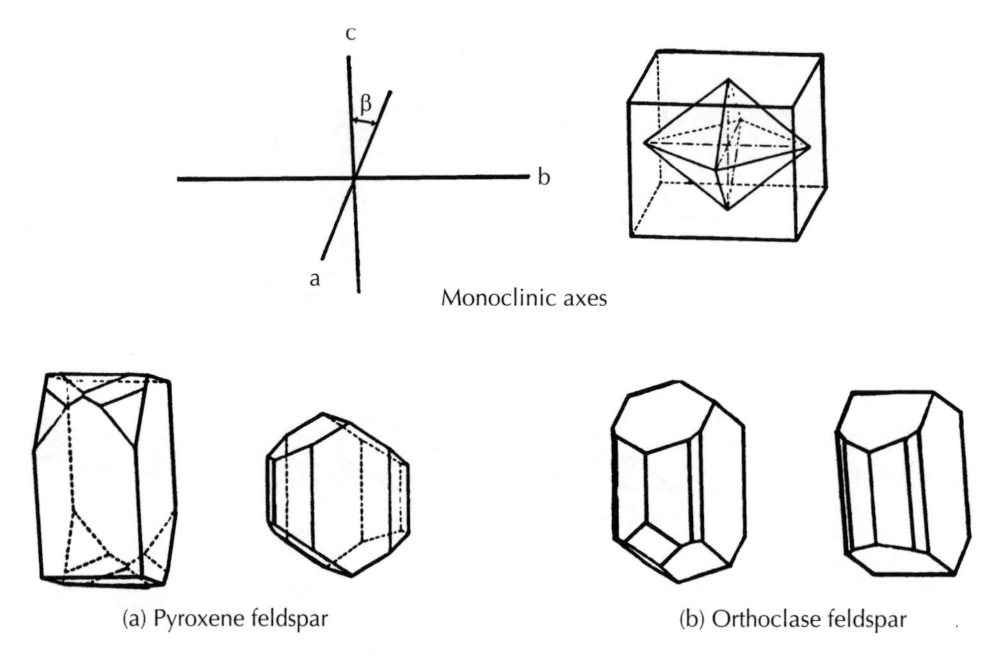

Figure 21: Monoclinic axes and crystals forming in the monoclinic system

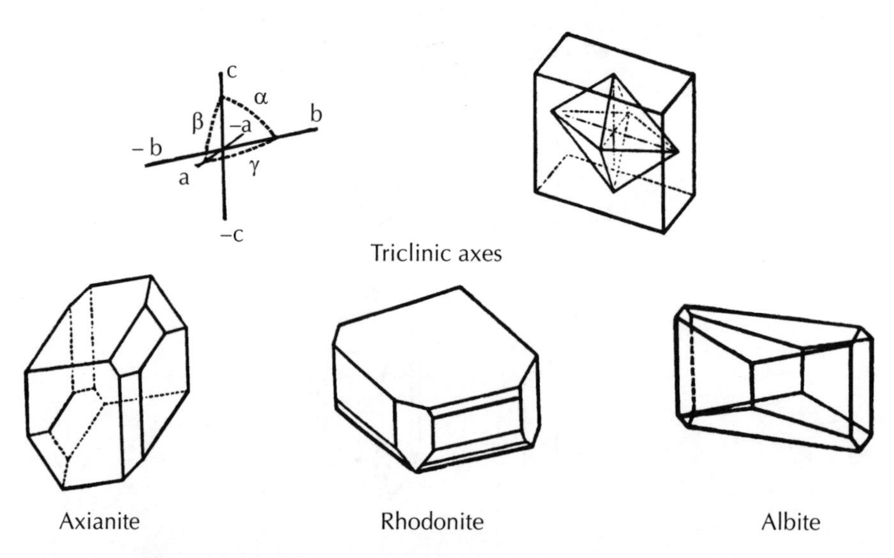

Figure 22: Triclinic axes and crystals forming in the triclinic system

Twin Crystals

Another group of crystals is made up of various representatives of each of the six different crystal systems. These are called twin crystals, and are made by two or more identical crystals growing together in certain patterns.

The first type of such twins are called *penetration twins*. In a penetration twin, illustrated by the minerals fluorite and staurolite in Figure 23, two or more complete crystals appear to actually penetrate each other. In fact, these crystals tend to have a common centre and have simply grown from this centre in two separate yet intermingled growths.

It is possible to have repeated twinning along common faces of several crystals, giving rise to circular-appearing crystals, which are called *cyclic twins*. Examples of these are chrysoberyl (Plate 17) and staurolite, illustrated in Figure 24. Other twins are shown in Figure 25.

Quartz produces another type of twin crystal – two crystals growing in the same space, yet which appear to be only one crystal. This type of twin is called a right-hand crystal, as opposed to the 'normal' quartz crystal, which is a left-hand crystal. These names derive from the tendency of the tetrahedral-shaped quartz molecules to arrange themselves in spiral patterns. In the left-hand crystal the spirals turn to the left, but in the right-hand crystal, the spirals turn to both the left and right. There are no quartz crystals where the spirals turn only to the right.

This is an area where there is a great deal of confusion by esoteric writers about crystals. The right-hand crystal is identified by the presence of a lozenge-shaped face or faces present to the right of the largest pyramid face of the crystal. If the face appears to the left of the pyramid face, it is a left-hand crystal. Most quartz crystals are mixtures of both.

Figure 23: Penetration twins

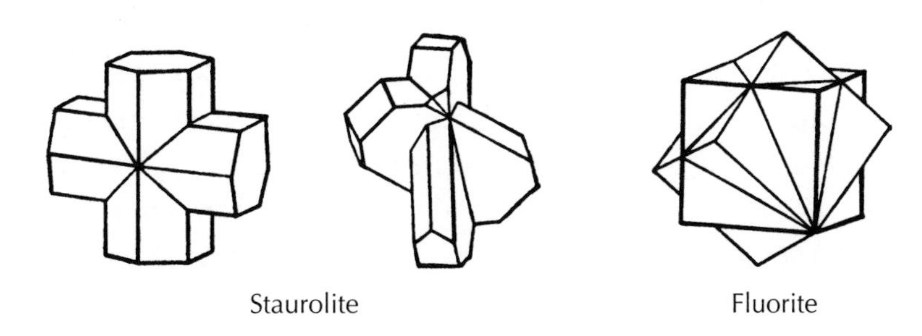

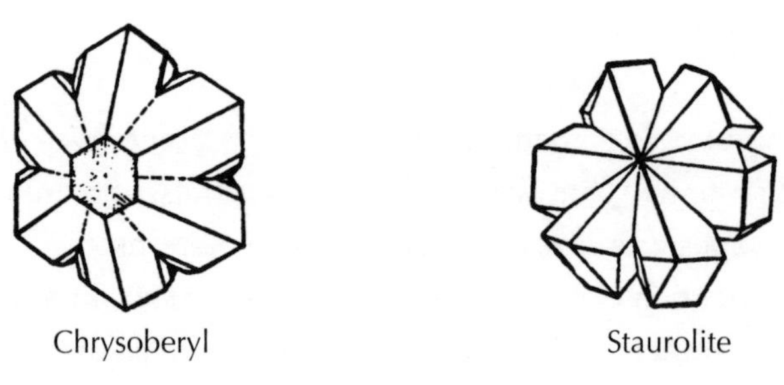

Figure 24: Cyclic twins

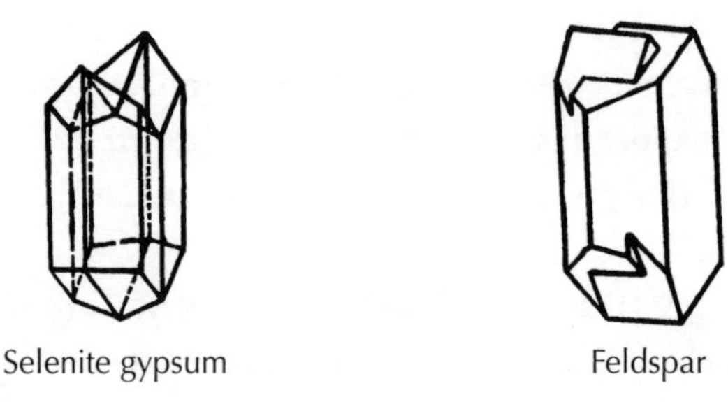

Figure 25: Other twin crystals

Figure 26: A left-hand quartz crystal

Distorted Forms

Crystals of the forms illustrated throughout this chapter are idealized forms and occur in nature only under ideal conditions. In Figure 27 the distorted crystals more commonly found in nature are shown. It must be remembered, though, that the laws of symmetry by which the crystal systems are derived apply to the position of their faces *relative* to the crystal axes, and not to their actual dimensions. Therefore, even a distorted crystal still represents the basic elements of symmetry just as much as an idealized one.

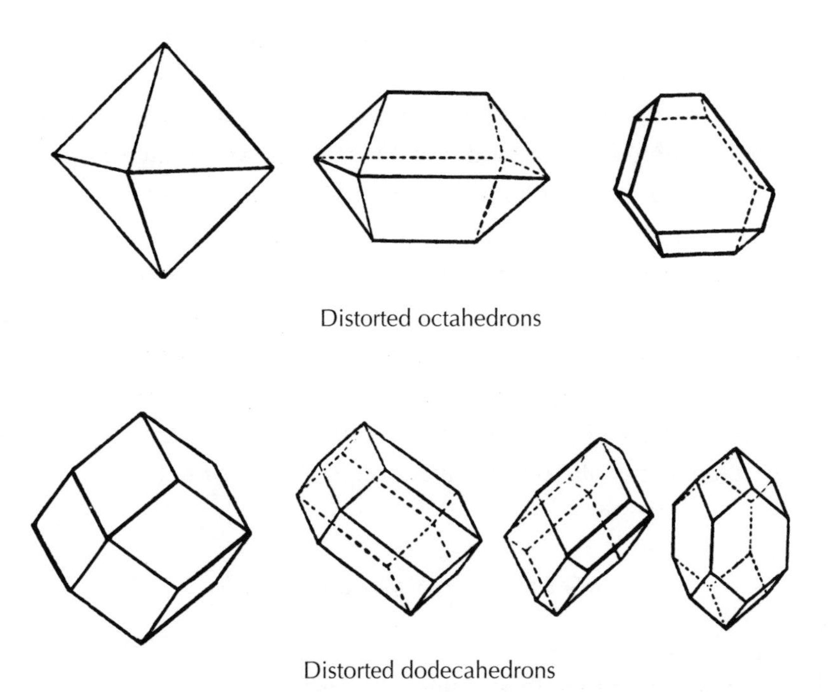

Distorted octahedrons

Distorted dodecahedrons

Figure 27: Distorted forms of crystals

Inclusions

Crystals may have numerous types of internal 'imperfections' within themselves, many of which are not visible to the naked eye. One of the most common types is called an *inclusion*: any foreign body enclosed within the crystal. These are extremely common and may take the form of crystals of other minerals, bubbles of gas or liquid. The so-called black spots which appear in diamonds are nothing more than minute crystals of the minerals graphite or olivine that formed at the same time as the diamond and became attached to one of the forming faces at some stage of the growth of the diamond crystal.

Another common example is in a crystal such as the star sapphire or ruby, where microscopic crystals of the mineral rutile have arranged themselves in certain patterns within the sapphire crystal. When the crystal is cut and polished in a certain direction relative to the crystal axes, the reflection of light from these tiny particles of rutile forms a star pattern.

III – CLASSIFICATION OF MINERALS

While crystals are classified by their geometry, minerals are classified by their chemical composition. Remember that a crystal is always a mineral (and, according to the definition, characteristic of that mineral), but minerals do not always form crystals. Our definition of minerals stated that minerals were always of a definite chemical composition, and this is how we classify them (see Table 1).

A mineral is always classified first by its chemical composition, and then by its characteristic crystal form. Thus titanium dioxide TiO_2 is always an Oxide (Group V); its mineral name is rutile, and it is then described as crystallizing in the Tetragonal system. Thus TiO_2 is always rutile, but only when it forms crystals are they Tetragonal. It remains rutile whether it is in crystal form or not.

Table 1 The System of Mineral Classification

I	Native Elements	
II	Sulphides, Selenides, Tellurides, Arsenides, Antimonides	
III	Sulpho-salts	Sulpharsenites, Sulphantimonites, Sulpho-bismuthites
IV	Haloids	Chlorides, Bromides, Iodides, Fluorides
V	Oxides	
VI	Oxygen salts	1. Carbonates 2. Silicates, Titanites 3. Niobates, Tantalates 4. Phosphates, Arsenates, Vanadates, Antimonates, Nitrates 5. Borates, Uranates 6. Sulphates, Chromates, Tellurates 7. Tungstates, Molybdates
VII	Salts of organic acids: Oxalates, Mellates, etc	
VIII	Hydrocarbon compounds	

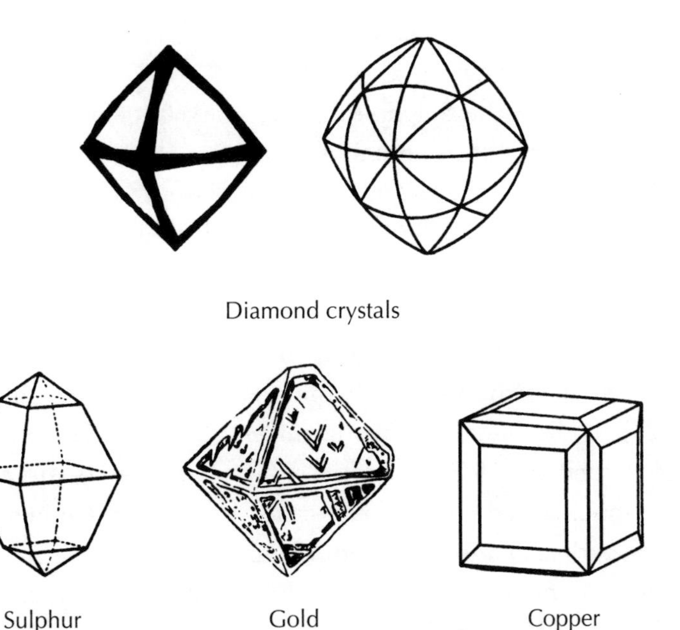

Figure 28: Crystals of Native Element minerals

Let's take a closer look at each of the mineral groups shown in Table 1, and the crystals you are most likely to encounter from each of them.

The first group of minerals is simply called the Native Elements. These are elements that occur in nature uncombined with other elements. Typical examples are gold, silver, platinum, sulphur, copper and carbon (in the form of diamond (Plate 8) and graphite). Crystals of some of these minerals are shown in Figure 28.

In Group II the most commonly encountered crystals will come from the Sulphides. This group of minerals is simply a metal combined with sulphur. When the metal is lead, the mineral is galena (PbS). When it is zinc, the mineral is sphalerite (ZnS), and when it is iron and crystallizes in the Isometric system, it is called pyrite (FeS_2) or Fool's Gold. Under other geological conditions iron sulphide can crystallize in the Orthorhombic system, and it then becomes the mineral marcasite.

Pyrite and marcasite give an excellent example of how a mineral has to be categorized not only by its chemical composition, but also by its crystal form (remembering that, in the definition earlier, there was a characteristic crystal form for each mineral). If we have two minerals of the same chemical composition but forming in different crystal systems, they are two different minerals and are given different names. This situation occurs in other mineral groups, and will be pointed out as we go along.

Group III minerals, the Sulpho-salts, are unlikely to be encountered as large single crystals, and are not commonly available.

Minerals of Group IV, the Haloids, are formed from a metal combined with one of the halogen chemical group – chlorine, bromine, iodine or fluorine. In this group we find minerals such as halite (rock salt – NaCl) and fluorite, also called fluorspar (CaF_2).

The next group, Group V, are formed by the combination of a metal with oxygen; this group is the Oxides. If the metal is silicon, the mineral formed is quartz (SiO_2). If the metal is tin, the mineral is cassiterite (SnO_2). When it is aluminium, corundum (Al_2O_3) is created. When corundum occurs as a blue crystal, it is called sapphire. Red corundum is called ruby. They are identical except for their colour – both are varieties of corundum.

Although in terms of total volume, the feldspars are the most predominant mineral in the Crust, quartz has the greatest number of varieties. Mineralogists divide the varieties of quartz into two separate classes: vitreous (meaning that they have a glassy appearance), and cryptocrystalline (i.e., that they are made up of microscopic quartz crystals). Because the crystal user will encounter quartz in many of its forms, these are described here.

Table 2 Varieties of the Mineral Quartz

Vitreous

Rock Crystal – Colourless, or nearly colourless quartz

Asteriated or Star Quartz – Contains inclusions of submicroscopic needles of some other mineral, showing a star pattern when polished

Amethyst – Clear purple or bluish violet; colouring probably due to ferric iron

Rose – Rose red or pink, commonly massive, rarely occurring in crystals over 5mm in size; colour perhaps due to titanium

Citrine – Yellow in colour, resembling yellow topaz

Smoky Quartz or Cairngormstone – Smoky yellow to dark smoky brown, varying to brownish black; Morion is the proper name for nearly black varieties

Milky – Milk white and nearly opaque

Sagenitic – Enclosing needle-like crystals of rutile, or black tourmaline; or other minerals such as asbestos, hornblende or epidote

Cat's Eye Quartz – Exhibits opalescence but without prismatic colours; Tiger Eye is also a variety. The gemstone just called Cat's Eye is a variety of chrysoberyl

Aventurine – Internally spangled with scales of mica, hematite or other minerals

Cryptocrystalline

Chalcedony – Having the lustre nearly of wax; transparent to translucent, colour white, greyish, blue, pale brown to dark brown, black; also shades, with other names

Carnelian (Sard) – A clear red chalcedony, pale to deep in shades; also brownish red to brown

Chrysoprase – An apple-green chalcedony, the colour due to nickel oxide

Prase – Translucent and dull-leek green

Plasma – Rather bright green, sometimes nearly an emerald green. Heliotrope, or bloodstone, is essentially the same stone, with small spots of red jasper in it, looking like drops of blood

Agate – A layered chalcedony. The colours are either banded, irregularly clouded, or due to visible impurities such as in moss agate, which has brown or green moss-like forms distributed through the mass. The bands are delicate parallel lines of white, pale and dark brown, blue and other shades. They are sometimes straight, but are often wavy or zigzag, and occasionally circular. There is also agatized wood: natural wood replaced by agate

Onyx – Like agate and consisting of layers of different colours, but the layers are in even lines and the banding straight

Sardonyx – Like onyx in structure but includes layers of carnelian (sard) along with others of white or brown

Flint – Somewhat like chalcedony, but more opaque and of dull colours. The flint of chalk formations consists largely of the remains of diatoms, sponges and other marine organisms

Jasper – Impure opaque-coloured quartz; commonly red but also found in yellow, dark green and greyish blue

Touchstone or Basanite – A velvet black siliceous stone or flinty jasper, used on account of its hardness and black colour for testing the purity of precious metals

There are other varieties of quartz, but these are the most common and they are names that the friends of the Mineral Kingdom are likely to encounter.

Another type of silica, similar to quartz but made up of layers of microscopic balls of silica and containing water in the structure, is Opal. There are many varieties of opal, but the most commonly encountered are precious opal, exhibiting a play of delicate colours, and fire opal, which is hyacinth red to honey yellow, with fire-like reflections. The majority of opal is common opal, which is usually transparent to translucent, and milky white, yellow or olive green in colour. There are other varieties of opal, but these are the most common. Within Group VI, the Oxygen Salts, an important sub-group is the Carbonates; here carbon and oxygen combine with a metal. If the metal is iron, the mineral is siderite ($FeCO_3$); if the metal is zinc the mineral becomes smithsonite ($ZnCO_3$). The metal may also be calcium, which combines with carbon and oxygen to form either calcite or aragonite ($CaCO_3$). Chemically, both minerals are identical, but in calcite the crystals form in the Rhombohedral division of the Hexagonal system and aragonite crystals form in the Orthorhombic system. As with pyrite and marcasite, this is an example of how identical chemical substances are classed as different minerals when their crystals (and hence their internal atomic arrangements) fall into different crystal systems.

In Group VI, the Phosphates are of particular significance to the human body. Bone tissue and tooth enamel are both made of the mineral apatite (Plate 1). Apatite is made from calcium and fluorine combined with phosphorus and oxygen. A crystal of apatite is shown in Figure 19. Another phosphate mineral is an iron/magnesium aluminium phosphate called lazulite, crystals of which, when dispersed in calcite, form the rock lapis lazuli. Another phosphate gem mineral is turquoise. It is usually massive in form but crystals are occasionally found.Within the Group VI Sulphates we find the mineral barite (also called barytes). This is the metal barium combined with sulphur and oxygen ($BaSO_4$), a crystal of which is shown in Figure 20 and Plate 10. Gypsum, the crystalline variety of which is known as selenite, is also a sulphate, but with water in the crystal structure. A twin crystal of selenite is shown in Figure 25.

Also found in Group VI is by far the largest family of minerals on the Earth – the Silicates. Although there is a vast range of compositions which are frequently very complex, X-ray investigation has shown certain basic facts about atomic structure in the Silicate group, and their intricate compositions. The most fundamental structural unit of all Silicates is a silica tetrahedron, with four oxygen atoms surrounding each atom of silicon. But these SiO_2 groups may be linked together in various ways to form an indefinitely extended series. The basic silicate tetrahedron is shown in Figure 29. But silica itself – quartz – is not included in Group VI, because it is an oxide of the metal silicon, and therefore is a Group V mineral.

The largest group of crystals in the bulk of the crust are the feldspars, which fall into two groups. The first is made of various combinations of potassium and sodium, in combination with aluminium and silica. The potassium and sodium content can vary from zero to 100 per cent, and the name that is given to any particular feldspar in this group is dependent on its potassium : sodium ratio. The two major sodium feldspars are orthoclase ($KAl\ Si_3O_8$), which crystallizes in the Monoclinic system, and microcline (Plate 4), which has the same chemical formula but which crystallizes in the Triclinic system. These feldspars are generally

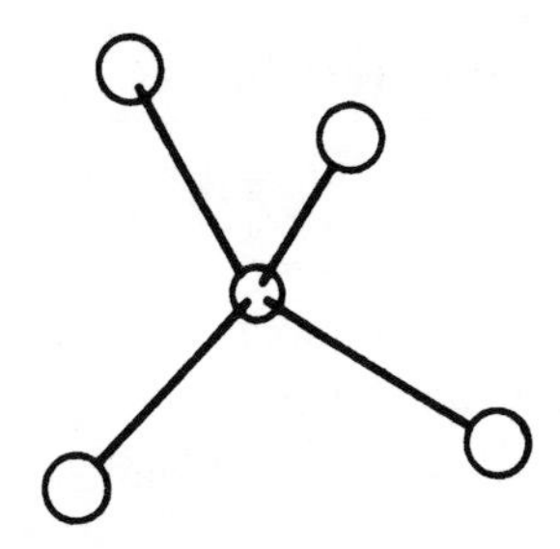

Figure 29: A silicate tetrahedron

pink in colour and are the minerals that give granite its characteristic pink hue.

The other main group of feldspars is based on sodium and calcium, which vary in percentage ratio just as the potassium and sodium ratio does in the first group, above. Crystals of these two groups of feldspars are shown in Figures 21 and 22.

Another important group of silicate minerals commonly encountered is the garnet group. In number of varieties it is second only to quartz. Table 3 shows various types of garnet, and their chemical make-up. The basic structure (all crystallizing in the Isometric system) of each group of garnets is the same, with one or more metals freely substituting in the structure. In the case of the aluminium garnet, the calcium, magnesium, iron and manganese all substitute for one another, and thus we seldom find an absolutely pure pyrope garnet or an absolutely pure almandite garnet, as there is always a certain amount of intermixing. Crystals of garnets are shown in Figure 16. Although garnet is usually thought of as red, it may also be colourless, yellow, brown, black or green. The name garnet comes from the Latin word *granitus*, meaning 'like a grain', and directly from pomegranate, the seeds of which are small, numerous and red – like, in fact, the common occurrence of garnet: as numerous small, seed-like grains mixed in with other minerals within the rock where they formed. The name almandine probably refers to the ancient city of Alabanda, where almandine garnets were cut and polished.

The garnets and feldspars are two of the major mineral series within the silicates. Other silicate minerals the crystal user may encounter are zircon (see Figure 17 and Plate 16), staurolite and topaz (see Figure 20, Plates 3 and 19), tourmaline, or beryl, which is usually found in its blue-green variety called aquamarine (see Figure 19) or – if lucky – in its pure green form, emerald.

Table 3 The Garnet Group

I – Aluminium Garnet		
Grossularite	Calcium-Aluminium Garnet	$Ca_3Al_2(SiO_4)_3$
Pyrope	Magnesium-Aluminium Garnet	$Mg_3Al_2(SiO_4)_3$
Almandite	Iron-Aluminium Garnet	$Fe_3Al_2(SiO_4)_3$
Spessartite	Manganese-Aluminium Garnet	$Mn_3Al_2(SiO_4)_3$
II – Iron Garnet		
Andradite	Calcium-Iron Garnet	$Ca_3Fe_2(SiO_4)_3$
	1. Ordinary	
	2. Magnesian	
	3. Titaniferous	
	4. Yttriferous	
III – Chromium Garnet		
Uvarovite	Calcium-Chromium Garnet	$Ca_3Cr_2(SiO_4)_3$

Another series of minerals within the silicates that might be encountered, although probably not in distinctive crystals, are the micas. The micas form very thin, flexible and transparent to semi-transparent sheets. As with the garnets and feldspars, the micas form a complete group of minerals within themselves, all of which contain aluminium and silica, and may also have various combinations of potassium, magnesium, sodium and lithium. They also all contain water within the crystal's structure. The common name by which several of the transparent species are known is *isinglass*, which was often used as the transparent 'windows' in old wood-burning stoves.

Other silicate minerals which are often encountered, but that do not usually form large single crystals, are serpentine, talc and all of the various clay minerals such as kaolin.

The last two groups of minerals, VII – Salts of Organic Acids, and VIII – Hydrocarbon Compounds, are not discussed since they do not form crystals of any size.

In this chapter, we have examined how crystals and minerals are formed, studied and classified. In the next, we will see how the failure to understand these processes has led to almost all of the common misunderstandings about what crystals are, and what they can – and cannot – do.

CHAPTER 5

CRYSTAL MYTHS AND REALITIES

✧

No man ever became great and good except through many and great mistakes.

Cicero

This chapter on crystal myths and realities is much longer on myths than on realities, for the simple reason that there are many more myths than realities taught about crystals! Not only that: the realities are simple, crystal clear, and exactly to the point – unlike most of the myths. Entire books based on misconceptions about crystals can be found!

One thing that is often totally misunderstood in 'esoteric' circles is that, because crystals are at the very foundation of the material universe, the laws of the physical universe are utterly and completely bound up in them. In the purest sense, they are the laws of physics and chemistry made manifest. Because this is so, there is no way that they can be used to violate the laws of physics and chemistry. Nor can they do so themselves. Nor, indeed, can they be *made* to do so, regardless of the supposed intentions of the user – although if the user purports to be 'spiritual' (i.e., in harmony with the nature of the universe), why would they wish to do so? But that this is observed time and again in 'spiritual' groups and individuals suggests a lack of understanding of the nature of reality as made manifest in the crystal. The purpose of this book is to suggest ways and means of moving closer to that inner reality through the concrete reality of crystals. It all stems from the same Source.

MYTH 1: 'CRYSTALS STORE ENERGY'

So, let's take a look at some of the common misunderstandings about crystals. We begin by remembering our discussion about chemical bonding in Chapter 2, and that the forces which tie a crystal together are in perfect balance and harmony. A crystal is in a perfect state of equilibrium – in its *resting* state it neither gives off energy nor takes it in. The evidence for this is quite simple: if it were taking in energy, it would be growing; if it were giving off energy, it would be shrinking. Thus crystals do *not* sit there giving off 'healing energy'. It is physically impossible. As it turns out, crystals absorb and emit energy constantly – principally light and heat – but they are doing so in perfect balance. That is, the amount of energy given off is exactly equal to the amount of energy taken in, and thus the crystal remains unchanged. (There is one group of crystals where this is not true – the crystals of radioactive elements. Here, energy is being given off all the time, but the crystal does change.)

This misunderstanding of their balanced energetic nature leads to the myth that crystals store energy. They can't.

By its nature a crystal is in perfect energy balance; every atom in that crystal is held very rigidly and very accurately in place by enormously well-balanced energies. If the atoms which make up the average crystal were the size of footballs, then there is no way that you or I could place those football-sized atoms, even with the most accurate surveying instruments, as accurately and as precisely as they are placed inside a crystal. If any energy comes to that crystal, it either doesn't absorb it at all, or, if the energy does go into the crystal, then by its very nature, the crystal must immediately get rid of an equal amount of energy in order to keep itself in balance.

There is no way energy can be stored in a crystal. A crystal is sometimes regarded as some sort of sponge into which vast quantities of electricity may be poured and stored and then squeezed out for use at some future time. Once we understand the balance of energies that takes place within a crystal, we can see the utter impossibility of such a belief: a crystal gives off, in another form, exactly the amount of energy that is put into it, and at virtually the same instant.

An effect known as the *piezoelectric effect* (pronounced 'pie-ay-zoh-electric'), which is observable as a flash of light given off when a crystal is struck with another object, is a genuine property of certain crystals that is the foundation upon which the above and many other common misunderstandings are based. This effect is produced by the stripping of the electrons from the outer atomic shells when a crystal is subjected to stress. A crystal of quartz easily demonstrates this effect. If a quartz crystal is laid on its side and struck with a mallet, the structure is compressed momentarily. What we observe is a flash of visible light. What we do not see, unless we have special sensors, is that the crystal has also given off a burst of electricity. This effect – giving off visible light – was well known to ancient man: quartz crystals are often found in American Indian camp sites, usually well-battered.

We use this property today, but don't strike the crystal with a mallet: we prepare precisely made slices of quartz crystal to compress mechanically; each slice is also connected to electronic measuring devices. In compressing the crystal structure (and we are talking about a compression so small as to be almost unmeasurable), we are pushing the atoms slightly closer together and freeing the outer energy shell electrons from the need to bond quite so tightly. As we do this, electrons are freed from the outermost shell and move to the surface of the crystal. This transfer of electrons from one shell to another or, in this case, out of the shell entirely, is also connected with a quantum of light (*see page 39*). So, we not only transfer free electrons, but we also release the amount of light energy that it takes to 'hold' the electrons in the outer shell. The inner electron shells do not seem to be affected: all the effects discussed in this chapter only take place in the outermost shell.

Remember, this effect only takes place while the crystal is being compressed, and only until all the available free electrons have been released. Once the compression is held at a certain level (like being squeezed in a vice), and once all the electrons at that level of energy have been released, there is no further discharge. As in the case of our mallet, once the pressure is released, the crystal springs back to its original dimensions, and replaces its lost electrons by either drawing them back from the surface of the crystal, or by drawing free electrons from the air (where there are plenty of them). The crystal also re-absorbs enough light energy to 'glue' the electrons back into their proper shell positions. Even in a dark room, there is sufficient light available to do this, although there is not enough to register on the human eye.

The amount of pressure you can put on a quartz crystal with your hand is so tiny that it would be difficult (if not impossible), even with the most accurate instruments, to measure the amount of electricity being given off. And it is just electricity; you can get the same stuff out of your wall socket, so there is no need to squeeze a quartz crystal to get it! In fact, crystals are so incompressible that if we were to take a quartz crystal an inch long and about a half-an-inch in diameter, and we wanted to squeeze it down to about half of its original thickness, we would have to stack a weight equal to approximately 5,000 railway locomotives on top of that crystal. You can imagine how hard you would have to squeeze a quartz crystal to get anything out of it whatsoever!

It is possible to reverse this process. Rather than compress the crystal to give off electricity, we can put electricity (i.e., a flow of electrons) into the crystal to cause a momentary expansion of the structure. What happens is that the influx of electrons momentarily overloads the outer shell, and the atoms drift slightly apart. However the electrons in these new positions are not stable, and they almost instantly break away to move on to the next plane of atoms. As they do so, the atoms that have been forced apart snap back into their original positions, until the next set of electrons comes along to repeat the cycle all over again. This alternating expansion and contraction of the crystal structure, then, is nothing more than vibration. If you had very sensitive fingers you could feel the crystal vibrate physically. Or, if we put enough high energy electrons (a higher amperage) into the crystal structure, we could actually blow it apart – obviously not an experiment that many of us would be very happy to perform.

This ability of the crystal to vibrate has some other interesting twists; for example, because the atoms in crystals are so precisely placed, if you put the same electrical energy into two pieces of crystal which are exactly the same size, each crystal will give off exactly the same vibration.

This rate of vibration (called a *frequency*, because it is measured in the number of vibrations per second) is a property that is widely employed in technology, particularly in quartz resonators for frequency control, in crystal pick-ups for gramophones, and in pressure gauges. Some readers will remember the old crystal radio sets, the crystal of which was nothing more than a slice of quartz. In the earliest two-way radio sets, unless both sets used crystals of the same thickness (i.e., the same frequency) they were unable to 'talk' to one another.

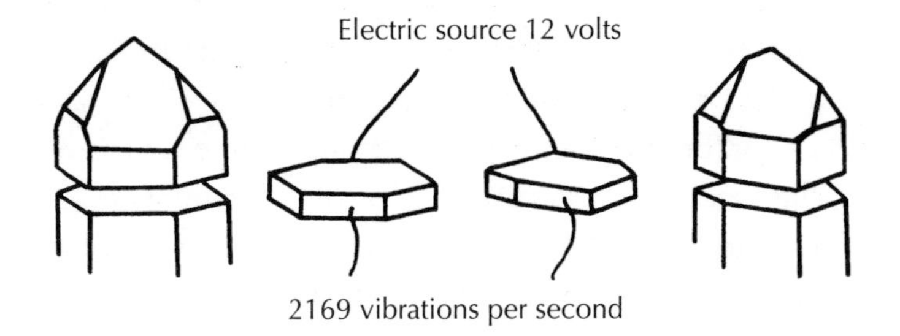

Figure 30: Quartz plates of identical dimensions from two different crystals

Many of you will be making use of this same property even as you read this book – in the workings of your quartz watch, which contains a tiny slice of synthetic quartz. The battery puts electricity into the quartz crystal. Because the quartz crystal will not absorb the energy, it has to give off an equal amount of energy to keep itself in balance – the mechanical energy of vibration. The rate at which a given crystal vibrates per minute is known. So, in your watch you have a little quartz crystal, a battery, and a computer that counts up the vibrations. The computer knows how many times the little piece of quartz will vibrate in a minute. When it has vibrated that many times it clicks over the minute counter; and when it has done that 60 times it clicks over the hour counter, and so forth. But the energy is not being stored in the crystal; it is being given off in another form.

MYTH 3: 'CRYSTALS ACT AS RADIO TRANSMITTERS'

Another area of misunderstanding, in relation to quartz crystals in particular, is the role that they play in electronics. The fact that quartz resonators are used in radio transmitters and receivers and in amplifiers does *not* mean that they *are* amplifiers, transmitters, etc. It is purely their ability to control vibrational frequency that is made use of in electronics. But that is *all* that they are used for, and they only make up a small part of the mechanism of the transmitter or amplifier. Thus, we are not likely to find cavemen, or Egyptian priests for that matter, sending one another radio messages on quartz crystals. Some writers seem to believe that you only have to stick a crystal in your ear and dial Peru! Nor do crystals store light (for the same reason that they cannot store electricity); nor do naturally occurring crystals convert light to electricity – a misunderstanding of the artificially grown crystals of silicon *metal*, which do not occur in nature and which seem to be frequently confused with quartz (quartz being made of silicon and oxygen).

You will hear all of these various qualities attributed to quartz, as if quartz were the only thing that has these properties! A lot of other minerals do exactly the same things that quartz does. Most of them do to some degree, but the mineral tourmaline does all of the electronic things that quartz does, and it does them even better. The reason that we don't have tourmaline watches, or that tourmaline is not used in most other electronic applications (although it is used in a few), is that tourmaline is not cheap – as you will have noticed if you have ever tried to buy a tourmaline ring. It is 50- to 100-times more expensive than quartz. And also, at the moment, we don't know how to grow it synthetically. Almost all the quartz that is used in electronics is synthetic, grown in a laboratory. Therefore it is relatively cheap and it does all the above things well enough (but not as well as tourmaline).

The other minerals that do exactly the same thing as quartz are not commonly available either, nor are they as easy to grow in the laboratory.

Pyroelectricity

Pyroelectricity is the name given to the effect of the application of heat to crystals. It has been known for centuries in India and Sri Lanka that tourmaline, when heated in the embers of a fire, first attracts ashes and then repels them. This phenomenon is due to electrical charges accumulating on the surface of the crystal, and occurs in the same crystals that show piezoelectricity. The effect appears to be closely related to piezoelectricity in that crystals, when heated and cooled, expand and contract and are in a state of strain. It is in fact quite difficult to differentiate between pyroelectric and piezoelectric effects.

It appears that as the crystal is heated, distortion of the cell lattice takes place, possibly due to the number of electrons moving into higher energy shells as a result of the increased heat energy in the crystal. As in piezoelectricity, certain electrons are energized enough to break loose from the outer electron shells and, once again, float to the surface of the crystal. There is an easy demonstration of this electrical property achieved by heating tourmaline. A clean, dry crystal of tourmaline is heated to about 200°C and then passed a few times through the flame of an alcohol lamp to dissipate the surface charges. It is then placed on a glass plate to cool. As it does so, a mixture of powdered red lead and sulphur is sifted over the crystal. The red lead goes to the negatively charged surfaces, and the sulphur to the positive areas. As the crystal completely cools, it will re-absorb electrons into their proper structural positions, and the crystal will go back to its original dimensions. When it has done so, the lead and sulphur powder will drop off.

ERRONEOUS CONCLUSIONS

Having looked at some of the basic myths and misunderstandings about crystals, we should now look at some of the conclusions that have been drawn from these misconceptions.

A direct result of the various misunderstandings about the behaviour of quartz crystals under compression leads to a whole new series of misunderstandings about how quartz-bearing *rocks* behave under compression. The example usually seen in most writings is that of granite, which in some instances may contain up to 50 per cent quartz. It is assumed that since quartz crystals give off a momentary electrical charge when they are rapidly compressed, then the quartz grains in granite must do the same. This ignores two very important factors:

a) that the energy properties of single crystals are highly directional in nature, and if forces are applied other than in very specific directions, nothing happens; and
b) the quartz crystals in granite are not well formed and they are orientated almost at random; i.e., the crystallizing axes point in virtually all directions.

In a piece of granite used in building construction, such as in the King's Chamber and roof supports in the Great Pyramid at Giza, the compressive forces themselves are highly directional, and relate to the amount of stone that is piled on top of it. It would be very surprising indeed if even 1 per cent of the quartz grains in the piece of granite (and remember, these are quartz *grains*, not crystals) were aligned closely enough to the compressive direction to have any chance whatever of producing an electrical charge. And, once the compression stabilizes, there is no further energy that can be given off. In other words, once the energies have balanced (i.e., when the last block was put on the pyramid), nothing further happens.

In various 'esoteric' articles, the ceiling blocks in the Great Pyramid are described as 'capacitors' or 'rectifiers', and were supposedly carefully positioned and connected via copper wires or rods to the outside of the Pyramid. There is no archaeological or historical evidence of this whatsoever, nor would such 'capacitors' have worked even if they were connected as supposed.

Many writers propose energy properties that relate directly to the amount of stone that is piled on top of quartz-bearing rocks, like granite, when they are used in building construction. If these rocks do possess such incredible energy properties, then why do we not see evidence of this at the places where the greatest compressive load is being applied to them – the mountains themselves¿! Rather than perhaps a hundred feet or so of rock piled on top of the granite blocks in a pyramid, we sometimes have thousands of feet of rock piled on top of granite. According to the thesis of these writers, in this situation the quartz-bearing rocks should be producing bolts of electricity like a power station! In fact, of course, they are giving off precisely – nothing.

To be sure, the construction materials used inside the Great Pyramid were very carefully chosen, but not for their ability to generate vast amounts of electrical energy.

This supposed property is also projected onto stone circles. Without a doubt the stones from which these were made were again very carefully selected for their overall properties, and they definitely cause localized disturbances or accumulations of various types of energy. Once again these effects are attributed to piezoelectricity, which (it is often claimed) originates because the bases of the stones project into underground water flows. This belief encompasses two areas of massive misunderstanding – the nature of underground water flow in the first instance, and the nature of the hydrostatic effect (or water pressure) in the second.

There seems to be an assumption by some of these writers that underground water flow takes the nature of rivers or streams on the surface – that there are large volumes of water presumably flowing through cavities in the rocks below. Although this does happen on rare occasions in cave systems, the likelihood of it ever happening anywhere near a stone circle, and particularly where the bases of the stones would protrude into the water flow, is almost non-existent. Almost all rocks are slightly porous; they are rather like sponges, and they have minute air spaces between the various particles that make up the stone. These pore spaces are the largest in sedimentary rocks, a typical example of which would be sandstone. But porous space in these rocks seldom exceeds 10 to 15 per cent of the total volume, and the pore spaces themselves are rarely as large as half the size of a pinhead! Thus in underground water flow, we are not talking about a vast torrent, but a slow oozing of water from one pore space to the next. Even in the relatively porous sands and gravels of unconsolidated material, the rate of flow seldom exceeds a few feet a day. Hardly a raging torrent! Nor do such underground flows take on the characteristics of surface streams, flowing in very narrow, ribbon-like patterns. Underground water flows as broad sheets of water, sometimes miles wide, all seeping in the same direction.

It is suggested that the bases of the stones buried in the ground are subjected to great pressures from these same underground waters. No one appears to have read the excavation reports on stone circles such as Stonehenge and Avebury. In few instances have the bases of the stones extended below the water table (the highest level to which underground waters rise) for any significant depth. Hydrostatic pressure increases with depth of water, and it would take depths of several metres to generate any significant amounts of pressure. You can demonstrate this for yourself the next time you are in a swimming pool: dive down to the bottom of the deep end, say about three metres, and see if you are crushed by the pressure.

OTHER QUARTZ MYTHS

Because a great many of the misunderstandings about crystals involve quartz, let's look at a few more misconceptions about it.

'Quartz is "special"'

Perhaps the major myth about quartz is that it is somehow 'special'. As we saw in the previous chapter, one particular belief is that it is the most abundant mineral in the Earth. The mantle makes up two-thirds of the Earth, and therefore we would expect that any mineral prominent in the mantle would be a likely candidate to be the most abundant. And this is true.

However, there is no quartz in the mantle. The minerals in the mantle are very dense, and quartz is fairly light – if there ever has been any quartz in the mantle, it has long since been squeezed up to the crust. But quartz is not even the most abundant mineral in the crust. There are hundreds of times more feldspar in the crust than quartz. There are 2,500 different minerals – quartz is only one of them.

'Quartz is used in computers'

Another myth about quartz is that it is used in computers. *No* quartz is used in computers. Crystals of silicon metal are artificially grown and are the so-called 'silicon chips' that are used in computers. The confusion arises from three similar-sounding words: silic**a**, sili**con** and silic**ate**. Quartz is the mineral name for the chemical silicon dioxide, or silic**a**; sili**con** is a metal, as noted above, and silic**ates** are a group of several hundred minerals (to which quartz does not even belong, because it is an oxide) which contain silica as one of their components.

'CRYSTAL' MYTHS AND MISCONCEPTIONS

There are several other types of 'crystals' that should be mentioned, some of which will be useful to the user of crystals, and some which will not.

Crystal glass

Let me just briefly mention another use of the word 'crystal', because yet again there is a tremendous amount of confusion about this word. It is often applied to a type of glass. Now 'glass' is actually a very specific scientific word, which has a very precise meaning. Glass is a liquid that is so solid it won't flow at ordinary temperatures. So window glass is actually a liquid; it is just very thick at normal temperatures. I met a glazier in Australia who told me that in removing glass from very old buildings, it was actually possible to measure the difference in thickness between the top and bottom of the pane – there had been that much flow over a century or so. The characteristic of a liquid is that its atoms are arranged in no patterns whatever; it's totally structureless. So to use the word 'crystal', which means totally and very precisely structured, and the word 'glass', which means absolutely no structure, means we use words that have absolutely opposite meanings – rather like that old joke, 'military intelligence'.

If you had anything made from 'crystal' before about AD 1300 (like a 'crystal' bowl for example), it was made from a piece of quartz crystal. When very colourless glass was made – glass that was as colourless as natural crystal – it became known as 'crystal glass' to differentiate it from ordinary glass. In order to differentiate the natural stone, then, it was called 'rock crystal', as opposed to 'glass crystal' or 'crystal glass'. These names came into common use around AD 1500. Because the properties of crystals are a consequence of their structures, structure-less 'crystal glass' has none of the properties of natural crystal. This doesn't mean that it can't be enjoyed for its own beauty.

Liquid crystal

Liquid crystals are similarly of little immediate importance to the crystal user. These are semi-solids in which the molecules of the liquid are arranged in regular patterns. Many types of living tissue are composed of liquid crystal, and it is thought that much of the memory-storing capacity of the brain is made up of liquid crystals. These crystals are generally microscopic in size, and although of great importance generally, are of little specific use in the terms in which we have been speaking of crystal usage.

Artificial crystal

Many different types of crystals are grown artificially, and most of these take on the same forms and mundane energy characteristics of natural crystals. The aspect of these which makes them generally unusable for crystal enthusiasts, however, is that at a subtle level the crystal takes on a great deal of the energy of its growth environment. The growing environment of an artificial crystal is very clinical and sterile, and is far removed from any sort of natural environment.

Crystals other than quartz are being grown from materials and in forms that are not found naturally and which therefore violate the laws of natural matter. In other words, we have 'forced' these crystals to grow against their own nature. Obviously, crystals grown in such environments are not likely to harmonize well with natural energies.

Several types of crystals are regularly grown in the laboratory, including quartz crystals for the electronics industry, ruby crystals for lasers, sapphires for bearings and substitute gems, emeralds for gems, diamonds for industrial use, and rutile, cubic zirconia and garnet as diamond substitutes. In the latter case, the garnet grown is yttrium-aluminium garnet, which does not occur in nature (nor does cubic zirconia). They are colourless, have a high refractive index, and are two of the 'forced' crystals mentioned above.

The Russians have successfully grown silicon crystals (i.e., silicon *metal*) in an orbiting laboratory in zero-gravity conditions that allow extremely pure crystals to form – if one can consider such forced growth as pure. This is not to suggest that laboratory-grown crystals are totally without use. As we know, a crystal incorporates much of the energy of its growing environment into its form; so imagine, if you will, a quartz crystal grown with a group of people continually directing pure love into it as it grows!

Crystal forms and appearance

The external forms of crystals are regarded as significant by some. There is definitely a relationship between the shape of a crystal and static electricity, as static electricity tends to accumulate on the points and edges of crystals. Unfortunately for those who attempt to draw conclusions about this, static electricity also accumulates on the points and edges of everything else. Whether it is the point of a pencil, the tip of a cat's tail, the peak of a house or church steeple, in each instance there will be a static electricity accumulation. This is very noticeable in drier climates, especially when two people walk across a room with a shagpile carpet to kiss one another – there is often a bolt of static electricity a quarter of an inch long or more as they get close to one another, and often from distinctly uncomfortable portions of the body!

If this focus on outer shape had any substance to it, then we might expect to carve quartz crystals (or at least the shape of quartz crystals) out of blocks of wood, and for them to behave exactly as natural crystals. Obviously this does not happen, because in a crystal the outer form is a direct consequence of the inner form. When lumps of a mineral like rose quartz are cut into the shape of crystals (as almost all rose quartz 'crystals' offered for sale are) the shape has no effect on its properties. The quartz might as well just stay lumps. There is nothing wrong with that, but let's not pretend that they are crystals.

There is another external property of quartz that has been made much of – *striations*. Striations are parallel lines running across the prism faces of quartz, which some have decided are like the bar-codes on packaging. Apparently these are messages from the past encoded onto quartz crystals by the ancients before they buried them hundreds of feet underground, and somehow fused them to the walls of veins. Leaving that part of the idea without further comment, striations are natural features created in the crystallization process. It is the pull of forces within the crystal that creates them, as temperatures and pressures within the vein vary. During one set of conditions the crystal produces prism faces; with slight changes in conditions, rhombohedron faces start to form. The striations are, in fact, incomplete rhombohedron faces. There is no mystery whatsoever about them.

Another myth is that crystals have to be 'perfect' in order to be useful. The word 'perfect' is usually taken to mean that they have to be transparent, with no chips on them, and that they've grown in a really lovely form.

Nonsense. They can be cloudy, they can be chipped, they can be battered and beaten and they are still perfectly useable. What makes crystals do what they can do is their atomic structure, their pattern, their inner nature rather than their external appearance. A bit like us, in fact. Some of us are a little more battered on the outside than others, some of us aren't quite as pretty on the outside as others, and yet inside we are all beautiful, we are all perfect, we are all whole, we are all in harmony in our deepest inner nature. That's exactly the way a crystal is. If it wasn't perfect it wouldn't be a crystal.

The question of 'perfection' comes up a lot in crystal courses. Perfection is in the eye of the beholder. Think about this for a while: in the eye of the Creator of all things, everything is perfect. Maybe we need to learn how to see things that way, rather than to see the 'imperfections' resulting from our own prejudices.

A crystal term you'll run into that is made much of is *double termination*. The word termination just means the point on a crystal, the pyramid-shaped end of the crystal (see Figure 18). In some quartz crystals (in fact you'll find it on all kinds of other crystals as well but, once again, it is usually applied to quartz), there is a point on both ends. The term for this is *double terminated*. There is an idea that those crystals develop both ends at the same time, and are therefore something special!

Sorry, again this is wrong. Most of the double-terminated quartz crystals form when the crystal breaks off from the cavity in which it is forming and just grows another point on the broken end. No big mystery about it at all.

Another term you'll come across are 'male' and 'female' crystals. This originates from American Indian mythology and was originally connected to turquoise. Mother Earth is seen as being green – connected to the green of growing things; and Father Sky is seen as being blue. Turquoise comes in green and blue varieties and therefore the green turquoise was assumed to be feminine, or Mother Earth turquoise, and the blue turquoise was assumed to be masculine or Father Sky turquoise.

If we ourselves embody a great deal of feminine energy we might well experience crystals 'giving off' that sort of energy – assuming crystals give off energy (which, of course, they don't; they are only reflecting our own energy back to us).

From a purely cynical standpoint (a very accurate one in this particular case), the term 'feminine' is usually applied to the milky, cloudy quartz crystals. The crystal miners in Arkansas, Brazil, and most of the other places where quartz is produced, had mountains of milky crystals lying around that they couldn't sell because nobody wanted them. Everyone wanted the very clear ones. Conveniently, the milky crystals are suddenly special 'female' ones, and now they have a high market value. They couldn't give the things away a few years ago. This doesn't mean that the milky crystals are not of value – they are still crystals, and therefore still perfect. But let's please stop our need for a lot of nonsensical terms to justify what is.

(There is more of this by the way: the whole idea of birthstones was cooked up by the 19th-century Victorian jewellery industry to sell certain stones that were in abundance at that particular time. If you look into the lists of birthstones, you'll see that there are almost as many lists as birthstones, and they are all different! If you trace the lists that have appeared at various times in about the last 80–90 years, the stones that appear on the list at any given time are the ones that just happened to be quite abundant at that time!)

YET MORE MYTHS AND MISUNDERSTANDINGS

Several publications have suggested that the Earth itself is a crystal, based on the geometric form of an icosahedron combined with a dodecahedron. Various purported positions of the intersection of faces and crystal edges are drawn on the Earth's surface, and then these various positions are studied to try to find archaeological evidence of particular activity along these lines.

Unfortunately for this theory, the Earth is predominantly covered with water and many of these lines and points tend to fall in and across various oceans. The various archaeological artefacts that are described as forming concentrations around certain points often cover as many as 500–600 square kilometres on the ground surface. Not only that, the most fundamental aspects of crystals are completely ignored – that they have precise internal arrangement, and precise external symmetry. A quick glance at a globe or map of the Earth, will soon inform the reader of exactly how symmetrical the Earth is. Even if we were to use other criteria, such as the size, shape and distribution of continental plates, we would find once again that the Earth is anything but symmetrical.

Several 'teachers' around the world are 'manifesting' various gems for their disciples, apparently out of thin air. Any halfway competent magician (or, more correctly, illusionist) can do the same thing. One such illusionist in Las Vegas was even 'materializing' live tigers on stage. The only difference is that these illusionists are not claiming to be spiritual masters.

The more telling point concerns the 'gems' themselves. I have had an opportunity to examine some of these, and there are several curious things about them. One 'messiah's' gems are almost all cut into the shape of famous diamonds – but they are not diamond. Such diamond replicas are easily obtained on the commercial market, but they are usually cut from quartz. These indeed appear to be quartz. One of the other 'gems' is a replica of the Hope Diamond, which is blue. This one is cut from synthetic sapphire. Are they running out of the real thing on the Other Side?

The stone cutting process

Not only is there a lack of understanding of geology and mineralogy but also of the most basic processes of the lapidary or gem cutter. This lends itself to some rather extraordinary interpretations of certain artefacts from the past, and in particular artefacts with a high degree of emotional impact – such as the crystal skulls which have been 'found' in Latin America.

Some writers tend to view these skulls as isolated artefacts, and do not place them in the context of products of a civilization vastly experienced in stone working and carving. The fact particularly overlooked is that these very same cultures which allegedly produced the skulls were producing intricate carvings in jade – equally as complex technically and even more difficult to execute. Even an amateur lapidary knows that jade is ten times more difficult to shape and carve than quartz crystal.

These writers, and indeed the 'scientists' who have studied these skulls, seem to have the typical layman's misunderstanding of the processes of gem cutting. This usually involves an image of a little old man sweating over a stone that he is about to cleave with a blade and a mallet, and then fainting dead away when the stone falls in two perfect pieces! In fact, this particular process is done very rarely, and almost always with large diamonds that would take months to saw. Virtually every other type of stone is simply sawn into the desired shape using a diamond-impregnated saw blade, and then ground into final shape on lapping wheels.

It is this misunderstanding that allows the researchers to be 'amazed' that the skulls bear no particular orientation to the crystallographic axes, which would be necessary had they been shaped by cleaving rather than by ordinary grinding methods. Quartz has *no* cleavage, and therefore will not shatter (as the researchers suggest) if the shaping process is not very precise. Truly, the only thing that would have been amazing is if the skulls *had* been oriented to the crystallographic axes.

The researchers also conclude that, since there were no marks present to suggest it, no metal tools were used. As a professional lapidary, I would be very interested in seeing what sort of marks one looks for as evidence of metal tools. If a piece is properly executed, there should not be *any* evidence that tools were used! However, from the lack of these marks, the researchers then conclude that these skulls were probably chiselled into shape using diamonds! Diamonds, although hard, are also quite brittle and shatter easily enough if subjected to sharp blows.

Even if metals were not available (and they probably were not), sand drills were. The sand drill is a device commonly used by primitive people even today in various parts of the world for drilling holes in beads and ornaments. In this process a bow drill is used, and the drill 'bit' is often nothing more than a cactus spine that is fed a slurry of fine mud or sand at the point where it enters the rock. As quartz is quite easily ground away by this method, at least compared to jade, one can easily imagine tools of this type scaled up for grinding and shaping larger pieces. Using certain types of hard woods and fire-hardened bamboo, metal tools are totally unnecessary.

The rough forming of these skulls would have been partly accomplished by sawing or by *cobbing*, a process of chipping off small pieces until the rough shape is achieved. Cobbing was used to rough-shape quartz crystal balls in Japan until well into the 20th century. The tool that may have been used for sawing is a mud saw, which once again has a modern equivalent. In this tool a single strand of wire (or hemp fibre or fire-hardened bamboo in the ancient tool) is drawn back and forth across the stone, often with a bow to hold the wire taut, and fine mud is fed in along the cut. This process is used today for sawing large jade boulders in Alaska, but with a large metal blade instead of hempen fibre. Some of these researchers have concluded that it would have taken approximately 300 man-years to have made one of these skulls. It would be very surprising if it took two men more than two months. There are a great many lapidaries in the world today who could duplicate one of these skulls in approximately that amount of time, using techniques that would have been available 1,000 years ago.

Rather more amazing to me than the crystal skulls are the cylinder seals that were produced in Mesopotamia several thousand years *before* these skulls were made, which are very intricately carved and need a magnifying glass to see all of the detail. Why is it so difficult for us to realize that so-called primitive man knew a thing or two about working stone?

As to the actual uses of these skulls, one need only look again at the culture in which they were supposedly produced. Oracular devices, such as 'talking' idols, were not at all uncommon in these cultures, and usually consisted of nothing more than a hole bored through the idol at the location of the mouth. The priest then stood behind the idol (out of sight) and gave the idol's 'pronouncements' to the assembled multitudes. As the one crystal skull that has a moving jawbone also has two small holes on either underside of the jaw (where wires were clearly attached), there is no reason to suspect this skull was anything else. As the human skull was held in particular respect, and even awe, in these early civilizations (as it is even today in ours), then it is easy to imagine the effect of such a 'talking' skull, especially when lit from below, as this particular skull was apparently designed to be.

There are a great many psychic phenomena that are described by people who have been in the presence of these skulls, and this is not surprising. Keep in mind that no matter what its shape, it is still a piece of quartz crystal, and therefore responsive to all of the various energy transformations of such crystals. Because the shape itself is highly emotive even in our 'modern' culture, a person in the presence of such an object will be generating significantly larger amounts of emotional energy than normal, not to mention the reflection of his or her own expectations.

There is one last point. Quartz crystal skulls were quite commonly manufactured in Europe in the 16th and 17th centuries. Not one of the skulls 'from' Mesoamerica has ever been found in authenticated circumstances.

Channelling

There is a huge amount of channelled information about these days, both about crystals and other things. There is an assumption that because something comes from a 'spirit' source, it is true. Nothing could be further from the truth. Of the material channelled about crystals, fully 90 per cent of it is factually wrong. For example, I was approached at a festival by some very nice and very sincere people who had channelled information about crystals, and they were very anxious to share it with me. To step backwards in the middle of the story, the word 'crystal' comes from the ancient Greek for 'ice'. The Greeks only used the word in reference to quartz, which was believed to be ice that had frozen so hard it couldn't melt.

The very first words from these folk's channelled source were: 'Crystal is just ice that has frozen so hard it cannot melt.' They were channelling a message from the spirit of an old Greek somewhere, who was telling them the absolute truth about crystal – to the best of *his* knowledge. There is much channelling from many sincere and 'truthful' sources – and most of it is completely wrong.

THE ORIGINS OF THESE MYTHS

Why do myths happen? How do they get started? We know that things can have the appearance of doing one thing, when in fact something entirely different is happening. We are frequently deceived by appearances.

There are things that happen with crystals that *appear* to amplify, that *appear* to transmit, that *appear* to heal, that *appear* to do quite a few things. But what is really happening is that our own *human* ability to heal, our own *human* ability to amplify and to focus our own energies, is being reflected back to us more clearly through the use of crystals.

We can take any number of personal development courses and the one thing that we will learn in every single one of those courses is that *clear intentions get clear results*. What greater reflection back to us of the most subtle and profound levels of our own inner clarity could there be than the very clearest expression of energy that exists in the universe: the crystal? When we hold crystals, when we use crystals, when we have them near us, we have reflections back to us at an intuitive level of our own inner clarity. When we form an intention coming from that most powerful level of clarity in ourselves, then we get clear results.

It looks as if somehow the crystal has done it. But crystals don't do anything except reflect. Just like everything else outside of yourself. It is *people* who are powerful, *people* who heal, *people* who are all of the things that we think crystals are. All the crystals do is reflect back to us. And, as such, they are immensely powerful tools for healing at a most subtle and deep level. But they are not doing the actual healing – this comes solely from inside ourselves.

Because we are out of touch with our Inner Being, the source of our own healing and our own power, when those things are reflected back to us in crystals, we don't recognize them as reflections because we don't recognize them in ourselves. We believe that the reflection is the reality.

Throughout this book, you will discover more about how you can use those crystal-clear reflections to become more and more in touch with the reality of who you *really* are.

CHAPTER 6

USING CRYSTALS

In the mountains of truth you never climb in vain. Either you already reach a higher point today, or you exercise your strength to climb higher tomorrow.
Nietzsche

So, what are the practical realities of crystals? In the simplest terms, they are tools to which the deepest, inner part of ourselves responds in a clear and potent way, without the need for mystical mumbo-jumbo. This happens regardless of whether we are aware of it or not, whether we know anything about crystals or not.

In 1981 I was involved in an experiment at a private clinic in London which used the biofeedback device called the Mind Mirror – essentially a EEG for reading brainwaves, but with the various levels of brain activity displayed in rows of lights on a panel, so that the patterns of the various levels are simultaneously visible. The subject was blindfolded and wore earplugs, to eliminate as many outside clues as possible. After entering a meditative state with the brainwaves stabilized, crystals were passed over the various chakra points (see Chapter 7 for more information about chakras and their importance). The crystals were taped to the end of a metre-long stick to minimize the amount of the researcher's aura being involved with the subject. The subject was unaware consciously of the point at which the crystals were passed through the aura. What was discovered was that as the crystals passed through the lower three chakras – the most earth-connected ones –

there was a strong flare of brainwave activity in the subconscious levels. The body was instinctively aware of the crystals' presence. The researcher's conclusion was that this was the 'recognition' mechanism at work, referring again to the 'like recognizes like' esoteric truism.

Other experiments with crystals clearly show their realities and expose the myths surrounding them. Many crystal books list specific uses for different crystals. How people really respond to crystals is clearly demonstrated, time after time, in an experiment I do in my courses. The participants are seated in a circle with their eyes closed, and are asked to hold out their right hand. I go round the circle and place a crystal in each open hand. Keeping their eyes closed, after a few minutes I ask the group what they are experiencing with the crystal. Out of a group of twenty, three or four will experience sensations of heat. Another three or four will have sensations of cold. For a few it will feel very heavy, and for another few it will feel very light. Others will feel as if it is getting larger, and some will feel as if has disappeared altogether. Some will see colours or other visual experiences, or have sensations in other parts of the body. So, out of the group of twenty, many will have exact opposite experiences, and others will have highly varied experiences. But . . . *they all are holding the same type of crystal.* This experiment can be repeated as many times and with as many types of crystals as desired; the result is always the same – a number of opposite reactions, and a wide range of other responses, although not necessarily from the same people who had a particular reaction the previous time.

Each crystal is a unique entity in itself. Although their inner patterns are identical, their external forms will all be different in some way. Like snowflakes, no two crystals are exactly the same, therefore their mirroring of energy will be slightly different. Even for the same crystal, because no two people are exactly identical energetically, its mirroring will be different. For one person it will mirror one thing, but for another person the same crystal will mirror something else. In this one experiment the wide range of reactions to exactly the same thing demonstrates clearly the nonsense that specific crystals have specific uses.

Another experiment shows that how we react to a given crystal – how and what it mirrors – depends on where it is placed. Again the participants hold their right hand open and flat. This time they place the crystal themselves. First it is placed in the centre of the hand, and the reaction sensed and noted. Then the crystal is moved to the tips of the fingers and the reaction sensed; then to the heel of the hand, and then to wrist, again sensing as before. Even this one small demonstration shows that an inch or so in the placement of a crystal changes our response to it. You can do these experiments at home.

How does this affect the uses of crystals listed in the various crystal books? By all means *try* the uses suggested, but be sensitive to the response and the result. They may not be as described. What works for one person may have no result at all for someone else trying exactly the same thing. That is the nature of energy healing.

There is another point to this as well – when coloured crystals are used, many of the properties ascribed to them are, in fact, their colour properties, and are not related specifically to the crystal involved – as the following two chapters reveal. However, if the combination of both the crystal and colour factors are kept in mind, they provide a very useful and powerful combination, as we will see.

PREPARING TO USE CRYSTALS

The use of crystals involves several distinct stages. The first of these is *acquiring* the crystals.

The most common method of acquiring crystals is to buy them. There is certainly nothing wrong with this, since you are simply exchanging the energy you have put into acquiring your money for the energy that the crystal has accumulated – at least metaphorically – in making its way to you. A crystal that has come halfway around the world has 'acquired' the energy of the miner, of the buyer, of the importer, and of the various forms of transportation required to reach the mineral seller. The exchange for money energy maintains the perfect balance of energy that characterizes a crystal.

As to where crystals can be purchased, the business pages of your local telephone directory is a good place to begin. Depending on the part of the world in which you live there will be several types of headings to look for. These may be 'Rock Shops', 'Minerals for Collectors', 'Lapidary Equipment and Supplies', or 'Mineralogists'. Many of the businesses listed under these categories will not have crystals available for sale, but they will probably know where you can enquire further in your local area. If you do not happen to live in a large town, it is possible that you will find none of these listings. If not, try to locate the business pages for the largest town near you and begin there. You may need to make a number of enquiries.

Crystals can often be purchased by post, but it is more desirable to make your own choice in person. The actual method of deciding which crystal (or crystals) is the right one is simple – only choose what you are drawn to. Forget that you are a Taurian or a Libran and that some book or other says you should have such and such a stone. You are a unique individual, and each crystal is a unique individual. Remember that this uniqueness is part of the subtle make-up of both you and the crystal, and the only way such energies can be sensed is through intuition.

Many people feel that they are not very intuitive, but almost every one of us has had an experience of a 'first impression' – something inside us that tells us there is something about a person or place that does not tally with what we are being told, or perhaps with what we feel we should be feeling about that person or place. Later events almost always prove the 'first impression' to have been correct. This is really nothing more than a flash of intuition – which our 'thinking' mind later talks us out of. Many readers will already have confidence in their intuitive ability, but for those who do not, what might be called the 'first impression method' is suggested.

This is very easy: just stand in front of a group of crystals, shut your eyes, relax, then open your eyes quickly and grab the first crystal that your eye is drawn to! This crystal will almost always be the one that is needed at that moment. In that instant, before the thinking mind can react, your intuition (which reacts instantaneously) has already flashed to the right choice.

If you are choosing crystals for a specific purpose (like healing or meditation), then have this purpose in mind, or even project it to the crystals, and see which one responds, which one you are drawn to. Some people will actually sense an energy response from a particular crystal, perhaps as a flash of light, a vibration, or even a sense of the crystal almost jumping up and down saying 'Me! – Me! – Me!' It is reflecting your inner need for that crystal right back to you.

In choosing crystals for whatever purpose, I have seen all sorts of methods proposed and demonstrated – bent coat hangers, muscle testing, etc. There is certainly nothing wrong with any of these, but as we are really looking into our own hearts, I suggest that in using crystals, we do precisely that! Every one of us deep inside ourselves has some sort of body feeling or sensation, usually associated with the heart, or sometimes the solar plexus, that says: 'This feels right.' In choosing crystals, I always suggest that you simply go for the 'feels right' feeling. You are really looking for a crystal that resonates in some way with your Inner Being. If you are choosing a crystal to reflect the healing aspect of yourself, then one particular crystal above all the others may resonate to that. Likewise with meditation, one particular crystal will resonate. Perhaps you have had the experience of going to a table filled with crystals, and among them there is one that 'speaks' to you. This will be a crystal that is in some way like you – a perfect outworking of that universal law of 'like attracts like' again.

Sometimes it is not possible to choose crystals in person, or you may be asked, or feel drawn, to choose a crystal for someone else. There is nothing wrong with this, as long as you choose intuitively again. A good method is to visualize the person for whom you are choosing the crystal, project that visualization to the crystals, and see which one responds.

Occasionally you may be drawn to a particular crystal without knowing why. It may be that if that crystal is for you, it is for some time in the future. This may be the only chance you and the crystal have to meet: when the crystal is finally needed it may not be possible to be physically present in the same place. Alternatively, the crystal may be for someone else – perhaps someone you have not even met yet, and you have an opportunity to acquire the crystal that they may never have. Again, intuition takes care of these situations.

If you are given a crystal, or are not sure why a particular crystal has been drawn to you (or you to it), meditation may provide the answer. It is sometimes tempting to have someone else choose a crystal for us, someone who supposedly 'knows' more than we do about them. Always choose for yourself – anyone who chooses for you has taken away your opportunity to expand your own awareness and intuition. Your guidance or inner feelings for yourself are always better than someone else's for you.

One last thing – there are several international magazines published in the USA that are dedicated entirely to the mineral collector. Two of these are *The Lapidary Journal* and *Gems and Minerals*. An enquiry at your local natural history or science museum could produce the names of journals available in your area. There are many advertisements for crystals of all types in these magazines, and information will be available about places to collect your own crystals.

FINDING YOUR OWN CRYSTALS

Although it is enjoyable to find your own crystals if and when possible, unfortunately this is difficult for many people. Not all areas of the Earth are blessed with good collecting areas, although it is surprising what is often available in your own locality. You can find out by making enquiries at your local museum, or through geological societies, or even the geology or earth-science department of a nearby university. You may also be able to find guide books written for the collector which describe various collecting localities. Such books are often available through mineral dealers. If you happen to live near a good bookshop, you may very well find some interesting guide books tucked away in areas dealing with geology and mineralogy.

In a number of countries, there are clubs for people who collect rocks and minerals. These clubs will have knowledge of, and access to, many good collecting locations. Ask about such clubs through mineral dealers, or try the telephone directory. These clubs are very popular in Australia, New Zealand, the UK and the USA.

If you are fortunate enough to live in or near an area where mining or quarrying has taken place, there are excellent possibilities for finding crystals in the waste rock. Always be certain you have permission from the landowner or mine operator to go and collect, and be aware that these types of locations can be extremely hazardous. Under no circumstances should you enter mine tunnels or underground workings, as they are often unstable and cave-ins and rockfalls can happen quite easily. Also be cautious when walking in such areas, as vertical shafts will often be overgrown and difficult to see until it is too late. It is not recommended to take children into such areas, but if you do, keep them in sight – and within easy reach – at all times.

The types of crystals that can be found in such locations are many and varied, although not all mines or quarries will produce specimens. Take a small hammer and chisel along with you for separating crystals from the adhering rock, and also take along a container of some sort to carry them back in. Don't depend on your pockets – they get full all too soon!

Whenever you are in countryside where rocks are exposed, look out for any changes in the appearance in the rocks, especially changes in colouration which appear as straight lines or streaks. Often these will be veins of a differing mineral, and can contain crystals.

Beaches and stream beds are also good places to find all sorts of rocks and minerals, although they are much more likely to be water rounded. This does not necessarily detract from their usefulness as spiritual instruments, and once again your own sensitivity and awareness will tell you which ones want to come home with you. If you have been drawn to this book, you may already have piles of rocks and crystals on every available shelf – they *all* want to come home with you, it seems!

BASIC CRYSTAL USE

Questions are frequently asked about various aspects of the use of crystals, especially that of *cleansing* and *programming*. You will find an enormous amount of information available on these two subjects in various crystal books, and there are nearly as many techniques as there are books. In truth, it doesn't matter what activity you undertake in any of these processes, as it is not the activity itself that is creating the response. As in all things in the world, the response is solely a result of your intention.

As I will talk about the mirroring effect of crystals throughout this text, I think it will be helpful to look at the various aspects of crystal use in these terms.

Cleansing

The first aspect is *cleansing*. If crystals are mirrors of the Self, then cleansing is nothing more than cleaning the mirror! Physical mirrors get fingerprints on them, they get cloudy, they get dusty – in other words they need to be cleaned in order to see a clear reflection. Crystals as mirrors are exactly the same.

What crystals are mirroring is energy, and therefore the reflections they give are energetic in nature. Likewise, that which keeps a crystal from giving a clear reflection is also energetic, and therefore the 'cleaning' of a crystal takes place at an energetic level.

As has been discussed, a crystal does not store energy, and yet, through its contact with humans, there is some sort of energetic shift that takes place within it – a change of consciousness, a change of the nature of the energy it embodies. There is a parallel within you. You still have exactly the same number and arrangement of atoms in your body before a profoundly enlightening experience, but afterwards, you are definitely changed. So too are all experiencing individuals on the Earth, no matter what Kingdom they are from. With crystals, this can be a result of being dug from the earth originally, from being handled by the miner, the various crystal dealers who have sold and resold it, or other people who have handled it or whose thoughts and intentions have been impressed upon it.

The act of cleansing the crystal is nothing more than returning the consciousness of the crystal – returning its reflectivity – to whatever state you wish it to be in. Often, this is returning a crystal to its natural consciousness, the one it had as it resided in the earth. At other times a crystal will be 'programmed' for a specific purpose. Programming is discussed below. It must be remembered, above all, that the physical activity of cleaning, whatever it may be, is not actually what has happened. The crystal is responding to the intention of the cleaner, and whatever physical activity is being used is merely a reinforcement of the intention of the person doing the cleaning, and it is that intention that the crystal is responding to. So, put the crystal in the moonlight, soak it in salt water, wipe it with eucalyptus oil, or whatever. Whatever activity you wish to perform reinforces your intention about the state of being of the crystal, and about the clarity of the reflections it gives back to you.

The actual technique of cleansing varies from individual to individual, and you will find a technique through experimentation that will feel right for you. You can just wash crystals in flowing water. Water is a universal cleanser and is effective in cleaning those energies that are undesirable in the physical body, whether it be the body of a person or the body of a crystal. Many of you will be familiar with the effect of salt water in cleansing your own body's aura, and a similar effect is seen on the 'aura' of a crystal. A word of caution though – do not use hot water on your crystals, as it is likely to shatter them. Always use water that feels cool to the touch, or cold water. You will find that even at room temperature, your crystals will feel cool to the touch, and the water temperature should match that as nearly as possible. While washing crystals, they should be held in the hand, and the holder should intend that all energy/consciousness that has been impressed upon the crystal and is not desired will be washed away, and that all the desirable energy/consciousness it has absorbed will remain.

Sunlight is always a great cleanser. If it is possible or practical to do so, leave your crystals in the sunlight, once again with the intention of cleansing any negative energies, and also with the intention of transforming undesirable consciousness into desirable consciousness. A few hours should be sufficient, but allow your own sensitivities to be the judge.

Some people suggest washing crystals in eucalyptus oil or surgical spirit (medical alcohol), or even breathing on them in a certain manner. Truly, it makes no difference: in each instance, it is the intention of the user to clean the crystal that matters, and it is this intention to which the crystal responds.

My own method for cleaning is to use a simple visualization, as all that is really necessary to clean a crystal is a focused intention. For me, a symbol of purity is clear mountain spring water, so I just visualize a flow of such water through the crystal, washing away anything that I don't want in it. With an unprogrammed crystal, I visualize washing away anything that was not part of the original nature of the crystal; but with a programmed crystal, I visualize it retaining its original nature plus whatever programme it has in it.

The question of when to clean crystals (apart from the initial cleansing) will largely depend on the intuition of the user, as well as on the use to which they are put. Crystals that are being intensively used, such as those used by a healer on a regular daily basis, will need frequent cleansing. It will probably be necessary to clean healing crystals each morning before the first patient, so that any energies accumulated overnight will be removed, as well as between each patient.

Programming

Programming is the act of selecting whatever energy reflection you wish to have come back to you from the crystal. So, when we programme a crystal for healing, we are really programming that crystal to reflect back to us our own human ability and capacity to balance and harmonize. Or, if we are using a crystal in a clinical situation, we are using it to reflect back to the patient their own natural abilities for self-healing. Once again, it is our intention that is creating the action here, and a crystal is merely acting as a reflector. If you programme a crystal for meditation, then you are selecting a reflection back to you of some higher aspect of yourself. We exist on many different levels, and it takes a bit of effort to bring some of those levels into our conscious mind. This is the function of meditation.

There is a certain amount of subtle energy already 'programmed' into your crystal that is a result of the natural environment in which it grew. Although this is not usually apparent in its physical form, with experience of discerning energies you will be able to tell, for example, a piece of quartz crystal that has come from Arkansas in the USA from a Brazilian one. In one you will find a very clear and high energy, in the other a much more diffused and less intense energy. Remember that in choosing your crystal in the first place, your intuitive reaction will automatically compensate for differences in the original growing environment, and you will always get exactly the crystal that grew in the environment necessary to harmonize with your own particular energy.

It is not really necessary consciously to programme all crystals, especially those carried for personal use whenever a need should arise. In this instance, the crystal is 'programmed' as it is used, and it is not desired that the crystal should retain the programme. It could be said that such a crystal is already programmed with the user's own energy, but this often takes place at an unconscious level.

Crystals that are used for a single purpose, such as healing or meditation, benefit most from conscious programming, where it is desired that the crystal should retain its programme. The actual process is simple. All that is necessary is to direct a thought into the particular crystal, intending that that crystal's energies should be focused for a particular purpose and that the crystal should retain that particular thought or intention within itself. During this process it is most effective for the crystal to be held in the hand of the user, since this will help the crystal to harmonize totally with all the mundane energies of the electrical 'aura', as well as with the highest spiritual consciousness. All of this will be imprinted into the crystal during the process of programming.

Protection

Another stage of crystal preparation could be called *protection*. This stage is nothing more than being selective about the reflections from the crystal, and in this case reflections which we *don't* wish it to give. My particular protective programme is to install the thought in the crystal that I don't wish it to reflect anything that is not in harmony with Christ energy. There are a lot of energies around in the world, energies at many different levels of life and different levels of being. The Christ energy is an energy that applies solely to the human race, but all other energies in the world are in harmony with it. If we think about it for a minute, the only inharmonious energies in the world are those created by the human race!

The question will naturally arise that if crystals reflect perfect balance and harmony, how can they reflect back that which is not? In a way, an analogy with your bathroom mirror is apt. When you look in the mirror, does it not reflect back everything? But when some of the things it reflects are not as they should be (Aah! Another bad-hair day!) we know *because of* the reflection that something is not right. So it is with crystals. When they reflect back something out of balance, the nature of the reflection calls our attention to it. One of the favourite exercises in my courses is to have each person choose a crystal that either makes the participant uncomfortable or, even better, one that they absolutely dislike. Then, by sitting and meditating while feeling the uncomfortable feelings, they get in touch with whatever aspect of themselves it is reflecting.

There is no reason whatever why all of these preparatory steps cannot be performed with a single thought, but in the beginning it helps to break things down into stages. Many of you may be using crystals already, and are undoubtedly familiar with these steps, and have perhaps developed your own variations on them.

I always suggest that people should choose and programme crystals for themselves. There are certainly a lot of people around who will offer to do both for you, but your deepest Inner Being always knows best about what is right for you. What we are all ultimately working towards in this life is to take full responsibility for ourselves and for our own lives, and this is another small way in which you can begin to do that. So what if you make a mistake? There is no way you can harm yourself with crystals.

Many users feel that personal crystals, i.e., crystals that are used solely by one person, are best kept out of sight and not handled by others, so that the large amount of personal energy involved with such a crystal is not disrupted. Such crystals often like to be kept in a dark place, such as a bag of black, blue or purple velvet, when not in use. Where others' energies are involved, crystals in general use (such as healing crystals) are often happy to be on display and to be handled by anyone. Again, your individual intuition will tell you how your crystals should be kept.

Some crystals are happy with certain other crystals, and not so happy with others. This probably has to do with the harmony (or lack of it) of their natural energies. Thus some crystals will feel content next to one another on a shelf, and some will not. In either case, it is no reflection on the crystals involved – it just is as it is.

USING CRYSTALS

There will probably be one direction or another that the crystal will naturally point in when in use. Different teachers say that the termination should point in one particular direction or another. In my experience with many workshop groups, there is *no* particular rule about this, except that there will be a certain way that some crystals will feel natural in the hand. This will vary greatly from person to person, so yet again, go by whatever feels right to you: lay the crystal in your open hand and rotate it through a full circle. There will be a certain point where it just feels *right.* It is this *right* feeling you are looking for whenever you work with crystals.

Where and how the crystals are placed or held has been the subject of a great many crystal books – and various placements and patterns are suggested. In some books they are laid out along the body at distances believed to correspond to different levels of the aura. In others they are laid directly on the body over the chakra points (see Chapter 7). In yet others, the crystals are held by the healer and moved in patterns across the body. There is nothing fundamentally wrong with any of these methods – except when they are done because they 'must' be done in some specified circumstance. Every single person involved in every single treatment – 'patient' or healer – is a different person every single time. Energetically we change from second to second – thus *every* 'healing' is in some manner different from the last. Secondly, and just as important, every condition being treated may be the result of any number of deeper causes. Thus every patient who presents themselves with the same symptoms is, energetically, coming from a different set of causes. All of this will be explored in detail in Part III, but for now we need to understand that the patient–healer interaction needs to be one of sensitivity to the needs of the individual patient, and not the repetition of a formula from a book. Energy healing differs from allopathic medicine in precisely this way.

So . . .

By all means use crystals in various patterns. By all means place them on chakra points. But, be sensitive to what you are doing, and *let that sensitivity* be your guide. Look for the *right* feeling. If you haven't read other crystal books, then when working with yourself or someone else, place (or hold, or move, or use) crystals as your feelings and sensitivities direct. You can't do any harm with them – there is nothing you can do 'wrong'. Does this mean that neither you nor anyone being treated won't experience any uncomfortable feelings through the use of crystals? Far from it. The healing process often involves distress and discomfort. This, too, will be explored in a later chapter.

To some this will all seem a little vague. It is. At least in the sense that when we try to lay down hard and fast rules, we involve our minds and not our sensitivities.

It is this very thing that separates us from our Source more than any other factor in the Western world – our tendency to live in our heads, rather than in our hearts. But this, too, can be sorted out using crystals, as we shall discover.

PART TWO

COLOUR AND CRYSTALS

CHAPTER 7

COLOUR AND COLOUR HEALING

by Lilian Verner-Bonds

WHAT ARE LIGHT AND COLOUR?

Light is a small portion of the electromagnetic spectrum, which includes X-rays, radio and television waves, microwaves, ultraviolet and infrared light waves, and many other waves. Waves, in fact, are the characteristic movement of these types of energy, always travelling in straight lines as they radiate out in all directions from their source. The distance between the crests of the waves determines which type of wave they are: television and radio waves have wavecrests a metre or more apart. Others are only billionths of a metre apart – gamma rays and cosmic rays. More or less in the middle of the spectrum is the tiny portion of waves we see as visible light.

Within this small portion of the spectrum are further gradations of wave spacing – the colours. The widest wave spacings are in the red end of the spectrum, and the narrowest in the purple. The other colours fall in between, with the order of their spacing following the colours of the rainbow. Just off either end of the spectrum are infrared and ultraviolet light, which are invisible to us but are visible to other creatures like snakes and bees.

Nature's intention is for all the world to receive an array of all the colours of the spectrum. Even in conditions of perpetual snow, the white snowflakes embody all of the colours. So what makes colour special? Most importantly, life on our planet evolved within that narrow range of the electromagnetic spectrum to which we are sensitive. Much of the spectrum is actually fatal to human life, for example microwaves on the longer side of the spectrum and X-rays on the shorter side. The

Earth's atmosphere screens out harmful radiations, which is why, when we damage the atmosphere with pollution, we are ultimately harming ourselves. The very evolution of the human body is intimately connected to colour.

COLOUR IN CRYSTALS

How atoms arrange themselves in unit cells is, as we discovered in Chapter 4, determined by two things: size, and electrical potential. Sometimes a 'rogue' atom will slip into the structure that is nearly the same size and electrical potential as the atoms making up the forming crystal, but not quite. (These 'foreign' atoms are technically called trace elements.) Because the crystal structure exists specifically for the purpose of creating perfect balance, it will attempt to balance the effects of the foreign atom by absorbing light energy. The light that is absorbed restores the balance, but only those wavelengths that relate to the specific energy imbalance are absorbed. The rest of the light escapes. That part of the colour spectrum that gets away is what we see – it is the colour of the crystal. As few as three or four foreign atoms per million are enough to cause colour.

As with bonding (see Chapter 4), it is the outer electrons that are involved; those of the deeper levels of the atom do not seem to be affected. These electrons may be the outer shell electrons of the atoms in the crystal lattice, or they may be electrons associated with defects in the lattice. Defects in the lattice which cause colour are called colour centres, or F-centres (from the German, *Farbe*), and such lattice defects absorb light. Lattice defects may be due to:

a) the presence of foreign atoms in the lattice
b) an excess of atoms of one element over that which is required by the chemical formula, for example, an excess of calcium atoms in a crystal of fluorite (CaF_2)
c) mechanical deformations of the lattice.

Foreign atoms in the structure

To see how the presence of foreign atoms in the structure causes colour we can look first at a hypothetical section of the mineral corundum (Al_2O_3), Figure 31a. Here an atom of chromium has substituted itself in the structure for an atom of aluminium. Chromium and aluminium atoms are approximately the same size, and the chromium will fit into the corundum structure in place of an aluminium atom – almost. As it turns out, the chromium atom is just slightly larger than the aluminium atom, and fitting it into the structure is rather like putting a size 6 foot into a size $5^1/_2$ shoe – it will fit, but it pinches! The pinch in this case is a disturbance of the bond energy surrounding the chromium atom, causing a slight distortion in the crystal lattice. It is this disturbance that frees electrons from one position and entraps them in others. These entrapped electrons then absorb the energy of certain wavelengths of light that pass through the atom and, in the case of chromium in the corundum structure, the only wavelength that 'escapes' is red, thus producing a red corundum – which we call ruby. Exactly how the electrons 'trap' energy is not known. As one professor of physics remarked, this question belongs perhaps more to the realm of philosophy than physics.

If the foreign atom in this same corundum structure is titanium, the only light which escapes is blue, and we call the stone sapphire. We discover one other interesting situation. Rubies are almost always smaller than sapphires, and there are very few large rubies known in the world. Experiments have shown that chromium, even in minute percentages, inhibits the growth of crystals. Thus the presence of chromium automatically ensures that the crystal it is colouring will be smaller than it would have otherwise been.

Figure 31b, shows an imaginary structure of a crystal of quartz (SiO_2). In this instance, an iron atom has substituted itself for a silicon one in the structure, but again it is not quite the same size as the silicon. Once again, a slight structural deformation has taken place in the lattice and the freed electrons in this instance are trapping all of the colours except violet, turning this piece of quartz into amethyst.

Figure 31a: a chromium atom present in corundum
Figure 31b: an iron atom substituted into quartz

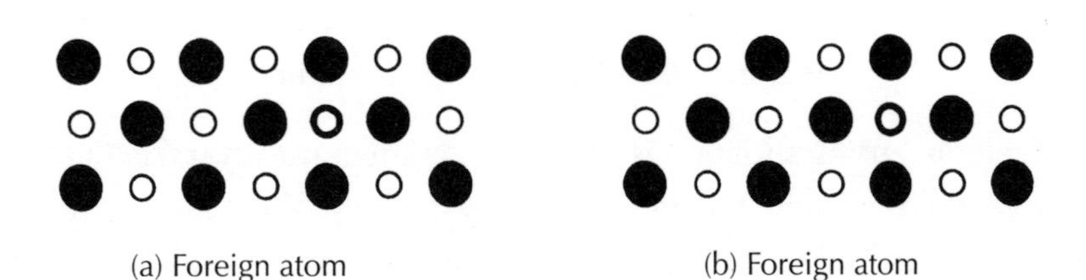

Sometimes, although a particular crystal has entrapped foreign atoms, until some outside agency such as heat or radiation is applied to the crystal there is no colour change. This happens in quartz where an occasional aluminium atom has substituted for a silicon atom. Unless this crystal has grown in an area where there is a certain amount of natural radioactivity in the rocks, the crystal will remain colourless. But if it is subjected to even a relatively small amount of radiation, the crystal will assume a range of colours from yellow-brown to black (producing citrine and smoky quartz). Much of the smoky quartz on the market has been artificially irradiated to produce its colour.

Many gemstones are regularly heat-treated to change their colour, and within the last decade certain gems, such as diamonds, have had their colours changed by X-ray irradiation. In both of these treatments, when foreign atoms are present there is a change of energy state in the foreign atom, freeing extra electrons to absorb different wavelengths of light. An example of this is brown zircon, which is regularly heat-treated to turn it blue. There are also certain varieties of amethyst that can be heat-treated to turn them yellow-brown (citrine).

The number of foreign atoms in a crystal that it takes to cause coloration is relatively small – only a few atoms out of every million normal atoms. How little it takes can be easily imagined by visualizing a three-metre-cube of quartz – the amount of iron that it would take to turn that quartz cube into amethyst is approximately the amount of iron in the head of a pin.

Excess atoms

The second of the circumstances that produces F-centres is that of an excess of one element over that required by the chemical formula. This is not a particularly common cause of coloration and seems to occur mostly in crystals with ionic bonding (*see Chapter 4*). Once again the extra atoms cause lattice deformations that trap light-absorbing electrons.

Mechanical deformation of the lattice

The third colour-causing situation is the deformation of the crystal lattice. This can be produced mechanically by pressure or by heating. Generally speaking, any disturbance of the lattice will produce vacant positions for the positively and negatively charged atoms. These types of F-centres are believed to result from a

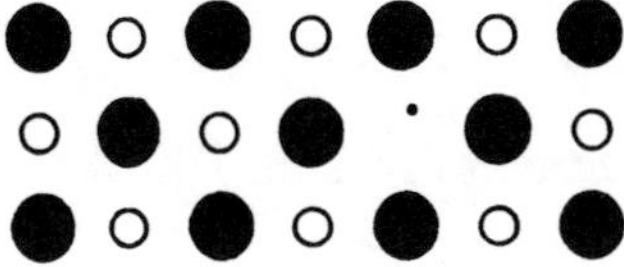
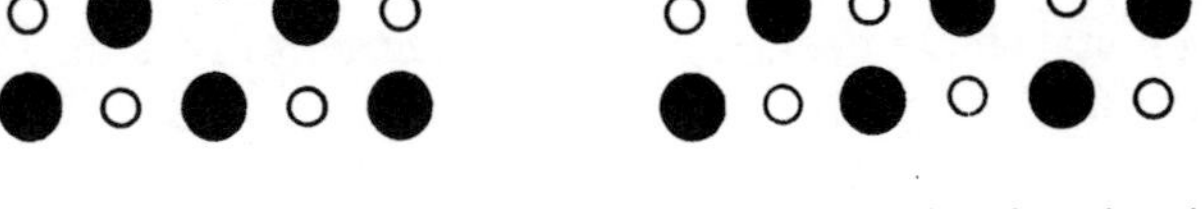

(c) Missing atom with entrapped electron

(c) Broken bond with entrapped electron

Figure 31c: A lattice with an entrapped electron
Figure 31d: A lattice with an incomplete bond

positively charged vacancy in the cell lattice, with an electron moving about in it. Another type of lattice defect that falls into this category is an incomplete (broken) bond, which can also serve as an electron trap. These situations are seen in Figures 31c and 31d. These stressed lattices and their ability to trap electrons behave very much like the stressed lattices caused by foreign atoms, above.

When colour is produced in an initially colourless crystal by irradiating it, it is supposed that some of its atoms have lost an outer electron that has absorbed a quantity of energy, thus allowing it to move about freely. In this case, if the lattice were perfect, the free electron would fall back into place when the excitation ceased, but lattice defects provide local energy levels into which the electron can move. When irradiation ceases, the energy distribution in the crystal will have been changed and F-centres that absorb light energy will have been formed. The crystal will now be coloured. Each positively charged atom that has lost an electron will now have a vacancy in its outer energy level. Such atoms are called positive holes – a term used much in connection with transistors – and will have the power to capture any new electrons that come along.

The silicon chips that are used in computers (and which are regularly confused with quartz in crystal books) are silicon *metal*, which is electrically unresponsive, and to which a small amount of a trace element has been added, usually phosphorus. This creates F-centres in the silicon, giving it its electrical properties. So, not only is quartz *not* used in computers, even the silicon metal that is used has to be tampered with to get it to do anything. Neither silicon metal or its alloys occur in nature.

CRYSTALS AND COLOUR

For centuries crystals have been used for all manner of reasons – healing being one of their prominent and positive activities – notwithstanding their beauty. We are drawn to crystals for various reasons, including their shape, their form – and their colour. I have seen teachers clutching a crystal before students, extolling on the qualities and properties of the crystal in hand and, without exception, virtually ignoring its colour content. But, simply, we perceive colours through the eye, which filters through to the brain, which in turn affects our body's chemistry.

Colour has a profound impact on us mentally, emotionally and physically; as colour is a major ingredient of your crystal, if the language of colour is understood, it can be correctly applied for the recipient's benefit. The colour and the crystal complement each other. The crystal reflects back to you the colour's information, and the colour's information in a crystal is extremely powerful.

How the dimension of colour in crystals is often totally missed, even by 'experts', is illustrated in the following story: I was listening to a radio phone-in programme between a woman caller and the interviewer, who was a crystal 'expert' promoting a book. The woman said she had passed a jeweller's shop-window recently and was drawn to buy a turquoise ring: 'I just had to have it, could you please tell me why?' The expert said, 'Maybe because you liked it, you felt you wanted it.' The woman replied, 'I'm recovering from a nervous breakdown.' 'I'm sorry you've been unwell,' said the interviewer. 'I hope you feel better soon' – end of call.

I felt it was a pity that the *colour* turquoise was not taken into account for the caller. If there had been a knowledge of what the colour turquoise can reveal, it would have answered her question. It is the most prominent colour used to heal the nervous system. The woman who purchased the ring was indeed working on her own healing by being drawn to the one colour through her crystal that could return her to health.

There are many ways of harnessing the power of colour. It can be eaten, worn, drunk, absorbed through your skin or eyes, visualized, and your home or workplace can be decorated and lit specifically with colour healing in mind. Coloured salt-rubs have been successfully used to help invigorate paralysed limbs; different coloured silks can be wrapped around the body; or coloured crystals can be brought into the aura.

COLOUR AND HEALING

Many healing therapies are built on the premise that the body's energy flows can be influenced in a positive way through outside intervention. While this is true for the relief of symptoms, final and complete healing is another matter altogether, as is explained in Chapter 9. It is also a mistaken belief that it is the nature of crystals to directly interact with these energies. Most levels of human energy are reflected by the crystal, but for interaction, we need to look to colour. It was because of their colour that crystals first came into use for 'healing'. Around 3000 BC the Egyptians used substances for treating illness that were the same colour as those produced in the body by the illness they were treating: yellow substances for jaundice, red substances for blood problems, purple substances for bruising, and so on. Coloured stones were among those things used. Yellow beryls were used for jaundice, bloodstone for haemorrhage, and lapis lazuli for the blue of restricted circulation.

Eventually it was believed that the wearing of the colour prevented diseases that produced that specific colour. Thus stones, with their permanent colours (unlike flowers or other organic materials) became especially valued. This is the origin of the use of stones as gems. But they were valued for their *colour*, not for their own intrinsic worth. As coloured glass became available the emphasis in coloured light shifted to this man-made substance, and stones became more valued as items of adornment, while still maintaining their mystique from their days of healing.[1]

In the following chapter, both colour psychology and colour healing are explored through the colours of crystals. As we can see, the colour of a crystal is a vitally important part of its whole make-up, as, indeed, colour is of ours. And why, when used together, colour and crystals are such a powerful combination – and why many of the 'traditional' uses of certain crystals are connected to their *colour* uses.

COLOUR AND ENERGY HEALING

What the physical body's relationship to colour is, and how colour can be used to keep the body in a state of harmony and balance – i.e., health – has been the work

[1] Lilian Verner-Bonds, *The Complete Book of Colour Healing* (New Arlesford: Godsfield Press, 2000)

of colour therapists and researchers for centuries. Colour healing both comes from and is an important part of the entire realm of energy healing. In the early part of the 20th century, physician Dr Dinash P. Ghadiali did much to promote the use of colour medically, healing with different coloured lights. He called his process spectro-chrometry, now known as chromotherapy. In 1903 Danish physician Neils Finsen was awarded the Nobel Prize for Medicine for his work on light and colour in healing disease.

The idea that the human body is more than just flesh, that it has components that are energetic in nature, has come to be more accepted, and that that nature is both reflected in and influences the functioning of the physical body. How we see the manifestation of energy within the human being, and the effects of energy healing, depend to some degree on what we are looking for. For example, the acupuncturist looks for the lines of energy flow within the body, and knows that the placement of needles at certain places within that flow have an observable influence on the physical body. Another way of seeing and understanding the body's energy flows is to observe the body's energy field, its *aura*. This is usually seen as a field of energy that extends beyond the physical body, occuring as a number of colours, the exact colours depending on the person's mood, state of mind and, more importantly, state of health. Another way of seeing the body's energetic nature is through the *chakras*, an Eastern concept which is used by many healers, and a popular way of experiencing the body's energy field. Chakra healing works particularly well in conjunction with crystals.

THE CHAKRAS

The coloured 'seven centres' of the chakras are points of focus of various levels of energy along the spine, neck and head. Because energy comes in many shapes and forms (such as heat, light, inertia, momentum, and so on), it follows that as physical, mental, emotional and spiritual beings, we too embody many different levels, and within those levels there exists a 'spectrum' of energies. The energies of colour (and thus its spectrum), are part of the environment in which the human body evolved.

At the respective ends of the spectrum are the purely physical energies that relate to the world of matter and reproduction – often described as 'dense' – and related to the red end of the colour spectrum. At the opposite end are the 'higher' energies: lighter, subtle, refined, and easily overlooked in everyday life – related to the purple end of the spectrum. In between are five other levels, each relating to a different facet of life: orange and yellow are considered coarser levels, with the energies of blue and indigo more ethereal. In the middle, and the point of balance, is the colour green. It has an exact correspondence in function to the heart centre, which we will explore in greater detail in later chapters.

Each chakra is located on the spine and appears like a vortex – similar to a cone that constantly spins – giving off energy that can be seen when it leaves the body as the aura. Although we cannot see these vortices with the naked eye, it is advisable to keep them balanced and topped up, so that they all rotate constantly in harmony with each other.

The chakras embody various human attributes that can be strengthened or emphasized through raising the energy of the associated chakra. The first three chakras are linked to the body's physical survival: the root chakra – pelvic bone – the colour red; the belly, the colour orange; and the solar plexus, yellow. The next three chakra spots are the heart, throat and brow (midway between the eyes). The heart is connected to the emotions – the colour green; the throat to communication, the colour blue; and the brow relates to the colour indigo, the first stage of your intuitive, physic abilities. The seventh chakra, the crown, is located at the top of the head, and is linked to the colour purple, the highest spiritual connection.

Pendulum healing for chakras

Crystals play a part here: chakras can be balanced by using a pendulum over each chakra spot on the body. A clear quartz crystal can be used as a pendulum for the purpose of reviving the energy centres, but if you want to better balance each chakra using colour, and to give them an extra boost, use the same colour crystal as the chakra wheel. Sitting in a chair, hold a clear quartz or coloured crystal on a chain or piece of string near each of these centres. The pendulum may swing wildly at first. If so, just wait until it settles down and stops, showing that the chakra is balanced.

Each of the seven chakra levels also relates to a gland of the body, and has a corresponding colour. The colours and their corresponding glands are shown over the page:

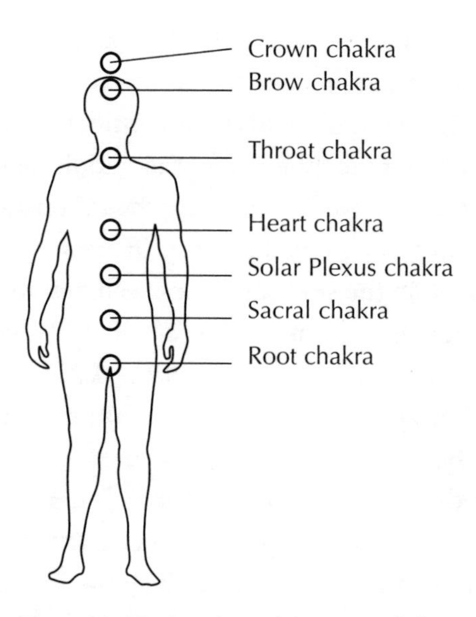

Figure 32: The locations of the seven chakras

Chakra	**Gland**	**Colour**
Root	Ovaries/Testes	Red
Sacral	Adrenals	Orange
Solar Plexus	Spleen	Yellow
Heart	Thymus	Green
Throat	Thyroid	Blue
Brow	Pituitary	Indigo
Crown	Pineal	Purple

You can keep yourself well by toning up your active endocrine system daily, incorporating colour energy through your crystal. Or, you can work on single chakras only, using a different colour for the chakra. For instance, use a blue-coloured crystal over the yellow chakra centre to counteract upset stomachs and to relieve the pain of ulcers. To know which colours to use, see the 'healing' section for each colour in the following chapter.

COLOUR PSYCHOLOGY

The study of colour psychology has been undertaken by numerous eminent psychologists and psychiatrists. Psychoneurologist Dr Kurt Goldstein, a founder of Humanistic Psychology, was a leader among these. When he studied colour and its effects, he made a number of discoveries which underscored what Drs Ghadiali and Finsen, as well as colour therapists and other colour researchers, had worked with for years: that colours affect the entire human organism, and that each colour has a role to play. It was established that a good balance of colour was necessary for a healthy life. Dr Goldstein confirmed that colour-response is deep-set, and intimately entwined with the entire life process, and he also discovered that various mental conditions and psychological states have definite and varying responses to colour.

Other researchers have confirmed Goldstein's work, including Dr Robert Ross of Stanford University. He found that certain colours are allied to dramatic intensity and strong emotion, and Dr Maria Rickers-Ovsiankina confirmed even earlier work with the colour preferences of introverts and extroverts. Colour affects our sense of the passage of time, our sense of space, our senses of taste and smell, and it has been shown to be affected in turn by various sounds. Our entire organism is reactive to colour, and its effects go beyond the immediate sensation or sense of colour. Because we are so interlinked with colour, the entire state of our being can in some way be represented by the colours we embody. We know, too, that a person's psychological state has profound implications for their physical state – that the two are, in fact, inseparable. Colour psychology is thus intimately intertwined with health and healing.

CHOOSING A CRYSTAL COLOUR

The truth is there is no one perfect stone for everyone. All crystals have their own worth, messages and experiences to be encountered. Colour is also a medium to learn to exchange and interact with. Like crystals, there are no good or bad colours – only information to be gained. The exciting world of colour begins with exploring the avenues that can be shown to you if you are willing to be patient, by taking the time to delve into their mysteries. A key factor is how you interact with your coloured crystal, the value of which is personal to you. Each stone, whether you are comfortable with it or not, gives you insights.

If you are eager to delve into your intuitive, physic ability then use your left hand when choosing a crystal, as this is known as the side which leads to divine power, directly through the heart. Use your right hand if you want more mundane information relating to your life on a day-to-day basis. If you cannot decide which coloured crystal to choose, you can close your eyes when selecting. You will, on a certain level, still be choosing the coloured crystal that appertains to you. It just depends whether you trust yourself to do this! Or, when faced with a selection of stones, just pick up the one that most attracts you. Note if it is rough or smooth – a cut or uncut stone. If it is rough, it indicates that the information that will be given by the colour impact is in its early stages; whereas with a cut, smooth stone the colour's information is of longer standing.

Check the following chapter on colour for the understandings that that particular crystal colour has given you. Concentrate on the colour of the stone you are holding. Does it feel strong or weak? Experience any sensations that it may be giving you. You may have sensations in your hand; your mood could change. All of your senses can be involved. Whatever you receive, you will be shown something you need to know. If the feelings are uncomfortable, take into account the colour you have chosen to pinpoint why, as the colour will direct you. Do not despair if you seem to experience nothing at all. If this happens, regard the colour of the stone you have chosen as being perfectly balanced within your system at that moment. Always recognize the significance of the colour of the crystal, as the colour does count.

DIVINATION CRYSTALS – CRYSTAL AEROMANCY

Since the beginning of time man has been obsessed by curiosity to forsee the future. One of the best and most popular methods of gaining insights is to use a clear quartz crystal in the shape of a ball. Crystal ball gazing is called *scrying*, which is derived from the Anglo Saxon 'descry', to see. This art has flourished in various forms all over the world for at least 3,000 years. The Mayans used crystals and they were sacred to their god Tezcatlipoca. In Mexico there was a temple dedicated to this god, and the walls were entirely lined with mirrors. Mirrors made of obsidian or pyrites were frequently used for divination purposes and pronouncing judgments. The Incas also used such mirrors, and clear crystals were most popular with the Indians of Northern Central America, who used to polish up a specimen and consult it.

Whether you use an expensive quartz crystal ball to conjure up a glimpse into the infinite or a mineral mirror, the surface must be clear and able to reflect back to the gazer 'inner space'. A clear crystal works with the Brilliance, so it has every colour captured in it. Do not use a smoky quartz crystal as this colour will delay and hinder seeing. To become really sophisticated you can acquire a coloured crystal ball to focus on particular attributes; for instance, use a green crystal for answers regarding relationships or a yellow one for work prospects. You can also keep to a clear crystal ball for your general scrying work and, rather than buying extra crystals when focusing on specific areas, just put the appropriate coloured cloth underneath the ball to reflect the colour through it, to pinpoint particular issues. Use the list below to select the appropriate colour. Simply gaze into your crystal ball, relax, and see what it can foretell for you.

Another technique, if you don't have a crystal ball, is for you to hold a crystal of the appropriate colour while meditating on a specific question or problem related to the life area represented by that colour.

Red	Travel, children, sex life
Orange	Work, career opportunities, divorce
Yellow	Intellectual accomplishments, examinations, the media
Green	Romance, money, finance, marriage, general health
Blue	Healing, literary opportunities
Indigo	House moves, psychic potential
Purple	Leadership qualities, artistic possibilities, self-employment

Light travels at 186,000 miles per second. As long as there is light there is a movement of energy. With all colours arising from this brilliance, it is not surprising how powerful colour healing can be.

CHAPTER 8

COLOURED CRYSTALS PSYCHOLOGY

by Lilian Verner-Bonds

THE PSYCHOLOGY AND HEALING OF COLOUR

In this chapter we will look at the colours of crystals and the messages those colours hold for us. Under each colour are listed crystals that are found in that colour. Some may appear under several colours, since they can occur in a variety of hues. Where a mineral variety takes its name from its colour, like amethyst in quartz, or sapphire and ruby in corundum, the variety name will be listed.

When we talk about a colour we refer to the *hue*, the single, definitive colour, expressed scientifically by its diagnostic wavelength. We work from the basic seven spectrum colours, and denote their shades and tints. All tones of a colour share the colour's basic qualities, but they are modified by whether they are a shade or a tint of the colour.

In the descriptions that follow are a number of colours and their shades, tints and combinations. They are described in terms of their psychological and personality meanings, which are also the meanings of the colours themselves. Read the characteristic as either personality or colour, as appropriate to how you are using it at any particular point. Their healing potential is also described. Colour is in many ways like a language: the more you practise it, the more proficient you become with it.

Tints are pale colours, with more white in them than the main colour, making them stronger for healing, and making the personalities that embody them much lighter than those relating to the pure hue. In healing, for example, pale pink is more powerful than the basic hue of red, because of the abundance of white in it.

Shades are darker, the basic hue mixed with black. Generally tints are considered positive and the shades negative; but the negative can be equally useful, because it directs us and tells us what we need to look at, especially where our personalities are concerned. The more a person embodies a shade, the more their life is hindered; hence, the characteristics of shades are described as 'hinderences'.

This chapter will enable you to locate and identify the colour aspect of a crystal for all its information. The basic-hue personality given below will heal on all levels. The light tint will speed up healing because it has the Brilliance with it, which makes it more powerful – so use it sparingly, particularly when working with children or the elderly. The dark shade will slow the healing, but is beneficial for a slow introduction of the colour.

You can use any method of colour healing, or just simply close your eyes and visualize the colour, or focus your eyes on an object of the desired colour. You can also imagine the air being filled with the correct hue, shade or tint, and just breathe it in. Learn to incorporate the colour of your choice (the one that is within your crystal) into your life for a fuller understanding. Grasp the wealth of healing opportunities that can be yours when you embrace colour's magnificence.

To use the information in this chapter, first select a crystal and experience it. Then look at the charts below to get a full understanding of what you are working with colour-wise. Remember, a great deal of insight can be coming from the vibration of the colour of your stone.

How to use the colour meanings with a crystal in hand

This example uses a ruby red crystal.

1. Focus

Tune into the crystal's colour energy. The act of choosing a crystal for its colour focuses your response to that crystal specifically on the colour's vibration.

2. Experience

You have acquired a red crystal. Ask yourself: 'How does this crystal feel to me? Is it cold to the touch, or maybe warm or burning? Am I happy, comfortable, or not? Are there any other sensations?' Be aware whether it is a physical sensation or an emotion that is being reflected back to you.

3. Physical red level

Locate red in the charts. Red is a hot colour and if you are feeling cold whilst handling your crystal it could give an indication that you have low blood pressure. Red foods, drinks and appropriate daily exercise will help to regain health, plus a red decor and clothes can be of benefit. (*Note*: always check with a doctor if you are thinking of starting a workout programme.)

4. Emotional red level

Red being a warm, volatile colour usually means that when the red vibration within our bodies is balanced, we are able to express appropriate anger. A cold sensation with a red-coloured crystal would indicate a suppressing of emotion. A good old-fashioned anger release, like hitting a pillow or shouting out loud, could free and release tensions. A happy mind makes for a healthy body.

Always check your personal experiences with any coloured crystals that you encounter, and be aware of the colour attributes, both positive and negative, given below that relate to you. The colour aspect of the crystals will help to pinpoint relevant issues and show you the way ahead.

THE COLOUR CHARTS

Brilliance: crystal-clear cosmic light

We examine first the Brilliance: the transparent, crystal-clear light from whence all colours spring forth. Brilliance is the clear light of universal healing. Space may appear empty but it is full of invisible colour. Each colour overlaps itself to form the seven colours of the rainbow. Every colour is contained in equal parts in the Brilliance. These colours give us our dark shades and pale tints. Crystal clear light gives a glimpse into the transparency of the infinite light. No shadows hide in the clarity of brilliance. It is the great reflector. All that enters its beams will be recorded and shown back to you. Reflection is the key gift that the transparent crystal contains. Look within yourself if you want information. Use your clear quartz as a crystal ball and become a scryer – one who dares to look and see the truth. In seeming nothingness there is everything. The clear light contains its coloured messages: seek and ye shall find, all will be revealed to you.

Use the Brilliance to get in touch with spirituality and intuitive understanding. It is soft, gentle and introspective. Within it is a natural enthusiasm that nurtures and brings compassion; it bonds and trusts. Its benefits are dissipated when imposed upon, or overwhelmed by outlandish behaviour.

Brilliance in crystal is fragile, like a fine piece of porcelain. It will not assault the world, as it always knows what is, so it becomes calmness and tranquillity. It is the purpose of life. Crystal-clear brings in gentleness and security. Its beauty has no problems because it clears away any cloudiness in a person's internal colour-energy field. Crystal brilliance inspires, as it constantly gives you a clean sheet in life. It clears away all blots and stains to expose corruption, whilst maintaining perfect balance and perfection. However, access to the unseen realms revealed by brilliance will be withdrawn if the user takes advantage of the brilliance or rejects its benefits through their behaviour.
Brilliant Crystals: Quartz – Diamond – Danburite – Calcite – Selenite – Apophyllite – Halite – Topaz

Healing Clear Brilliance

Brilliance has the ability to be a cure-all – fling open the windows and doors, and let the sunshine in. A clean sweep of light allows the body and psyche to renew themselves and start again. Crystal clear will always show you the path to take – it represents the light at the end of the tunnel.

White

Basic White Personality

White is the combination of an equal amount of all the colours of the spectrum, the same as the clear brilliance. But with white, there is a density: if you hold up a white sheet to the light you cannot see through it. White's basic personality is efficient, even if a little cold. White has a tranquillity that conjures up hope. White always strives towards a purity of spirit, regarding all mankind as equal. White has an all-forgiving nature, even though it strives to unearth and expose all that is untrue, shedding light in dark corners. As a colour, white encourages growth and new ideas. It is the great opener that allows expansion and creativity. It removes one's blinkers, so that the truth can be seen, bringing about unity and harmony for all.

Dark – Hindrance of White

Off-colour white can show that a person feels they have fallen from grace. They have suffered at the hands of inequality, bringing frustration. Isolation occurs, often with a feeling of emptiness or a barrenness of spirit.
White Crystals: Moonstone – Milky Quartz – Aragonite – Common Opal – Selenite – Calcite – Muscovite

Healing White

White governs the lymphatic system. It is extremely good to keep the lymphatic system clear. Visualize a white stream filling the body and travelling around to clear the lymph sites. Concentrate on the groin area, underarms and the stomach. White helps to keep the skin nice and moist. It is a lubricant that keeps the body supple, and a great tonic as it contains equal amounts of all the colours within it. White light clears and cleans; it is particularly beneficial for clearing bacteria in stagnant areas. White helps to restore anything that seems faded. White is a universal antiseptic.

Red

Basic Red Personality – Root Chakra

Red is the greatest energizer of the spectrum. This hue promotes courage and the will to overcome. Action is a key red word – it just hates to hang about. The red personality is the pioneer, pushing forward against all the odds with zest, energy and drive. Red has a desire for justice, but it is practical and will ensure that justice is seen to be done. Red will go to war if necessary. Pure red at its best is a fine leader, and a born strategist. A lover of humanity, red will sacrifice him or herself for others. The use of red energy is very good for starting up a business. The constructor, it can build great things from very little. Red will seize the day always.

Shade – Hindrance of Red

Red in its negative state can become too pushy – the bully – and inclined to draw to itself more conflict than most. With its quarrelsome tendencies, it must always win the argument and have the last word. Negative reds are either too forceful by

temperament or suffering from pangs of guilt or shame. They have a tendency to act before thinking things through.
Red Crystals: Ruby – Garnet – Tourmaline – Rutile – Cinnabar – Rhodachrosite – Spinel

Tint – Light Pink Personality

The pink character is affectionate and kind – it is the colour of universal love. Pink has the power to melt and dissolve past hurts and pains. It can pour oil on troubled waters. Extremely sensitive by nature, pinks must arm themselves against the harshness of life's events. They are very easy going and forgiving. They often feel a need for protection, when in fact, they don't need it. They are inclined to be impetuous, and are very responsive. They give out unconditional love wherever it is needed.
Pink Crystals: Diamond – Tourmaline – Morganite – Garnet – Dolomite – Rhodonite

Healing Red

Red is connected to the circulation. A great pick-me-up for the blood, it increases the circulation. It can help to clear furred arteries and anaemia. It is a healing colour for any sexual imbalances – the great nurturer which can get rid of hang ups and excess emotional baggage. Red aids a sluggish digestion. As it stimulates, it is useful in cases of paralysis, particularly when combined with physiotherapy. Red can cause irritations, so use it sparingly and never use it for heart conditions. Red quickens, so it will tune-up slow metabolisms.

Orange

Basic Orange Personality – Sacral Chakra

Orange is the colour of assimilation, able to absorb the goodness from life. Orange is made up of red and yellow so it will have tendencies from both these colours contained within it. Determination is a strong factor of orange. It is the best colour to use to remove fears of any kind. Athletes relate to this colour – they will practise until they get it right, which is right along the lines of orange's energy. Orange will not let sleeping dogs lie: it will always bring to the fore any unresolved problems. It breaks down barriers by focusing on the physical necessities of life. It possess the ability of putting things together again when all seems lost. The orange personality is warm-hearted and generous, but it can be hindered by an inferiority complex. Orange is extremely optimistic and very friendly.

Shade – Hindrance of Dark Orange

Dark orange can be inclined to think that everyone is against them, and often have a chip on their shoulder. They are inclined to take on more than they can fulfil. They believe life has let them down, and that they have been thwarted – but it's never their fault.
Orange Crystals: Dark Citrine – Zircon – Realgar – Calcite – Vanadinite – Wulfenite – Garnet – Spinel – Topaz – Orthoclase

Tint – Light Peach Personality

Pale orange, the peach colour, works on a gentler level than the major hue of orange. Peach has impetus, but it is a little cautious. It checks that it is safe – it *always* checks first. The peach personality likes to be polite. It can be inclined to give a lot of love out for no return.
Light Peach Crystals: Peach Beryl – Topaz – Calcite

Healing Orange

Orange can heal hidden phobias. It can help remove fears and psychological paralysis. It is a good healer for all shock symptoms, bereavement and grief. It supports torn ligaments and is an aid for infertility. Kidney complaints benefit from orange, as well as broken bones. It is excellent for the relief of mucus and catarrh. Use orange as a stimulant to increase appetite in treating anorexia. Orange is particularly good for the relief of menopausal symptoms.

Yellow

Basic Yellow Personality – Digestive Chakra

Yellow is the brightest colour of the spectrum. An inspiring colour mentally, it reasons and works things out in the mind. Yellow stimulates the intellect and is very interested in the media and world affairs. A lover of variety, if nothing is happening the yellow personality will set things in motion. Yellows are great ideas people, full of visions and originality. They are good at starting projects, but may not be around to complete them because they have moved on long ago – the chase is better than the catch. They have an inclination to neglect themselves, because the variety that spontaneity brings forth sweeps them along an imaginative path.

Yellow is full of fun, laughter and joy. They are the great jesters and the communicators who can work through mental intuition.

Shade – Hindrance of Dark Yellow

This colour can be extremely tense and sarcastic. They mix low self-esteem with a lack of confidence. They are over-analytical, evasive, critical, and have an extremely rigid outlook, yet they themselves tend to be lazy and inefficient. They can nag and complain when unhappy.
Yellow Crystals: Diamond – Citrine – Apatite – Sulphur – Brazilianite – Sapphire – Scheelite

Tint – Light Yellow Personality

The pale yellow character is practical and able to cut through red tape – the great eliminator. They are very fair and reliable, very broad-minded, mentally agile, and have a tendency to take a back seat once they have put the wheels in motion. They question what is, so that a better understanding can be gained.
Light Yellow Crystals: Citrine – Topaz – Spodumene – Scheelite – Topaz

Yellow Healing

Yellow is the great cleanser, good for releasing toxins from the body. It is helpful to relieve constipation and digestive disorders, and heals skin problems and the nervous system. It removes negative thinking and phobias as it sharpens the mind, making it excellent for depression and weariness of the spirit. Yellow helps you pinpoint the situation, bringing about the solving of problems.

Gold

Basic Gold Personality

Gold is wisdom accumulated from experience, the colour of old memory. It represents the senior citizen that really has something worth saying – the ripeness of maturity, regardless of wrinkles and creaky bones. The gold personality is not a victim, it will not be put upon. There is an honour with gold. It knows how to put action into motion because of the knowledge it has of mankind. Gold does not dwell on the past – it releases it, believing that what you do today is what counts. It is the colour representing forgiveness without denying self worth. Gold always unites. The United Nations' energy colour is gold.

Shade – Hindrance of Dark Gold

Dark gold believes in inherited worth, because it believes materialistic strength will set it apart from law and order. As gold begins to believe in its own superiority, it becomes very conceited. Liberation of the masses becomes a fear for gold, as they prefer suppression for the majority, but a special place only for their superior selves. They are forever chasing the key for eternal youth to the extent of missing out on today. Positive gold reassures – depressed gold is lost for all time.
Gold Crystals: Gold – Pyrite – Marcasite – Topaz – Barytes

Healing Gold

Gold will help all chronic skin complaints. It releases any parasitical disorders such as fleas and worms. Apply gold to scar tissue because it is stronger than yellow. It can be beneficial for stimulating an under-active thyroid and very successful with depression of all kinds. It acts as a filter to remove toxins, particularly from the kidneys. Use gold for haemorrhoids. It also aids digestion, enabling a balanced liver function. Mentally it will clear doubt and give a reason to live, as it radiates enthusiasm and vitality, and clears emotional hang ups.

Brown

Basic Brown Personality

Brown is the colour of recycling. A state of brown is the fallow field. The brown personality is the salt of the earth. Loyalty ranks high on the agenda – they would rather die than let you down. Great as employees, they like to remain in the background, diligently completing their tasks. They love to hold the fort. They are great as right-hand men because they have no desire to eclipse the boss. There is always an underlying sorrow about brown, a grief for what was, coupled with a fear of what is yet to come. They believe in yesterday and have a reluctance to let go of the past. But great potential resides here – it's only in hibernation, dormant – the awakening is yet to come. Brown has the badge of life – it knows that it has the seeds for next spring, even when winter seems to be dragging on. Brown has extreme patience; it allows growth to take its own time. Brown is safe because it knows when to dig in.

Shade – Hindrance of Dark Brown

Dark brown can sometimes feel it is unable to make any progress, primarily because it will not embrace change due to fear. Stubbornness is a hurdle because it is a stickler for doing things the right way only – which often results in not doing anything at all. Traditionalists to the extent of missing out on the new, they will not acknowledge themselves; they only believe in the proven. They are often emotionally uptight because of a reluctance to face tomorrow.
Brown Crystals: Tourmaline – Staurolite – Zircon – Barytes – Topaz – Idocrase – Siderite – Sphalerite

Tint – Light Tan Personality

The light tan personality chooses to process every step, examining every inch of the way. They like to establish a firm foundation, although they are definitely open to dare to take a risk. Like the snail, they get there in the end. Very hard working, but with more flair than their sister browns. They like to be rewarded fairly for the work produced, but find it difficult to acquire what's due to them.
Light Tan Crystals: Orthoclase

Healing Brown

Because brown can be the best friend you'll ever have, it is the colour of the great comforter. It will make you feel safe and secure, in a safe haven. Very calming and soothing, it is the remover of hassle and tensions. Brown is the great supporter; it is for the person who seek asylum from life's hurley burley. It supports you to let go of the old so that you can germinate and encounter the new. A good colour to use whenever you have to stand still to take stock before starting out again. Brown has the properties of manure – it is not always pretty, but it brings enrichment and new growth through its nutrients.

Green

Basic Green Personality – Heart Chakra

Green is the middle colour in the rainbow. Made up of two colours, yellow from the hot end of the spectrum, and blue from the cool, it is the bridge, the gateway. Green is the balancer because the two colours contained within it enable the person who relates to green to see both sides of a story. Harmony is the aim of green, as it stabilizes. Green holds the key to problems seen, it leads you to the core. Green does not follow any roles – it likes to create better ones. Green is connected to materialism – money. It can bring in prosperity for all. It also represents the great host and entertainer, and greens particularly love gardening and animals.

Shade – Hindrance of Dark Green

Dark green can become the emotional dictator. Or, the other way of dark green (as there are two sides to green) is an inclination to always do things at the expense of themselves. Paranoid about health issues, they can become the hypochondriac. Greediness or the miser is dark green at its worst. Shady green can struggle with jealousy and extreme possessiveness. They usually have a very strong physical constitution, but they are often on an emotional merry-go-round, particularly with emotional upsets.
Green Crystals: Emerald – Malachite – Dioptase – Apatite – Sapphire – Epidote – Olivine – Zircon – Jade

Tint – Light Green Personality

Pale green represents fresh starts and new beginnings. It reflects back youth's hope and inspirations. It encourages others to begin new adventures, and loves to have a try at new romances. Light greens have a childlike personality, appearing immature, but nonetheless full of enthusiasm. On one hand they are the idealist who has a social conscience, yet at the same time they are very practical. A tender and gentle character.
Light Green Crystals: Jade – Garnet – Smithsonite – Prenite – Amazonite

Healing Green

Green is the great healer and balancer. It heals pains of the heart as well as affairs of the heart emotionally. It strengthens strained relationships. Beneficial for claustrophobia and any physiological illness. Green helps to centre oneself when the nerves seem shattered. It soothes headaches and biliousness, stabilizes bleeding, calms the hyperactive, and is a good general detoxifier.

Basic Turquoise Personality

The turquoise personality is extremely cool, calm and very balanced, but there is a fire burning underneath that cool exterior. Turquoise has a discriminating eye. They are very self-sufficient and, when they want to be, extremely ambitious. If you have chosen a turquoise stone is it telling you that it is about time you jumped off the fence. Turquoise always nudges you to get on with it. It is hard for the turquoise personality to take sides, as they are always open to the possibility that each is right. The greatest love affairs you'll ever have relate to the turquoise colour. This colour often struggles for emotional control. Their main qualities shine in personal relationships. Togetherness with a partner is the desire of the turquoise character. They hate being single. Rapport with animals is a particularly turquoise trait.

Shade – Hindrance of Dark Turquoise

Dark turquoise can be cold and stand-offish, but in an effort to communicate they may appear boastful and unreliable. An emotional manipulator *par excellence*, and given to false flattery, they are narcissistic by nature. There is an inclination to have affairs, as they cannot decide which person they really want. They wither and collapse if their object of desire passes on and leaves them. They waste unnecessary time day-dreaming, waiting for that perfect partner that never comes.
Turquoise Crystals: Turquoise – Smithsonite – Aquamarine

Tint – Light Turquoise Personality

Pale turquoise is the light of love on a one-to-one romantic level. There is a craving to enjoy life. In their everyday working they can become the Jack-of-all-trades-and-master-of-none; nothing really interrupts their search for personal love. They are inclined to concentrate on acquiring that single mate, the love of their life, which they are adamant will bring them utopia. They are capable of extreme charm and divine love-making. They keep looking for a sensual, spiritual soul mate.
Light Turquoise Crystals: Aquamarine – Turquoise – Smithsonite

Healing Turquoise

Turquoise can be a slow healer, but persevere with it, as it will get there in the end and will eventually work. It is a good colour for healing the emotions and pains of the heart. It is great for soothing and healing the nervous system. It is helpful for minor skin rashes and problems, and also for light fevers and infections. It is an excellent colour for encouraging self-questioning, and can be instrumental in straightening out affairs of the heart. Turquoise is the only colour that will allow you to think of yourself first instead of always fixing everyone else. It is the great comforter for anyone who feels alone and unlovable.

Blue

Basic Blue Personality

Blue is the colour of truth. Blue starts to move away from the physical body towards the more spiritual aspects of life. It is a very peaceful colour that produces contentment. Honesty is a key attribute of the blue personality. They hate arguments and quarrels and will go to any lengths to avoid confrontation. A person expressing a lot of blue traits is able to bring order out of chaos. Blue has a need for both self-understanding and emotional understanding. Blues prefer plain speaking – there is an ability here to influence others. They are able to stretch themselves to go just that little bit further. Emotionally loyal, blue is the mark of the healer.

Shade – Hindrance of Blue

Dark blue can become the recluse, too timid to venture beyond their own front door. Inclined to become stuck in a rut and tend to act the door mat. People take advantage of the dark blue personality and they resent it. Very often overworked and underpaid. Can become pathetic, with a meanness of spirit, when dark blue is upset, and even deceitful. Can be completely suppressed for fear of speaking up. Life's experiences have usually been learnt the hard way.
Blue Crystals: Sapphire – Sodalite – Lapis lazuli – Spinel – Zircon – Kyanite

Tint – Light Blue Personality

Pale blue has the ability to inspire; it lifts up the spirits. It gives great support and encouragement to release ourselves from constraint and restrictions. It can help people to understand that which cannot be changed. Great ambitions can be

sparked off by the tint of blue. A helper for the helpers, light blue people always can be found encouraging others.
Pale Blue Crystals: Diamond – Barytes – Turquoise – Celestite – Topaz

Healing Blue

Physically, blue will increase weight gain as it slows the metabolism. It is very useful for a number of child ailments such as teething, ear infections, sore throats and fevers. Blue is also very beneficial for arthritis and rheumatism. Blue may be used to help bring down high blood pressure, and draw out bruising. It is also a mild-to-medium painkiller. It calms inflammation, and is particularly useful in the relief of stomach ulcers. Incontinence can be decreased by the use of blue. The bereaved and terminally ill find comfort in blue's consoling rays.

Indigo

Basic Indigo Personality

The colour indigo retunes our vibrations – it is the great reformer. A person relating to indigo will create rules where they don't exist. Law and order, which also includes duty, will be at the core of indigo's motivation. Indigo always beckons you to step into the threshold of the mysterious. The indigo sky and oceans hold the secrets of the great unknown. The rich indigo personality becomes totally devoted to any project that they embark upon. Once committed they become extremely dogmatic – they would rather die than give in. Indigo characters live along the lines of all or nothing – indigo never has a middle way. Indigo will always hold the fort, it always comes up trumps. They are extremely conscientious.

Shade – Hindrance of Indigo

Indigo's darker character can display a very moody temperament. A weakness towards blind devotion is indigo's failing. They can become the spiritual fanatic, unable to listen to anyone else's opinions. They have no respect for their bodies as they feel they are immortal. They have a tendency towards an addictive personality. Indigos love rituals; the problem is, they quite often forget what the intention behind the ritual was in the first place.
Indigo Crystals: Sapphire – Kyanite – Azurite

Healing Indigo

The indigo colour gives excellent results for any chest, bronchial or lung complications. It is good for migraines and sinus problems. It is the strongest pain-killing colour of the spectrum – best used for adults: only use it in extreme cases for children. Indigo helps in the relief of varicose veins, boils, diarrhoea and swellings. A very good colour to use for insomniacs. It is also useful for any neurological pain and for some eye disturbances. It is believed to be the great tissue regenerator, and is the best colour to protect the psyche and the etheric body.

Grey

Basic Grey Personality

Grey is made up of black and white, which can cause a wavering of the mind, the 'shall I or shall I not' quandary. Greys feel they are never first, it's always someone else's turn. Grey fears its own lack of definition. Adversity seems to follow grey however hard it tries to evade it. Nonetheless, grey develops persistence, putting the grey personality in good stead when the going gets tough. Grey does have hope, and constantly expects that the best is yet to come. They will never rush into any project or falsely commit on any situation. Grey desperately tries to bring calm and sanity when situations get out of hand and turn nasty. They prefer to live a nice, quiet, respectable life so that they can have space. They dislike rough behaviour.

Shade – Hindrance of Grey

The dark grey personality has a fear and a melancholy that tomorrow will never come. Disease and illness spring forth from dark grey. Poverty is a grey colour – a struggle to break the grey chains of restriction. Old age and frailty is constantly in the back of dark grey's mind. The bony skeleton reminds them of the inevitable dust yet to come. Prison is dark grey. Dark grey is the child who is abused – a smashing of youthful joy and exuberance.
Grey Crystals – Metals: Platinum – Marcasite – Arsenopyrite – Galena

Tint – Light Grey Personality

The light grey personality battles against all odds. They are able to count their blessings even when they may appear few. Light grey has accepted its lot in life

and is determined to search for the reason in all things. They will seek the light that will enable them to adapt and move on.
Light Grey Crystals: Arsenopyrite – Marcasite – Galena

Healing Grey

Grey as a colour for healing is the only vibration that gives prior warning that ailments and illness are about to manifest themselves. Grey suggests trouble about to brew. Positively, grey indicates that something needs to be addressed. Not all is lost, as it leads the way if healing is needed. Grey represents anything that is about to break down. Mould is grey, and the basis of one of the greatest life-saving antibiotics of our time.

Black

Basic Black Personality

We each have within us a light and a dark side. The black side is not necessarily negative. It represents, in a positive vein, mystery, visionary ability and the mystic secrets. Black holds all the colours of the rainbow within it, so it is worth daring to look into the dark chasm to explore the power of black. The black personality will not be rowdy or noisy; it tends to be engaged in deep contemplation, pursuing higher philosophical thoughts. Black personalities are rather inclined to keep their emotions bottled up, preferring them to remain dormant. As all is contained within they have access to all possibilities, truly a star in the making. Black has the comfort to retreat if it wants to, as when we slide into slumber every night. The challenge for black is emerging from the chrysalis. The black character will make enormous sacrifices if they feel convinced it is the proper pathway to follow. Black loves control, but it wields it more subtly than red personalities, by playing mind games. Talented in all areas relating to intuition and the forces of nature, black loves unraveling the unseen, and awakening physic sensitivities. Black is all-powerful and has all the resources it requires, so long as it allows the light in, enabling its magnificent traits and abilities to be used for the benefit of the universe.

Shade – Hindrance of Black

Inclined to keep any knowledge gained for the betterment of themselves only. They are able to absorb almost anything without giving it out again. They can

become the recluse that denies and restricts themselves to the point of insanity, and even death. An overload of black can bring out the worst aspects of the will, resulting in regression.
Black Crystals: Jet – Biotite – Tourmaline – Magnetite – Hematite – Goethite – Star Sapphire – Cassiterite

Healing Black

Any black spots in the aura can give indications of some maladjustment or illness. It can be mental or physical. Black can be wonderfully liberating, as it removes doubt. Black reveals your vices and virtues. In the black of our dreams comes forth a wonderful flow of information, illuminating issues for us. From this seeming no-man's land springs forth the seeds for rebirth. Black is great for putting oneself on hold whilst disturbances are sorted out. Problems can be dealt with under the influence of black, allowing a 'stand still' period to occur, and providing a space to investigate. Black is safe and hidden, a comforting place to retreat for limited periods before springing back into action.

Silver

Basic Silver Personality

Silver personalities yearn for spiritual harmony. They have quick minds which do not stand still, constantly changing like the waxing and waning of the moon. Silver loves glamour and is drawn to the movie world. They aim for the stars. Silver loves to fantasize; these fantasies can become reality if they can just earth themselves. Silver is the thread of cosmic intelligence. It conjures up the power to reflect; it illuminates. Silver people have an unbiased nature, and are perfectly happy to allow others to have their own opinions without any desire to bring them round to their point of view. Silver always remains in a fluid state. They are lovers of the sea and all tidal movements.

Shade – Hindrance of Silver

Dark silvers have a quicksilver temperament, and can be very slippery, hard characters. They can be elusive and have a very odd attitude to society and its workings. Dark silver finds it difficult to get a grip on what actually is. This shade of silver should never be under-estimated, as still waters run deep – and strong.
Silver – Metal: Silver – Platinum – Arsenopyrite – Marcasite

Healing Silver

Silver as a healer helps to quell erratic emotions. It is a natural tranquilizer, and enables one to endure pain. It calms the hormones and allows the physical and mental functions to flow freely. Silver is good for regular function of the kidneys. Mentally it helps reflect distortions so that corrections can be made. Bathe in the moonlight to receive its cosmic, soothing balm, which releases fruitless yearning. It teaches us that mistakes are not necessarily negative – the greatest teachings come from our mishaps. It can help absorb negativity, setting a person free from restraints.

Purple

Basic Purple Personality – Crown Chakra

The colour purple corresponds to the highest elements of human nature. Purple's main province is the brain, controlling both the mental and the emotional aspects that, in turn, conduct the physical. Those who relate to purple are not generally good mixers in public, although they have plenty of charm. Purple is embodied by the self-employed person unhappy at being an employee. It is the personality of the leader and master, the loner who marches to the beat of a different drum. Purple can produce the highest gifts in the creative world – musicians, poets and painters can be found here. Its personality traits are gentleness and power; combining the two is the challenge. Purple is the greatest protector, with a spirit of mercy. They are the great teachers. As purple is made up of red and blue it contains within it characteristics of both these colours. The colour blue helps someone let go and move on: movement which is made possible by red's influence. Purple has action with wisdom.

Shade – Hindrance of Purple

The dark purple personality is inclined to be pompous, as they desire royal recognition. They are the spiritual social climbers, who love to hold an audience, giving their soul-enlightening sermons. They are self-indulgent and over-bearing with delusions of grandeur, and they are not able to recognize their true spiritual path. Purple at its darkest shows suicidal tendencies. Depressed because they were not born into families with influence, recognition for their blood line is crucial to enable the dark purple to survive. Desperation occurs if they were born into a low position in the pecking order.
Purple Crystals: Amethyst – Sugilite – Apatite

Tint – Light Lavender Personality

Pale lavender has a light disposition and a very buoyant temperament – a happy spirit gaily tripping through life, merrily having a good time. Even so, they possess a deep understanding of destiny for themselves and others, and are able to perform regression work and to connect to anything associated with the past. They see with vision beyond the physical eye. They are much stronger in mind, body and soul than the impression given.

Healing Purple

Purple is the healer of all conditions appertaining to the brain. Always apply purple light to the head area on the back of the head only. Use purple sparingly for children, as it is a little heavy. Purple has the ability to control hunger pangs. It relaxes the muscles, including the heart. It is a good colour to slow down overactive kidneys. Purple also releases menstrual cramps, and removes pressure and sensitivity to pain. It decreases bleeding and haemorrhaging. It provides tremendous support for the eyes, neuralgia and general inflammations of the nervous system. It calms the emotionally erratic. Lavender is a great aid for assisting the person who desires to delve into their physic ability.

MULTI-COLOURED STONES

Opal

Basic Opal Personality

Opal is made up of microscopic balls of silica with water in the intervening spaces. It functions as a diffraction grating – the size of the silica balls determines the colours that appear. Similar to the pearl, it exudes all colours, but the white background holder of the colours is densest. It has the ability to bring down to earth all the personality colours contained within it. It is not ethereal or elusive, but activates the colours' energies. Great ideas are contained within, and an ability to juggle many ideas at once. Those who relate to it are extremely creative, i.e., the talented mogul – the one who desires to have it all!

Shade – Hindrance of Opal

Consistency is a problem for dark opal's character, as there is a difficulty with committing and staying. They can be inclined to start projects up that flourish for a while and then flounder – like a pyramid-selling company. They are always biting off more than they can chew. They are hyperactive when young, and although they appear strong, they can crack with age.

Opal Stone: White-based opals – Grey-based opals – Black opals

(Note: Many opals on the market are just thin slices of opal sandwiched between two pieces of quartz. These are called doublets or triplets. From the standpoint of colour there isn't a problem, but be aware that you are not buying a solid opal.)

Healing Opal

Opal exudes incredibly uplifting qualities. It amplifies all that is intended – in a colour sense. Their vibrant colours bring forth fruit from seemingly barren land. They embody a fullness of promise, and create excitement and expectation. Use the gem as an innovator. It will kick start all of the endocrine/glandular system. It is a rejuvenator of cells. Use it as a multi-coloured tonic for the lymphatic system.

ORGANIC GEMS

Organic gems are not by definition crystals. But they are generated within the Mineral Kingdom as mineral structures created by organic means. Coral, for example, is created as fibrous crystals of aragonite. Your tooth enamel is made of fibrous crystals of apatite. Despite their organic origin, their colour content is still relevant when viewed from the healing possibilities – mentally, emotionally and physically.

Pearl

Basic Pearl Personality

Pearl's colours include white, cream, pink and black. The pearl personality's nature is soft and gentle, with a roundness of perfection. Similar to the oyster's shell, the person who relates to pearl's characteristics will have an open or shut temperament – an all or nothing attitude. They are very sensitive and will 'clam up' if bored or threatened. The subtle mixer socially, they are never pushy. They can appear low key at first as they are not flashy, but close up they have a lustre that far outweighs others.

Shade – Hindrance of Pearl

A prized pearl gleams brightly. The duller the glow, the more prone the temperament is towards an uneven disposition. They become unreachable because everything irritates them. They might refuse to answer questions even if it could lead to destruction. They prefers to remain dormant where nothing germinates or grows, and are not interested in anything – not even themselves.
Pearl Stones: Sea pearls – Freshwater pearls – Mother of pearl – Cultured pearl

Healing Pearl

Pearl houses healers on all levels where subtlety is required. As pearl is related to sea water, it gently clears the system. It is good for regulating digestion where a tendency for gall bladder disease occurs. It helps to balance the constitution by creating rhythmic motion and movement.

Amber

Basic Amber Personality

The amber personality makes its presence felt but not seen. Privately they are good company, but you may only be presented with one side of them. They are often experienced by others as possessing many personalities. They are very interested in others and what makes them tick, and they always seem to know something that no one else does. They make great gamblers, as they always have that hidden card up their sleeve. They are quietly assured and extremely kind; but on another level they have experienced it all before – which enables them to bring unassuming wisdom to everything they deal with. Amber is nature's solidified honey of remembrance. Ambers are single minded with extreme powers of focusing. Open-minded and receptive, they are interested in just about everything, and have an innate sense of how nature's order works.

Shade – Hindrance of Amber

The dark side of amber relies on logic only to preserve the status quo. The dark amber-related person prefers to talk, because they are not interested in feelings. They can appear stuck-up and narrow-minded, believing only that which can be seen. They are usually unable to figure out their path in life.
Amber Stone: Amber/ yellow/ brown – dark citrine

Healing Amber

Amber personalities are prone to headaches and digestive problems, but as amber is a great nature lover, the countryside atmosphere will aid nausea and indigestion. The amber-coloured stone will support the system and strengthen general well-being when organic methods are being employed, such as vegetarian foods and herbs. This colour will encourage the entire body to become in tune with the elements: earth, air, wind and fire. It is the earth-balancer that produces a healthy attitude.

Coral

Basic Coral Personality

A gentle soul. Coral's personality challenge is to find its rightful place in this life. They always seem to be at the mercy of everyone else. They need others to generate energy, but they are very willing people, even if a little timid. They love to socialize, but never seem to be in the right place at the right time. Yet corals understand the order of the universe, and are very willing to play the game – the problem is nobody else seems to be. They have an extremely beautiful nature, fragile and delicate. They are great listeners who will help anyone in trouble. Even so, they have razor-sharp minds that can severely chastize when they feel a wrong has been done.

Shade – Hindrance of Coral

The dark coral can find it difficult to get the basic requirements that are needed to survive. They experience alienation as no one seems to understand their plight. Coral gets frustrated when it finds that it gives out a lot of attention to others for no return. They are plagued by past hurts that return to haunt, but they themselves cannot let past happenings become dead and buried. They are great

evaders of the issues. They can crumble when they are uncared for and feel emotionally starved.
Coral Stones: Pink Coral – Rhodachrosite – Rhodonite

Healing Coral

Coral can be good for healing mild anaemia, bladder conditions and childhood colic; it also soothes whooping cough, causing the chest to strengthen. Coral will support the bronchial tubes, encouraging an even contraction and expansion of the breath. It has a fluid rhythmic effect upon the system, bringing bodily functions back into line.Coral is a good safety-net colour to use when applying other colours, methods and techniques.

PART THREE

MAN AND MINERALS

CHAPTER 9

THE HUMAN PLAN, DISEASE AND HEALING

✧

Difficulties are things that show what men are.

Epictetus

In Part One we looked at crystals from 'first principles', the very energy roots of their existence contained within the atoms which make them up. In uncovering these principles, an understanding of crystals emerged that allowed us to see through many illusions about them – and to uncover the simple but immensely profound truths crystals embody. We will now look at our own human nature in the same manner. As we do so it is important to keep in mind that the Universal Mind that created crystals also created us, and that both man and minerals are part of the *same* thought. Not only that, but that thought manifests itself in patterns – patterns of energy in various relationships with itself. *Energy* and *relationships* – as true for man as they are for minerals!

First, let's look at our own thoughts about ourselves, to see where, if anywhere, there is a correspondence with Universal thought. Eastern and Western thought form two distinct polarities. These poles may be described as 'inclusive', and 'exclusive'. Eastern beliefs tend to be all-encompassing: an understanding of mankind as an integral part (but only a part), of the greater whole of the Earth and Cosmos. Western thought tends to exclude those people and beliefs that are not part of a specified belief system: Christian thought tends to exclude all but Christians, etc. Thus it becomes easy in the West to separate everything from everything else:

nature is separate from man; God is separate from man; we are separate from each other; spirit is separate from the material world; the ethics of business are separate from the ethics of personal interrelations; and so on.

In the Eastern view, nature is the bosom from whence we come and whither we go. Nature produces man out of itself; man cannot be outside of nature. I am in nature and nature is in me.[1] We have been taught in the West that God is a force outside of our lives. In the East, on the other hand, the accent is on inner experience: on one's *own* experience, not a faith in someone else's experience. The various spiritual disciplines taught are ways to the attainment of unmistakable experiences – ever deeper, ever greater – of one's own identity with whatever one comes to know as divine, as the God within.[2]

The word *buddha* means, simply, awakened, or awakened one, or the Awakened One. It is from the Sanskrit verbal root *budh*, to fathom; to penetrate to the core; to come to one's senses. But a buddha is one awakened to identity not with the body but with the universal dimension of one's self: the knower of the body; not with thought but with the knower of thoughts, that is to say, with consciousness. A person in Buddha Consciousness[3] knows, furthermore, that his value derives from his power to radiate consciousness – as the value of a lightbulb derives from its power to radiate light. What is important about a lightbulb is not the filament or the glass but the light it radiates. The bulb is but a vehicle for the light, as the body is but a vehicle for consciousness. What is important about each of us is the consciousness that shines through us. When one lives for that, instead of for the protection of the bulb – the body – one is in Buddha Consciousness. In the West there is an emphasis on, and identification with the body. When something goes wrong with it, it is seen as the malfunctioning of an organic piece of machinery, not as a tool of a Higher Power that is made manifest within us for a higher purpose than purely the functioning of the body itself. This higher understanding can be stated as a series of interacting principles:

[1] Dr Daisetz T. Suzuki (a Japanese Zen philosopher), quoted in Joseph Campbell, *Myths to Live By* (London: Bantam, 1972).

[2] From Joseph Campbell, *Myths to Live By* (London: Bantam, 1972).

[3] Buddha Consciousness is just one term. Others, like self-fulfilled, self-actualized, enlightened, or at-onement, are equally valid.

1. The collective Universe, both manifest and unmanifest, is God. That which God creates within the Universe is ultimately in fulfilment of God's needs and wishes, which may or may not be knowable to man.
2. The Earth and its Kingdoms, collectively called 'Nature', are both manifestations of God and God made manifest, and fulfil a need of God.
3. Accordingly, the Earth and its lifeforms *are* God, and are inseparable from the rest of the Universe which *is* God.
4. Man is a facet of God made manifest through Nature. As a creature of Nature, and as a manifestation of Nature, Man is thus inseparable from it.
5. Man was made from Nature, not Nature from Man. The presence of Man within Nature is thus an extension of the needs of Nature.
6. Because God is all that exists, Truth is an attribute of God's being. That truth is expressed as Earth and its Nature. Thus Nature is Truth unto itself, with or without the presence of Man.
7. Because Man is an extension of Nature, Man cannot experience his own truth outside of Nature.
8. It is Man's self-imposed separation from the Truth, both of Nature and of himself, that permits Man's 'inhumanities', both to himself and to Nature.[4]

The fully-realized human is one totally at one with his innate, animal nature, the nature fully in harmony with the ebb and flow of the natural rhythms of the world around him. Indeed, he is not fully human if he is *not*.

NATURAL MAN/ANIMAL MAN

Western civilization has generally believed that the animal in us is a bad animal, and that our most primitive instincts are evil, greedy, selfish and hostile. This negative attitude to animality was derived largely from very early animal studies, when the results were applied rather indiscriminately to humans. Indeed, the mis-application of early animal studies was made easier by the early beliefs about the nature of the human subconscious, where it was equated to the supposed animal nature, and was deemed to be the place where psychological demons dwelt. 'Nature, red in tooth and claw' was, and largely still is, the commonly held belief

[4] From *The Guiding Principles of the New Millennium Church*, with permission.

about animal behaviour, despite nearly a century of study that suggests otherwise. There has been even more misunderstanding about animal behaviour than about human behaviour, and this has led to severely erroneous beliefs about our own animal nature. This flawed understanding of our human animality is, according to psychiatrist Abraham Maslow, a mistake:

> . . . so crucial, so tragedy laden, that it may be likened in historical importance to such mistakes as the belief in the divine right of kings, in the exclusive validity of any one religion, in the denial of evolution, or in the belief that the earth is flat.[5]

Charles Darwin so identified with the negative view of animal nature that he saw only competition in the animal world, the 'survival of the fittest', and totally overlooked the cooperation which is much more common. Unfortunately, 'survival of the fittest' is still a popularly held view of animal nature. In his book *The Lives of a Cell*, Dr Lewis Thomas sets the record straight:

> Most of the associations between the living things we know about are essentially cooperative ones, symbiotic [mutually dependent] in one degree or another.[6]

Numerous studies have been done of human animality in addition to those quoted here, and among all of them there is one salient feature: *nowhere* is there a suggestion that the human animal is a 'bad' animal – quite the contrary. There is, likewise, agreement on another important point: that those human behaviours usually attributed to our animal nature – brutishness, greed, hostility and so on – occur *when our animal nature is thwarted.*

When a society requires us to live detached from our biological, natural, animal self – as Western societies do – when social restraints are relaxed, such 'bad' behaviours *do* appear. But they are *not* the behaviours of the animal self – they are the behaviours that occur as a consequence of the repressed pain of being forced to live an unnatural life.

Because God is *Nature, there can be no return to God through unnatural living.* When we deny our animal ancestry and the biological, 'animal' needs of the human animal, we deny an essential part of our nature and cut ourselves off from a vital

[5] Abraham Maslow, *Motivation and Personality* (New York: Harper and Row, 1987), p.31.

[6] Lewis Thomas, *The Lives of a Cell* (New York: Bantam, 1974), p.6.

link to our own life-force. We are all programmed by our biology, like it or not. We are not all that far removed as a species from our savannah-dwelling ancestors. Our cells are their cells, our instincts are their instincts. Our ancestors survived by co-operative hunting (today it is called working), while the women tended the fires (today called home-making). There are still woolly mammoths to be slain (the big contract), still predators lurking (the taxman). All that has changed are the costumes! Most of the ways our societies are organized, from our family structures to the structure of corporations, has – or should have – a firm grounding in our biology.

THE ROLE OF THE BODY AND THE EMOTIONS

It has been said that the body is the temple of the spirit. Because Man's own truth is expressed through nature made manifest as the body, it is even more accurate to say that the body is the perfect embodiment of spirit. Your body, with all its apparent flaws, aches, pains, illnesses, emotions, feelings and limitations, is the perfect reflection in flesh of the state of your oneness with God within you. All that has occurred in your life to bring you to your current state of physical, mental and emotional being is the outworking of your own personal plan to bring you to inner reunion with God. As we will discover, the messages our physical body sends us through its illnesses, feelings and emotions are clear pointers to healing our relationship with God – *if* we are able to listen to and correctly interpret the messages.

The emphasis is therefore on the 'Natural Man'. One of the most severely damaging illusions of Western culture is that humans are somehow removed from our biological, species-specific, instinctual nature. When unhindered by our conditioning, we instinctively know what is right for us and what fulfils our needs, just like every other species on Earth. When the inherent needs of the Natural Man *are* met, there is a feeling of rightness, a body-feeling. Without the sense of being right, one has no sense of how much one ought to claim of comfort, security, help, companionship, love, friendship, thinking, pleasure or joy. A person without this right sense often feels there is an empty place somewhere within.[7]

When instinct-directed needs are *not* fulfilled, we feel pain. Unfulfilled needs are signalled by pain for a very good reason – they are those needs that specifically

[7] Jean Liedloff, *The Continuum Concept* (London: Penguin, 1986).

promote the survival of our species. They are the needs that are, in the largest sense, God-given, in that they are the needs that completely fulfil Man's embodiment of his own particular dimension of God. Just as the physical pain of a physical injury signals an urgent need for attention to that part of the physical body, emotional pain signals that urgent attention is needed to fulfil other needs: the need for comfort, or love, or attention, or to be held – the emotional needs that are just as vital to our survival as the physical needs. Needs that are appropriate to Natural Man.

In order to protect ourselves from overwhelming feelings, from emotional pain (the original and most overwhelming of which was the sense of being separated from our Source), we erect defences. While these defences 'protect' us, at the same time they limit us. Every defence is also a limitation of our life-force, and another barrier between ourselves and our Source. The walls that defend us, equally imprison us. It is the closing off of our own hearts.

Our defences come in 'layers', as we discover in the next chapter. The process of opening the heart is not so much one of healing what is inside, but rather of systematically dismantling our defences to reveal what is already there. Because our defences are layered, and each of these layers utilizes a different portion of our being, each layer requires different techniques and points of focus in its dismantling. Thus opening the heart is really the processes that take place when patiently and systematically working through our pains, our fears and our angers, to find the real Self beneath – the Self that is always struggling to emerge. In the following chapter, we put crystals to work as reflectors of the deepest patterns within our hearts, the place where our Inner Being dwells. And in the exercises throughout the remainder of the book, we use crystals to highlight (and thus open up to healing), the barriers we have erected to the free flow of universal life from within us.

Our drive to re-unify with the Source of our being, operating through its repository of experience, the Self, is very tenacious. We would hardly have survived if it were otherwise. In the end, it will not and cannot permit us to leave restrictions to our life-force in place. Yet at the same time, those restrictions create the very growth experiences that we live a particular lifetime *for.* To resolve them we are internally led to various life situations that help us to heal old pain, to complete our unfinished phases and to dissolve our barriers to our Source.

We are aided by this in that we live in a world made of 'mirrors'. Everything that exists in our world serves in some way to mirror ourselves back to ourselves. The process of living on the Earth is the process of discovering who we are as creatures of the Earth – and, ultimately, to return to our Source with that knowledge, which becomes part of the Self-knowing of the Source itself. These processes are well known, and are the same for everyone, varying only in degree. Enlightened psychologists like Erik Erikson, Abraham Maslow and Carl Rogers have mapped the patterns of our development in detail – patterns that perfectly reflect the Universe's own patterns. The role of books and courses like this, and other courses and therapies that promote personal growth, is to become catalysts and accelerators of what is an already existing natural process. Crystals have a powerful role to play in this process, as the exercises later will clearly demonstrate.

Your Inner Being, the real You, has only one goal: self-completion. To this end, your Inner Being will use whatever is necessary to complete itself – including making you ill, if you refuse to see any of the other reflections of self-knowing in the world around you. Likewise, the Inner Being will draw you very strongly to any mirroring situation that will lead you to greater depths of self-discovery. We have physical mirrors to look at our physical bodies and see how things are progressing; we have a physical body that makes itself ill when it is trying to tell us we need to look at our state of harmony with our true inner nature.

ILLNESS

This chapter is about 'healing', yet there can be no true healing until the nature of disease is understood. That we have not understood its nature is, in turn, the result of our failure to understand the role of disease in the wider picture of the relationship of the human species to the natural world, both on the Earth and beyond. The most important realization about healing is that the *relief of symptoms* is not *healing*. You can take an aspirin for a headache, but it does nothing to treat the brain tumour causing it. You can use a crystal to relieve a symptom, but unless an inner shift of awareness happens, real healing hasn't taken place.

Just as it takes disharmony with your inner needs, which creates psychological and emotional pain and that pain's repression, to draw attention to the need to reharmonize oneself to one's deepest Inner Being, so too does the physical body draw attention to disharmony within it – by a method called disease. Illness is ultimately about healing the soul, about healing the real you. So illness is a gift that you give to yourself in order to help yourself become whole and at one with the universe again. There's no one who can fix you except you.

Dr Richard Moss relates the disease process to various levels of energy. Human beings exist at many energy levels: at the lowest level are the diseases that are clearly separate entities – viruses, bacteria, etc. These are easily distinguishable from our own body and *cause* malfunctions of the body, rather than *being* malfunctions of the body. High energy level diseases are those which are direct malfunctions of the body, such as cancer and heart disease, which are a result of direct cellular breakdown as opposed to an invasion of the body by outside organisms.

He likens the understanding of these two types of disease processes to Newtonian and Einsteinian physics. Newton had a basic and thorough understanding of the physics of slow moving, low energy bodies such as planets and comets. But applying the same ideas to atoms required a total shift of our understanding of the nature of physical reality. It wasn't until Einstein formulated basic relations between matter and energy, concepts that were totally unsuspected in Newton's day, that we were able to understand the workings of high energy levels of being – particles, atoms, and energy itself. The perceptual change we are now undergoing, especially in the West, is to understand that the human body does indeed exist at many levels, and that some of these levels are totally energetic in nature. Indeed, much disease *begins* in the energy levels.

The high energy diseases occur when we make choices that are not in harmony with our own highest energy level – the soul level of our existence wherein are generated the inherent needs. They come from unresolved, deep-level conflicts between our ideas about living, and our own inner knowledge of how we *should* be living. Simply to be told that these conflicts exist does not resolve them; the only way we can do this is to experience them. Primal Therapy and Bioenergetics are but two of a number of therapies evolved specifically to address such conflicts. In experiencing them we can make a perceptual shift in ourselves and thereby resolve and release them.

Cancer, in particular, is one of these high energy diseases, indicating an extremely deep level of inner conflict, creating enormous stress at the cellular level which, when combined with the numerous toxins available in our environment, produce cancerous cells. Dr Moss says about the development of cancers:

> We would like to continue believing that the human immune system . . . has all of a sudden stopped functioning, and allowed the development of the tumour . . . In fact, the human immune system may not be failing. Perhaps it is simply not subtle enough to recognize the force it is dealing with.[8]

Indeed, how could our immune system anticipate a situation where those it protects would, often deliberately, live lives against their own best interests, and even deny their own inherent needs?

Our diseases, especially high energy diseases, therefore become open doors – open invitations to us to shift our levels of awareness into levels which, ultimately, serve not only to heal our diseases, but to open our inner awareness to more subtle levels of ourselves, to resolve the conflicts that keep us away from our true inner Source. This is certainly the experience of numerous participants in self-development courses that I have been involved with – as deeper and deeper levels of Self-awareness occur, existing cancers tend to disappear.

In minerals that are hard and brittle and easily broken, there is a very high energy bond which, although it gives a great deal of rigidity, also makes it very susceptible to breakage. This sounds a bit like a certain personality type: the very rigid type of personality, very locked up in its own energy and beliefs, and therefore easily broken/subject to very high energy diseases such as cancer. (Contrast this with a flexible personality type, who is able to 'bend with the wind', and is therefore subject perhaps to lower energy diseases, if any at all.) Psychological research has shown this to be the case: the extremely rigid personality types, highly locked-up emotionally, and highly inflexible, are extremely high cancer risks. These types of individuals are also very locked-up in the heart centre and, once again, the incidence of heart disease is among them is alarming.

Illness is not something wrong with you. *Illness is something that your body is trying to tell you* to help you get right. Illness is something that's trying to heal you at a very profound level. *Illness is a symptom of something much deeper.* Because illness is a symptom, to just remove the symptom creates no real healing whatsoever. Unless the underlying causes are discovered and dealt with, the disease process will simply repeat itself somewhere else. The ultimate outcome of discovering why we have given ourselves a particular disease, comes from discovering what need in

[8] Richard Moss, MD, *The I That Is We* (Berkeley: Celestial Arts, 1981), p.57.

ourselves was being unfulfilled – where we were out of harmony with the patterns of our own lives. Congenital diseases occur because of the karmic pattern being worked through by the individual. The karmic pattern exists solely because of incompleted life lessons that separate one from one's Source.

Australian doctor John Harrison has been a pioneer in recognizing this in a medical sense. He says:

> Disease is both self-created and self-cured. Illness is the physical and psychological result of unresolved needs, not a malfunction of a machine caused by unknown or external factors. The client is needy, rather than sick, and has exercised an honourable option to him to take care of himself as best he can.[9]

He further emphasizes the point that this understanding of the disease process is very hopeful for the patient. As we become more and more familiar with our investment in developing diseases, we can begin to assume more and more control over diseases and over our personal destiny. Indeed – to become who we really are.

CRYSTALS AND HEALING

The most common use of crystals is in 'healing'. So, how do crystals 'heal'? The answer is simple: they don't. There is no external force that can make anyone take the inner steps toward reunion with their Source. Because our physical body is designed as a perfect reflection of our oneness, and because there is only one real 'healing' (the healing of our connection with our Source), then all 'healing' *must* come from the 'patient'. The 'healer' is only there as a facilitator. So, too, are the implements of healing, like crystals.

But crystals *appear* to have marvellous healing powers. So what is going on? Remember that old universal law that says: 'Like attracts like'? Another way of saying that might be: 'Like recognizes like'. If we see our own face in a mirror, we recognize ourselves. If there is something wrong with the picture – hair dishevelled, make-up smeared, we need a shave – we recognize what is *not* right, and correct it. But this only occurs if we know what *is* right. What if we don't

[9] John Harrison, MD, *Love Your Disease* (London: Angus and Robertson, 1984), p.4.

recognize the reflection? We know from recent studies of the brain that only about one-trillionth of the information reaching the brain ever gets to the conscious mind, therefore we are totally unaware of almost everything that goes on in our minds. Would it be any surprise then, that the mechanisms of healing, of intuition, of inner recognition, are not processes of which we are fully conscious? And what if we are so used to seeing what is wrong that we don't recognize what is right as even *being* us?

Everything in our world is a mirror, but different mirrors reflect different things. The mirror on the wall reflects one thing; the mirror of the crystal reflects another. But whatever the mirror, ultimately they reflect only *one* thing: the state of our Oneness with our Source. How do crystals reflect this state? Another restatement of 'Like attracts like' is: 'Like reflects like'. At whatever level your Being is reaching out for self-completion, it will attract the appropriate mirror to reflect your state of Oneness of that level back to you.

If 'like reflects like', what are crystals reflecting? For the answer to this, we need to look back to the crystal. What is a crystal? It is energy, in the form of atoms, arranged in a pattern; a pattern that is in perfect balance and harmony with itself. So what is it reflecting within us? Patterns within us that are the basic patterns of *all* creation; patterns that are whole and complete and in perfect balance and harmony – the basic patterns that are the *essential us,* the Inner Being, the Self. Thus the 'power' of the crystal is not the crystal's at all; it is yours, at your closest point of connection to the Source of your own Being. This is the 'real' use of crystals.

Real healing becomes sorting out one's inner beliefs and perceptions. Self-healing, ultimately, can be only one thing – self-discovery.

For some of us that is not very good news, because it makes us look inward, rather than outwards. It makes us look at ourselves. That is the thing most of us have the greatest fear of doing, and it is not easy. It's not supposed to be easy. Earth is a hard school. It is a university, not a kindergarten, and if you as a Being weren't ready for the hard course, you wouldn't be on the Earth in the first place.

A healer in the conventional sense can certainly help you in that process; however, every human being is a healer. Every human being has the capacity to help other humans find that point of wholeness within themselves. Remember, this often takes place on a subtle level, and the interaction between the 'patient' and the 'healer' mostly takes place on a subconscious level: at some subconscious level the person who is the 'healer' sets up a resonance with the person who is seeking to become whole within themselves and, at a very subtle level, something shifts.

However, it is not as if the healer is 'making' the other person well. Until the 'patient' is prepared at some level or other to make an inner adjustment, nothing can happen. Even God can't heal someone who doesn't want to be healed, and many of us have a lot of subconscious reasons for staying ill. In fact, from a psychological survival standpoint, there are some perfectly good reasons for staying ill. However, those reasons no longer serve us when we decide to start shifting within ourselves – to start becoming whole, harmonious, and at one with creation around us. The exercises in this book are specifically designed to create the sort of perceptual shifts that are necessary to start resolving inner conflicts within your Being. The good news is that, because of their high energy, shifts in perception (healing) can take place very rapidly as you shift into higher levels of awareness. The best news is that we carry within us the most powerful healing tool of all: that place deep within ourselves where the Source of all Being is beckoning to us.

Our own hearts.

THE HEART CENTRE

✧

The antidote to loneliness is not togetherness; it is intimacy.

Richard Bach *The Bridge Across Forever* (1984)

Dwelling within each of us is that perfect place that is always One with the Heart of God. It is called the Heart of Man. Both hearts not only beat to the same inner pulse, both hearts *are* the same pulse. The more we re-attain our inner harmony and natural rhythm, the more we reharmonize with the Source of our Being. Because our own heart *is* the heart of God, both our own manifestation of, and our experience of life becomes both the manifestation of and the experience of life *for* God. Opening the heart is to seek truth at its deepest level: the truth of who you are. And that truth is of your Oneness with God. Within the Heart Centre is the place where the fundamental patterns of creation are at their clearest, and it is the place most clearly reflected in those other fundamental patterns of creation: crystals.

Opening the heart is to discover the other levels of consciousness that already exist within yourself. The process of opening the heart is a process of gradual unfoldment to find the jewel within, the jewel of Truth – symbolized in some belief systems as the jewel in the centre of the lotus flower. At one level a jewel is a thing which is hard, fixed and immutable. It is an appropriate symbol. A jewel is composed of many facets, of many reflections, each one reflecting the constantly changing patterns of light and colour that surround it. Our experience of truth has many facets. It is constantly changing, as the world around us changes. And yet that which reflects it, the One Truth which is the love that is God, is always constant, fixed and immutable.

Thus our inner truths reflect the constantly changing patterns of our own lives. Life is an adventure; it is an exploration of what is and what may be. What your life will be in the future is only a reflection of what it is now, and the decisions and actions that you take now. It is constantly changing and constantly shifting – a continuous series of new reflections, reverberating from your own personal inner truth: the truth of God within you. As your heart reopens, as you begin to find and expose deeper and deeper levels of Truth, what will change most dramatically is your perspective.

Opening the Heart Centre is a process of transformation and change. It is to open ourselves to a whole new view of ourselves, not merely to polish up the old view so it looks even better. The living universe is a place of constant change – not to change is to stagnate: to stay frozen is, ultimately, to die. Sometimes it takes a dramatic event or realization to shatter us out of our rut. Otherwise, we keep travelling the same path, just restating over and over and over again our old and limited beliefs of who we are. It is this necessity to change in order to grow that ultimately draws to us a state of crisis.

As the process of inner seeking unfolds, there will be times when you are beset with fear, bewilderment and uncertainty. As the old and familiar (and therefore safe) ways begin to dissolve, we move into new ways of seeing things and new ways of doing things. Because these are unfamiliar, they feel unsafe and frightening. But as someone once said: Feel the fear and do it anyway.

We live in a world of paradox. We live in a world of form, and yet the essential aspects of our own being are formless; we are part of a universe moving into increasing complexity. A paradox can never be resolved by trying to find exact definitions, final truths or ultimate answers. Until we let go of our need to control and to resolve, we will be in a constant state of crisis as we move closer and closer to our own inner paradox. These crises will express themselves in many ways: through disturbances of the mind, through illnesses in the body, through stress, tension and breakdown. These are, on the whole, healthy processes, as long as we are prepared to use them as learning tools. The inward journey – the healing process – is one of balancing and harmonizing many apparently opposing forces.

As you progress deeper into the opening-up process, you will find that you have less and less need to define your experience, and are more content to just let it be however it is. The need to define, to interpret and to analyse all exist at one level of consciousness. The goal in opening the heart is to discover other levels of consciousness in yourself and to shift into those levels at will, according to the appropriateness of the situation in which you find yourself. Human beings exist at many levels. Because limitation is a necessary facet of living in matter, there will be some levels of consciousness that operate more efficiently in one set of situations, whereas others will operate more efficiently in other situations.

Crystals are a perfect tool of heart-opening, as we will see in the exercises at the end of the chapter. But they are not some sort of magic key that will suddenly and abruptly open the door to enlightenment. Enlightenment is a consequence of the efforts *we* make, not of the tools we use.

THE HEART CENTRE

We are all familiar with the heart as a mechanical device – a pump. As a symbol the pump is perfectly appropriate. It is from the heart that all nourishment is circulated to all parts of our physical body. The nourishment may be created elsewhere, such as in the respiratory or digestive systems, but it is only through the unceasing effort of the heart to circulate the blood that all of the benefits of other parts of the body can be felt throughout.

It is so at other levels of consciousness too. Although the benefits to our entire being may be generated elsewhere (even elsewhere in the Universe), those benefits only come to us through the Source within our heart.

The volume of language that has grown up around the various functions of the heart as a Source of Being is significant. We 'go to the heart of the matter' when we are talking about getting to the essence of something. The heart, then, becomes a reflection of our own pure essence. It also means the deepest level of our being, as in the expression 'you have reached my heart', or that we have reached the very soul. And the phrase 'with all my heart' means total commitment, commitment that comes from the very deepest level of our Being.

We speak of a person being open or closed, relative to the approaches of the world. We even see this in body language – puffing up the chest is a gesture of defiance, indicating that our heart is closed. The gesture of moving one's shoulders forward, as one would do in reaching out with the arms, can be seen as an open-hearted gesture, of reaching out. Paradoxically, either of these two gestures frozen into a permanent body posture will usually mean just the opposite.

We also associate expressions of love with the heart. 'To open your heart' means to be willing to take in the love of another person; 'giving your heart' means to fall in love. And, 'wearing your heart on your sleeve' means that you are openly showing your emotions and looking for love.[1] The heart, then, is an organ associated with feeling. The heart has a feeling of expansion with joy, or shrinking with anxiety or disappointment. And a broken heart is a feeling associated with a great deal of anxiety, pain or discomfort in the heart area. 'Broken' does not mean broken in two pieces, but rather a feeling that a connection has been broken.

Truly, the experience of opening the heart is of opening oneself to higher and higher levels of love – not just love on a personal or sensual level (although as one's heart opens those aspects of love also increase), but rather of achieving a higher energy state and a basic well-being that radiates from the inner Source. It is an outflowing from the Inner Being that embraces the whole Being, and radiates out from it to embrace everyone and everything that comes near. It is not a conscious act of embracing – it just is.

In Figure 33 we see the flow of energy from the Inner Being, the core of which is the heart.[2] In Latin, *cor* means the heart. The first channel of communication for the heart is through the throat and mouth. It is the new-born baby's first channel of expression as it reaches for its mother's breast with the lips and mouth. A baby doesn't reach out with the lips and mouth alone; it also reaches with its heart. In the act of the kiss, we have retained our awareness of this movement as an expression of love. But a kiss may be a gesture of love, or an expression of love; the difference is whether one's heart is in it or not, and that depends on whether the channel of communication from the heart is open.

The second channel for the heart is through the arms and hands as they reach out to touch. Here too the action can be an expression of love, or a gesture, depending on whether the feeling flows from the heart into the hands. Loving hands are highly charged with energy and have a healing quality in the touch.

The third channel of communication of the heart is downward, through the waist and pelvis, to the genitals. Sex is an act of love but, once again, it can either be simply a gesture, or a true expression of love if one's heart is really in it. If the

[1] Alexander Lowen, *Bioenergetics* (London: Penguin, 1975).

[2] *Ibid.*, with permission.

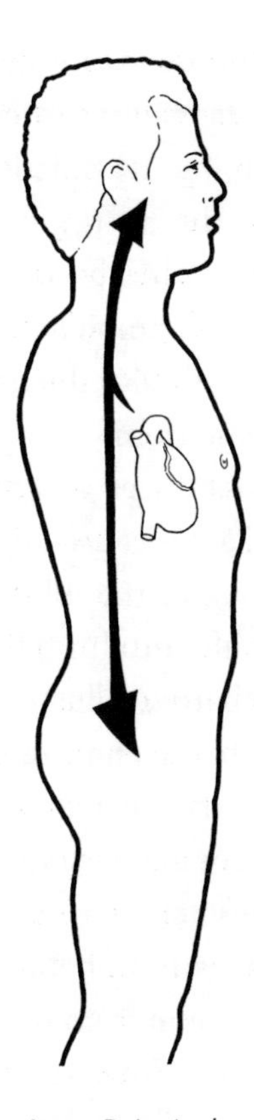

Figure 33: The Inner Being's channels of energy

feeling of love for one's partner is strong the sexual experience has an intensity that makes the orgasm an ecstatic event. In such a case, one can actually feel one's heart leap for joy at the moment of climax.

So, as the heart heals – becomes more open – all of the functions of human life become richer and fuller. If one wants to live fully and richly, it is only possible if one opens one's heart to life and to love. Without love – for one's self, for one's fellow human beings, for nature and for the universe – a person is cold, detached and inhuman. The lack of this love (i.e., an open-hearted connection with everything that surrounds us), leaves us with a sense of alienation and separation from the flow of life. That is because the flow of life within us is blocked, and the world around us merely reflects that fact to us.

In Figure 34, we see a love impulse coming outward from the Heart Centre through the various layers that surround the heart.[3] A blockage in any of those

[3] *Ibid.*

layers will cause a distortion in the flow of energy, so that by the time the love impulse reaches the surface (its personality expression), it can be totally distorted. If the blockages are severe enough, by the time love emerges at the surface, it can come out as hate! In many of us, the energy of love working its way outwards from our heart through the blockages has become so painful that we disassociate ourselves from it – in other words, the mind and the body have become separate. In this situation, we say that the head rules the heart.

But where do these barriers come from?

Primal Pain is the deep pain that arises when we are forced to live in discord with our natural rhythms. Primal Pain is caused by unmet inherent needs, the most potent of which is to live according to the inbuilt patterns that connect us to all that surrounds us. It is the pain of life torn from life. To protect ourselves from this pain, we erect one or more of the barriers illustrated in Figure 34, according to our own personal inclinations – they are the end-products of the process of repression. But the barriers that keep pain out also keep love in.

Because these are such strong energy barriers to the free flow of our life force, all that energy must be held somewhere in the body, or given expression in some other form. It can come out as various behaviour disorders – the anti-social behaviours incorrectly believed to come from our 'animal' nature; behaviours that are 'evil, greedy, selfish and hostile'. However eventually, because the energy is being biologically mischanneled, it will manifest itself as disease, as discussed in the previous chapter.

The manifestations of the barriers associated with the ego layer of Figure 34 are as follows:

a) denial
b) distrust
c) blaming
d) projection
e) rationalizations and intellectualizations.

Because our barriers are layered – each layer with a different energy charge – we must work through the same barrier more than once, each time releasing a different level of energy. That is why you will wish to repeat the exercises at the end of this chapter more than once. It is a reflection of your own movement into complexity.

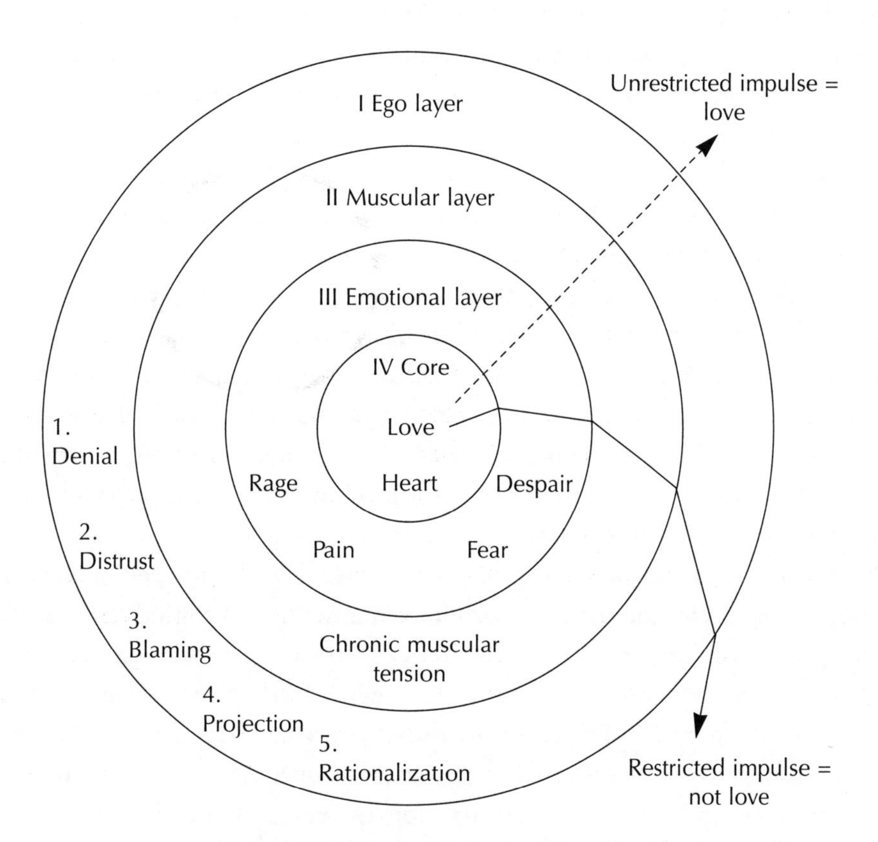

Figure 34: The barriers that surround our heart

In the muscular layer, we find the chronic muscular tensions that support the ego defences, and at the same time protect the person against the underlying suppressed feelings in the emotional layer, i.e., those that he or she dare not express. In the emotional layer, we find the suppressed feelings of rage, panic, terror, despair, sadness and pain. These are all of the feelings of Primal Pain that felt threatening to the heart, and thus have become suppressed.[4]

Finally, at the very deepest level of our Being, is the core or heart, from which the feeling to love and be loved derives. It is this that we are striving to liberate from the bondage of our own inner barriers. The love emanating from the core is the driving force for its own liberation. Love by its very nature demands free,

[4] *Ibid.*

unfettered expression. It drives us to the self-completion that is the dissolving of those inner barriers. It is to this purpose that our lives are shaped by this force. It is what drives us into relationships, to 'bring up that which is not love for the purpose of healing', as we discover in the next chapter. It is the source of the act-out (*see Chapter 11*) and of illness, physical and mental. These, too, are brought up for healing. It is the force that drives us to courses and therapies and books. It is the force that leads us into the forests and mountain tops, and into the deepest recesses of ourselves to touch the Divine within us.

The deepest core of our Being, then, where our soul resides, is love, and is our own source of love. One of the most difficult realizations is that we are our own source of love – it does not come from outside. No one can give it to us. And yet we desperately seek some perfect partner who will give us all of the love we deeply desire for ourselves. This course of action happens when our source of love is blocked off inside. If you are looking for love anywhere else, outside yourself, that is the clearest possible reflection of your deep need to seek it within you.

This book – as are all such books – is ultimately about opening the Heart Centre; taking down the barriers to your own inner flow – to find the One Truth within you: Love. Yet love, like truth, is a very misunderstood word, as the next chapter explains. Opening the heart is to seek Truth at its deepest and most profound level. And in finding that truth, what you will find is that you are already perfect exactly as you are: perfect, with all of your limitations. The purpose of limitation is its capacity to express distinction, to express uniqueness. You are who you uniquely are because of your limitations. If there were no limitations, everything would simply flow into everything else, and there would be no opportunity for unique self-expression.

This process of gaining greater access to the truth within you is frequently referred to as 'spiritual awakening', and it too has its own patterns.

SPIRITUAL AWAKENING

According to an Eastern story, when the gods decided to create the universe, they created the stars, the sun and the moon. They created mountains, seas, flowers and clouds. Then they created human beings. Finally, they created Truth.

Because the search for truth is the greatest adventure in the universe, the gods decided to hide truth, to prolong the search:

'"Let's put Truth on top of the highest mountain," said one of the gods. "Certainly it will be hard to find it there."

"Let's put it on the farthest star," said another.

"Let's hide it in the deepest and darkest of caves."

"Let's conceal it on the dark side of the moon."

'At the end, the wisest and most ancient god said, "No, we will hide Truth in the heart of human beings. In this way they will look for it all over the Universe, without being aware of having it inside themselves all the time."'

As one progresses inward, as one feels the impulse for change, there is often a feeling of urgency. Change is an ongoing process, and the 'goal', as some view it – to become such and such a person, or such and such a thing – does not exist. There is no once-and-for-all finished product. There is no final goal to our becoming, except the actual process of becoming.

We have talked about the opening heart, the unfolding process, the becoming process, as a process of dissolving and dismantling our inner barriers. On one level, we discovered why those barriers were put up in the first place. But there is another level.

We know that all things in the universe serve a greater purpose. So too do our inner barriers:

> God Supreme is everywhere, and yet without the experience of individuation, the separation, there would be an emptiness, a piece missing. There would be the totality without the consciousness to experience, to express, and therefore to become a part of that whirling universe of eternal creation.
>
> The separation from God began a journey of love. The individuating consciousness seeks, through the experience of human reality, to know itself fully and completely so that it can return to the Oneness with a greater light and a greater understanding.[5]

On the path to inner awakening and re-union, there are a distinct set of patterns that most people go through. They are the same patterns that have been described throughout. All things are a part of everything else, linked through rhythm and pattern. *My growth is a part of someone else's and someone else's is a part of mine.* 'I am

[5] Pat Rodegast and Judith Stanton, compilers, *Emmanuel's Book* (New York: Bantam, 1985), p.39.

not my brother's keeper' is paradoxical because we are at the same time all each other's keepers: someone else took the steps that evolved the processes and techniques that helped me in personal growth. My own insights as a consequence of that ongoing process will help others. It is an endless circle of growth and healing, if we allow it to be.

In the Macrocosm too, we realize that because each of us is an integral part of the Universe, our growth is part of the growth of the Universal Being. And as the Universal Being grows, so, too, must I. Is it any wonder the pressures for growth are so strong?

THE AWAKENING

The first stage of awakening occurs when we recognize that there is something beyond what we have been taught, something beyond the beliefs and values of our society. There is a feeling that 'there has to be more to life than this', even if we have everything that our society tells us is supposed to make us happy and fulfilled. That this is almost a universal first stage in the West is in itself a comment on our society. At first we follow the old and familiar pattern as we seek a new vision of ourselves: we follow a parent-figure or teacher. This can be a guru or other charismatic leader, a paternalistic religion, or an idealistic belief. But in all instances the authority for our life still comes from *outside* ourselves.

This is often the point where we make a whole or partial break with our past. We set out on stage two, the *quest.* Joseph Campbell calls these first two stages *separation* and *initiation*. We are still usually thinking in externals here, and the quest becomes an outer rather than an inward journey. We are often not clear what it is we are seeking, but our urgings tell us to go *somewhere* – India, Europe, anywhere but where we are. This is not a bad thing in itself. We discard the familiar, the safety nets, the excuses to stay stuck. However, at this stage there is equally a new opportunity to get stuck in a new place. Many become perpetual seekers, never standing still long enough to do any finding. But for those who do, there eventually arrives the stage of *discovery.*

The early discovery stage is another popular place to get stuck. As our awareness expands into levels that are often labelled 'psychic', our limited experience leads us to believe we have special gifts that others do not. When our egos get involved we can remain stuck here for a long time. When the doorway into other worlds begins to open, the light is so dazzling that we are frequently blinded by it – in many senses of the word. This is often a time of potent illusions. We glean fragments of Universal Truth, but our limited experience leads us to wild interpretations. These can be so enticing that it is a pleasant place to stay – stuck.

One of these Universal Truths is that we are *special*. It is absolutely true. But what is usually not seen at this point is that *so is everyone else*. 'Specialness' is not a bad thing; it is an attribute of Humanness that we all possess and need to acknowledge in ourselves, in order to become fully realized human beings. It is when we fail to perceive it in others, and set ourselves apart through our belief that it makes us different, does its realization fail in its purpose. *Anything* which creates or reinforces the illusion of separateness moves us further away from the truth, the essential Oneness of all.

Expansion and contraction cycles are an integral part of the awakening process. A new insight occurs, followed by a surge of growth; then there is a contraction inward to integrate the newly discovered dimension of ourselves. We all need our forty days and nights in the wilderness.

Another popular place to get stuck in during the discovery stage is to become a teacher. The urge to share our new worlds is a normal and natural impulse. The zeal of the newly converted is common to all belief systems. Indeed, when we reach real levels of inner truth, that truth *compels* us to aid others to reach the same levels of truth within themselves. There is nothing wrong with becoming a teacher, as long as we don't stop growing ourselves. But a teacher who doesn't learn as much from his students as he teaches them is missing something. There is an old saying: 'When the student is ready the teacher appears.' To which I would add: 'The problem is in telling who is who.'

Both this and the next chapter suggest that the opening process requires action – that something needs to be done. There is. Live life.

Life is the teacher. Life is the course. Our life evokes our character. All courses and techniques can do is give you new tools for looking at your own life, and dealing with the challenges you have drawn to yourself in different ways. Yes, do the courses. Yes, read the books. But remember that your everyday life is constantly bringing to you the lessons that need to be learned, the barriers that need to be dissolved.

Most of all we need to adopt a heroic approach to life – to, as the song says, look for the hero inside ourselves. It is there, in all of us.

EXERCISES

Through the following exercises you will have an opportunity to begin experiencing deeper and deeper levels of love radiating from the centre of your own being. During these exercises, it is not unexpected that you will experience physical sensations in the area of the heart. You may have great feelings of radiating warmth, feelings of softness, feelings of melting. And indeed, you may also experience physical pain. Should you do, there is no need for alarm. The psychological and energetic armouring that covers our heart is held in place by severe muscular tension in the chest area. As we begin to let go of the energetic armoury, those muscles will begin to relax. It is rather like the experience of setting down a heavy load that you have been carrying for longer than you wished – when you finally put it down, you notice how tight and cramped the muscles are.

This does not in any way mean that you should not seek competent medical advice should you feel any sense of discomfort or alarm about any of the physical sensations that occur in any of the exercises through the book.

The human mind works very much in symbols, and by creating appropriate symbols our subconscious mind will grasp them very quickly, and begin making the perceptual shifts that are necessary for our further opening. The first exercises are designed to do this. They follow the format of the exercises in the remainder of the book: first, a statement of the purpose of the exercise – what the exercise is intended to accomplish; second, the crystal for the exercise. A specific crystal is not suggested, because it will be different for each person; what is given is the purpose you should have in mind when choosing an appropriate crystal. Third, the programme: your focus of intention for performing the exercise. These programme steps are designed to help form clarity of intention. For most exercises, there will be some introductory material to help you to understand the function of the exercise in the overall growth and heart-opening process, and why it is necessary.

The first crystal exercises begin working directly with the Heart Centre. The first three are about gradually going deeper and deeper into your Heart Centre, to begin, first, to connect with it, and secondly to discover what resides there.

The first exercise is about cleansing the Heart Centre, and is designed to set in motion, subconsciously, powerful energetic forces in your own Being that will facilitate the remaining exercises in this book.

Heart Cleansing

Purpose

✦ This is an exercise for symbolically cleansing the Heart Centre. In it you are using the crystal as a symbol of the perfect Inner Being that dwells in the depths of your heart. We will be using a visualization technique to clear away anything that is clouding the perfect Inner Being – all thoughts, feelings and beliefs that are not in perfect harmony with who you are. This will all be seen in symbols; you may see inharmonious beliefs as tiny bits of rubbish, as black gunk, or as some sort of debris scattered about; just let your own mind create whatever symbol works the best for you.

Crystal

✦ The crystal for this exercise will be placed directly over the Heart Centre, and in the exercise you will be projecting yourself into the crystal. In choosing a crystal for this exercise find one with which you feel a deep heart connection.

Programme

✦ The crystal is programmed to reflect back to you the deepest levels of your own perfection and, by contrast, to see all of those things in your heart – in whatever symbols are appropriate to you – that keep it from being clear and clean and a perfect source of love to all of your being.

Exercise

✦ With the crystal in place over your heart, take in a few deep breaths and let them out slowly. As you do, become aware of your own heartbeat. Focus initially on the heartbeat, rather that the crystal. As you become more and more focused on your heartbeat, feel it as the centre of your being, as if everything that you are is focused in that beat. As you become more and more focused on the heart, extend your awareness to include the crystal resting on it.

✦ As you become more and more focused on the crystal, visualize the crystal becoming larger and larger, and your body becoming smaller and smaller. Eventually the crystal will become larger than your body, and you can then allow yourself to slip inside the crystal. It is as if we are stepping inside your own heart, symbolized by the crystal.

✦ When you are inside the crystal, take a moment to sense the feeling of utter balance and perfection there, and take a moment to just look around. Experience being in your crystal as if being inside a room – the facets of the crystal are the walls of the room. When you feel comfortable inside, notice that in one of the walls of the room (i.e., one of the faces of the crystal) there is a window. You can see this as any sort of window you like – a porthole, a large window, a small window – but in any instance one that can be opened.

✦ So, walk to the window and open it. As you look out of the window, you will see that what is outside is . . . the Cosmos. A whole universe of stars outside the window. The Universe is the source of everything in our Being – the unbalanced thoughts and beliefs, as well as the balanced ones. Our unbalanced thoughts and feelings are ones which have taught us: they are the things which have propelled us into learning. But as we begin to reach out to reharmonize ourselves with the Universe, we no longer need these things, so it is now OK to return them to the Universe.

✦ Now have a look around inside your heart crystal; looking for anything that looks out of balance, anything that is not in harmony. As mentioned, you may see it as rubbish or litter, or some sort of muck. You will find at hand whatever tools you need to clean with, so set to it! As you clean up whatever rubbish you find inside, just shovel it out of the window – return it to the Cosmos.

✦ As you go on cleaning, you will see the whole place becoming tidier; it begins to take on a bright and shiny brand-new sort of look. You may even want to take a cloth and polish it!

✦ When you have finished cleaning, close the window and return your cleaning tools to the proper place.

✦ When you have completed all of this, begin taking deeper and deeper breaths, focusing on your heartbeat. As you do so, visualize the crystal becoming smaller and smaller and your body becoming larger and larger, until they have both returned to their proper size.

The Crystal Cave

The cave is an important symbol for the heart centre, for just as you go deeper and deeper into the body of the earth in a real cave, you go deeper and deeper into the body of our own Being in a symbolic cave. This exercise is designed around the self-reflective power of crystals, and is a good beginning at truly looking at yourself and what is really there.

Purpose

✦ This is an exercise for deep self-exploration. It is for getting deep into the Heart Centre and for taking a clear look at yourself – including your own Shadow.

Crystal

✦ Place the crystal on your heart. Use a crystal that almost feels as if it were a physical mirror that you could actually look into and see a physical reflection of yourself.

Programme

✦ The programme for this crystal is to give a clear reflection of what is deep within your own heart – the rough with the smooth.

Exercise

✦ To begin this exercise, visualize yourself in a place out of doors, a place that might, for you, embody the words 'The Earth'. A place where you might find the entrance to a cave. Create the day to be a day that you would be happy to return to – sun shining, birds singing and so forth.

✦ The cave you are going to explore is a warm, dry and well-lit one. And what you will see as you go deeper into the cave is that the walls are lined with crystals, crystals of all sorts of sizes, shapes and colours. As you walk into the entrance of the cave you will notice the floor slopes downwards, so as you walk further into the cave you will be walking deeper and deeper into the earth. As you do, feel the living rock surrounding you.

✦ The light at the entrance will gradually disappear behind you as you begin to notice the crystals lining the walls of the cave – reflecting, sparkling, pure and perfect. Allow yourself plenty of time to get very deeply into the cave. When you are as deep as you wish to go, feel yourself in a large room, elongated like a central corridor of the cave. From this central room there will be little crystal-lined rooms, little grottoes, opening to the left and right.

✦ Before you begin to explore these rooms, it is important to have a clear intention to remember what you see, as there are several rooms to explore. The first one that you will explore is a chamber to the right of the central corridor. As you look into the chamber you will see it lined with crystals, and as you go into that room you will see certain specific reflections coming back to you from those crystals. You may see them as visual reflections, or you may feel them as psychic or intuitive reflections. What these crystals will be reflecting back to you are the best parts of yourself, your most positive characteristics, your most positive traits. Give yourself a few minutes to explore this chamber.

✦ When you have seen all that you wish to see, return to the central corridor of the cave, bringing with you memories of as many reflections as you could find in the room of positive reflections.

✦ Go now to a little room opening to the left of the central corridor where, once again, you will see a room lined with crystals. These crystals will also reflect something of yourself back to you, but in this room they will reflect the parts of yourself you really don't like to look at: your Shadow Self. As you go in and explore those reflections, be aware that many of those reflections of the disharmonious parts of you have also been very important learning experiences for you – until you identify and learn to love, and learn to work, with those parts of yourself you can never be a complete being. The Shadow Self is a vital part of who you are, and it is not a self to be done away with – it is a self to be embraced and integrated. Coming to accept ourselves as we really are is the *only* path to enlightenment and self-healing. So, when you have completed your exploration of the room of difficult reflections, return to the central portion of the cave.

✦ Once back in the central corridor, you will notice that the cave goes even deeper into the earth and, as you follow the cave further downward, you will notice the crystals get more and more beautiful. The reflections that come back to you are even more beautiful and profound, because these crystals, in the deepest part of your being, will reflect back to you the True You, the real Self. Follow the cave downwards as deeply as you can, until you come to the place where the largest and most beautiful crystals of all are; you will see, reflected back to you in those crystals, the great Cosmic Being that you really are.

✦ When you have completed the exploration of that deepest portion of the cave, begin your way back upwards, climbing until you reach the surface, until you return to the bright beautiful day outdoors, on this beautiful place called the Earth.

The Sacred Spring

Some years back I had an extremely deep meditation into my own Heart Centre. Since having the experience, I have met two other people who had exactly the same experience, otherwise I might have believed my own was just imagination.

All of a sudden I realized that I was deeper into the centre of my own being than I had ever been before (or have ever been since), and as I got deeper and deeper, I became aware of a glowing light. As I came closer to that light, I could see that it was a pattern; a pattern made from energy that appeared to be light blue in colour. There was a central structure to it, which appeared to be rods of light, and surrounding those rods of light were hundreds of dots of light, arranged in a very precise pattern. In that moment, I was aware that the 'rods' were somehow the core of the structure, and that each of the blue dots was an experience. I know that I was literally looking at the centre of my own being. It is a place we can all find within ourselves.

As in the previous exercise, you will use the cave symbol to go deeply into the core of your own Being, but this time you will experience the Well Spring of your own life. The depth of inner connection you can make in this exercise is profound, and it is one that you may wish to repeat a number of times as you progress along your inward journey. What you will discover as you do so is that the inner experience, although similar or identical in form each time, will have more subtle nuances, connecting with deeper subtleties of your own Being.

Purpose

✦ To get in touch with the deepest level of your own heart, the energy pattern that is at the core of your Being.

Crystal

✦ Choose a crystal for this exercise to which you feel a response deep in your Heart Centre. I suggest you look for a physical sensation in the heart for this one. In this exercise, the crystal is placed over the heart.

Programme

✦ To be drawn into the very deepest level of your own Being, and to see reflected back to you the energy pattern that is your Beingness.

Exercise

✦ In ancient times, the water source for a city was often within the city wall, and reached through a very deep well. These wells were often more than just vertical shafts – they were proper tunnels, with stairs leading down into them. Our sacred spring will be in such a location.

✦ Go in your mind, then, to some ancient place – a place where you feel a sacred connection. This can be a real place or an imagined one. Whatever spot you go to, find a doorway, a doorway that opens into a sloping tunnel, that leads to a sacred spring. Create the kind of doorway you might expect to find in such a location: an elaborate doorway, the entrance to a temple, or whatever image you might see for such a sacred place.

✦ As you walk up to the door, you may sense that you would like to do some sort of ritual, or some sort of personal cleansing, as you are about to enter a holy site. When you have done this ritual or cleansing, enter the doorway and begin walking downward. There is a passageway, a sloping tunnel that leads deep into the earth. It is a wide passageway, with stairs and a slope that is comfortable to walk down. It is warm and dry in this passageway, and it is spacious enough that there is no sense of confinement.

✦ As the light of day fades behind you, the lighting in the passageway will be provided by candles, giving it a warm and soft glow. You will hear the echo of your footsteps as you go deeper and deeper into the earth.

✦ Give yourself plenty of time, and really try to sense the depth – deeper, and deeper, and deeper, and deeper. Eventually, when you feel you have reached the very depths, you will begin to hear a gentle sound of water trickling. You know that you are approaching the sacred spring and the pool that lies at its feet. As you reach the deepest part of the tunnel, you will find that it opens into a large room, with a beautiful pool of candlelit water, surrounded by a sandy beach and by a number of seats. You are there by yourself, but you know that this is the same life source for many.

✦ Seat yourself next to the pool, and just feel the energy that comes upward with the spring – the waters of life. As you watch the pool, you will eventually notice that there is a faint glow in the water, which begins to get brighter as you watch it. You know that there is nothing to fear about what you are going to see, but you may certainly have other feelings that are appropriate to express.

✦ The glow becomes even brighter and you suddenly sense that something is rising out of the water from the very depths. As you watch, a glowing figure rises from the water. It is not in human form, being made up mostly of points of light, but you will be aware that radiating from this figure of light is an intense feeling of joy and love. You will realize that, in the depths of your Being, this is who you really are.

✦ There may be some communication from this Being of light or there may not, but in either case there will be a moment when you sense you have been in the presence of this Being for a sufficient amount of time. At that time, the Being will sink into the depths once again, leaving you alone in the candlelit chamber.

✦ When you sense completion, allow yourself time to digest your experience and, when you are ready, return to the surface. Allow yourself plenty of time to return, and if you have experienced any deep emotional feelings, lie down on the bed or the floor or wherever you are meditating, on your left side, and allow the experience to integrate itself.

✦ Be certain to write down every detail you can remember in your notebook as soon as possible after completing this experience, regardless of whether those details seem important at the moment or not.

Opening the heart, then, is to open oneself to the deepest levels of love. One of the most important ways we work through our inner barriers is to be in a situation where those barriers can be made visible, and can therefore be dealt with. These situations are called *relationships*.

RELATIONSHIPS AND RESONANCE

✧

Nature is upheld by antagonism: Passions, resistance, danger, are educators. We acquire the strength of what we have overcome.

Emerson

All things that exist in the Universe are *energy* and *relationships*. All relationships that exist in the Universe are manifestations of the five universal principles defined in Chapter 2. So it is with crystals, and so it is with human relationships. Since all relationships are created from the same universal patterns, there is necessarily a resonance between them at some level or levels. Our inner relationship with ourselves resonates in some way with the choices we make in life, be they choices of crystals or teacups or partners.

Those within all of the Kingdoms experience relationships. We have seen the relationships based on electronic or gravitational attraction that create stars, planets and galaxies; and the relationships between particles that create atoms, molecules and minerals. In the Plant Kingdom relationships become more complex and those relationships take on a more seasonal character.

The Animal Kingdom sees the development of relationships at a more personal and individual level than plants, especially as animals become more complex. Termites function as a single unit, with a level of social complexity not too far advanced from the collection of individually functioning cells that make up plants.

At the other end of the scale are the larger land and sea mammals, with levels of social and family relationship approximating our own.

We saw in Chapter 2 that one of the basic universal patterns is movement into complexity. One of the characteristics of creatures who themselves are becoming more complex, is that with increased biological complexity comes *an increasingly complex capacity for relationship*. And, that those relationships follow the basic patterns of Creation.

'Love' is perhaps the most confusing word in the English language. Love, for most, means a romantic feeling or a feeling attached to someone or something that is special to us. These are very real experiences of love – but what underlies them? Is it not the feeling we experience when we are in harmony with a person or place or thing? Is it not a feeling we experience when we are in a *right relationship* with the object of our love? It has been said throughout that our goal in attuning our lives to the rhythms, cycles and patterns of nature and the cosmos is to re-establish right relationship, to once again become a living *part* of the Earth and the Cosmos. Is not this right relationship love itself?

In Sondra Ray's book *Loving Relationships*,[1] one of the single most important points is that *'love brings up anything unlike itself for the purpose of healing'*. Love is the natural state of being – it is flawed relationships that create anything else: our relationship with our parents as children, our relationship to a spouse or partner, our relationship to God; and above all our relationship to ourselves, of which all other relationships are a reflection. Thus, as we heal our relationships, we heal not only our capacity to experience and express love, but we heal ourselves. However, the only way these flaws can be healed is for them to be seen. Therefore that which is not love makes itself visible – reflected in our lives – in order to return itself to a state of love. Further, love is the natural state of connection with the Source of one's own being. Healing our human relationships is a way to heal our separation from our own Source. We see, then, the importance of relationships, and why it takes a truly loving relationship to endure 'that which is not love'. All relationships, including that with one's own Source, follow the universal principle of expansion and contraction. Have you noticed how your personal relationships go through times of intense closeness, followed by times of 'apartness'? Aren't these 'apartness' times often associated with some feeling of hurt, resentment, or anger? That which is not love.

[1] Sondra Ray, *Loving Relationships* (Berkeley: Celestial Arts, 1980).

Growth is life. Lack of growth – stagnation – is a form of death. Growth of any kind brings times of discomfort and uncertainty. If love brings up anything unlike itself for healing, then a truly loving relationship *must* bring up anger and hurt. This is the natural order of things and it means that you have a good relationship. Does that sound the wrong way around? Do you believe that good relationships should be cosy and stable and that it is desirable for them to always be like that?

RELATIONSHIP PATTERNS

Ultimately, our relationship patterns tell us about ourselves. We see in our relationships, especially in our close personal relationships, the mirror reflection of our own upbringing and the patterns of relationships that shaped us. These patterns, set up through our relationship with our parents, are the patterns we have chosen to learn through in this lifetime. These are the 'barriers' described in the previous chapter. We choose a set of parents in the pre-conception state, when life-patterns are decided, specifically because they will set those patterns up for us, frequently (as it turns out), through their failures as parents. In fact, if our parents didn't fail us in some way, there would be nothing for us to learn: it is their failures that set up for us our learning situations. *We choose parents who will fail us appropriately, according to that which we need to learn.* These lessons may be structured through our birth trauma, childhood experiences, or other life-events. There is much talk of 'forgiveness' in relation to our parents' failures. The ultimate realization is that there is nothing to forgive: they did exactly what you chose them for.

None of this means that we should go into a relationship with the idea of changing our partner. It is utterly impossible to change anyone but ourselves. However, if you both enter into the relationship knowing the truth about relationships – that they are golden opportunities for growth – then the inevitable conflicts which arise can be dealt with in a whole new light.

As a consequence of the 'setting up' of learning by our parents, the unresolved issues each partner must face are the original relationship issues with their parents. There is a definite set of patterns that all of us have to varying degrees. Sondra Ray has noted these, and my experience as a therapist bears them out in eloquent detail:

* Pattern 1 – you tend to attract partners who re-create your parents' *personalities*.
* Pattern 2 – you tend to re-create the kind of *relationships* you had with your parents.
* Pattern 3 – you tend to re-create the kind of relationship your parents had *with each other*.
* Pattern 4 – as we are used to a lot of disapproval from our parents, we create disapproval in our partners.
* Pattern 5 – you tend to get even with your parents through your partner.
* Pattern 6 – because of guilt or self-disapproval, we tend to 'beat ourselves up' using our relationships.
* Pattern 7 – you will always find someone who fits your patterns.[2]

It is the nature of attraction that the two partners' issues will interlock. That is, your issues will be a part of your partner's issues, and *vice versa*. This is often referred to as a 'karmic' relationship. Karma is only 'cause and effect' in the sense that it is nothing more than an unfinished lesson: you and your partner are working on a different aspect of the same lesson or lessons. It is true that you and your partner may have chosen these lessons over several lifetimes – but it need mean no more than that. You are, at least for the time you are learning mutual lessons together, 'soul mates'. But in any lifetime you may have more than one 'soul mate', depending on the lessons to be learned, and how well you are each learning those lessons. If one partner learns and the other doesn't, then the purpose of your relationship will eventually cease, and you both need to move on. There is a real time of accelerated learning on the Earth at the moment, and that is why so many relationships are beginning and ending with such frequency. The caution here, though, is that many relationships end just at the point where the real issues arise, without the partners staying together long enough to resolve them. Such relationships are wasted opportunities.

Let's look at detail now at how some of the universal principles and patterns work out.

[2] *Ibid.*

In the time of coming together the real issues of a relationship usually do not arise until bonds have formed between the two partners – the first contraction phase of the expansion/contraction pattern – that are strong enough to endure when the going gets harder as those issues begin to arise. Three to six months is a fairly average time period for this stage. The strength of the bond that forms largely determines the depth of the issues that can safely arise. The bond must be strong enough to not break during the expansion period when the partners are furthest apart. Part of the initial bond-forming period is spent sizing each other up to see how well the other partner will react when the strains begin to show, when 'the honeymoon is over'. Many relationships end at about this time, as it becomes apparent that the partner will not be able to deal with what may potentially arise. Most of this 'sizing up' is an unconscious process. Figure 35a illustrates that phase of the relationship.

In the initial contraction stage of a relationship we begin to learn about our new partner – their likes and dislikes, something about who they are. This stage is laden with illusions with us acting out the parts we think our new partner wants, and projecting onto them the image of who we want *them* to be. Eventually, the realities begin to creep in. Paradoxically, it always occurs at the time when both partners are feeling closest to each other. Suddenly something happens to trigger feelings of anger, resentment, betrayal, or any number of equally unpleasant feelings. We have touched into the real issues of our relationship (Figure 35b). We wonder what has suddenly gone so wrong! The answer is that nothing has gone wrong. In fact it is going very right! You have become close enough for it to be 'safe' for those feelings to arise and to be worked through. The usual pattern at this point is to draw apart – the expansion phase – and to have a time of personal contraction, of drawing into one's self, to resolve what has arisen (Figure 35c).

When you can recognize what is happening, such times can be used constructively to further both your own and your partner's growth. Stay together and work at your issues unless you are absolutely certain that it is time to end your relationship. When and if it does become time, there is always a sense of completion – a sense that this person and I have nothing further to learn from each other. If you are staying together, allow each other the space to deal with what has arisen. And allow the relationship a healing time – lots of love-making, lots of talking, lots of sharing of experiences. Communication is of the absolute essence. Remember that

EXPANDED

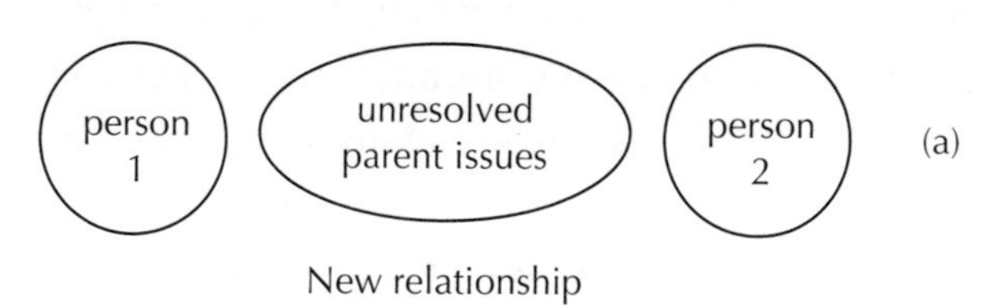

New relationship

CONTRACTED

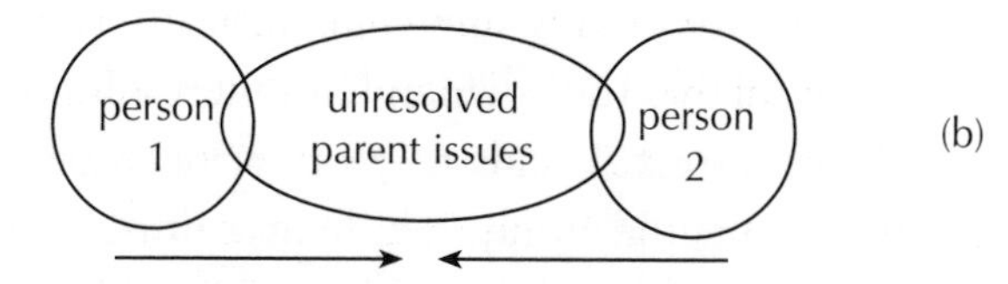

Bonds form drawing partners together

EXPANDED

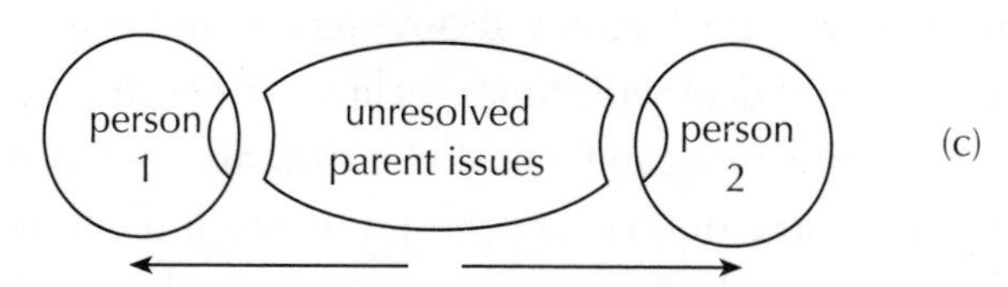

Bonds are stretched as each partner resolves issues that have arisen. Then the whole cycle repeats itself. Again and again!

Figure 35: The expansion/contraction pattern in relationships

relationships are about healing, and that your partner is trying to heal you, even when he or she is screaming at you!

You probably notice another expansion and contraction pattern in your relationships. You and your partner are either expanders or contracters yourselves! When a powerful issue arises, do you tend to withdraw into yourself and cut off communication – to contract? An expander, on the other hand, is not content to let an issue lie. They will pursue the contracter into the bedroom or the bathroom or wherever they have retreated to. The expander will be shouting 'Will you *listen* to me?' The contracter will be shouting 'Leave me *alone.*' These two types correspond to the two basic personality types identified by Arthur Janov, discoverer of

Primal Therapy. He calls these types *sympathetic* and *parasympathetic*, depending on which of the two modes of metabolic regulation is triggered in stressful situations. The sympathetic nervous system alarms and alerts, energizes and mobilizes: it expands. The parasympathetic system contracts: it conserves energy and demobilizes.

As you can probably guess, expanders almost always attract contracters, and *vice versa*. One of the reasons that opposites attract (just like positive and negative atoms) is that we need to develop some of the stronger attributes of our partner, which are usually underdeveloped in ourselves. The expander is attracted to a contracter because there are usually upwelling insecure feelings to be dealt with, feelings that are so painful that they demand instant resolution. Hence the demand to resolve it *now*. The contracter tends to be a person who buries his or her feelings, and allows them to surface only a little at a time. Again, these are painful feelings, and the contracter feels as if he or she will be overwhelmed if they cannot escape. Clearly the very existence of these patterns is a pattern in itself, in need of resolution. It is also a pattern that almost guarantees difficulties in communication unless both partners make an effort. The expander needs to make themselves slow down a bit and deal with the feelings of slowing down; the contracter needs to risk a bit more exposure and deal with those feelings. It doesn't happen overnight, but these are major patterns that can be healed if they are used constructively.

The expansion–contraction cycle is by no means limited to unpleasant experiences. We can be so used to our past relationships being unpleasant that in a contraction situation, when we are extremely close to someone, the pleasure can be so intense that we have to back off. We actually need to develop a tolerance for pleasure!

OTHER UNIVERSAL PATTERNS

The other universal patterns of *movement into density* and *movement into complexity* are also perfectly reflected in relationships. As expansion and contraction cycles repeat and we learn the lessons of our relationship, there is a deepening of the bond, an intensification of the relationship. Our relationship becomes more complex: new bonds form as we develop new dimensions of ourselves and our relationship; new areas open up for mutual exploration. Indeed, there comes a time in deep relationships where, if these things do not occur, the relationship ends. It eventually becomes apparent what *is* possible, and if the relationship does not have the potential to provide it, then it must end. It must be so because that which is possible always resides within us. In the words of Abraham Maslow, 'What we *can* be, we *must* be.' We cannot feel satisfaction with anything less.

Our own personal lives go through expansion and contraction cycles, forming our relationship with ourselves (our Selves). In an expansion phase we are actively out in the world, busy gathering new experiences. In the contraction phase we draw inward to integrate those experiences and to thereby gain a clearer picture of ourselves. These cycles may last for minutes or months.

Life is a trial-and-error learning experience. Many of us forget that, especially in Western societies where we are so competitive (even with ourselves) that making a 'mistake' means being a loser, and society only tolerates winners. In reality there is only one mistake that it is possible to make – to not learn from our mistakes. Rarely does anyone ever do anything perfectly at the first attempt. Making mistakes and learning to correct them is a vital part of human learning. It can even be dangerous to *not* make mistakes.

Many years ago I was a flight instructor. I had a student who never made a mistake. I would show him how to do something and he would do it perfectly first time. You might think that this would be the perfect student, but he was just the opposite. In the process of making and learning to correct mistakes, students learn to handle a wide variety of flight situations, and at the same time gain valuable insights into their own capabilities and the capabilities of their airplanes. If you never make a mistake, you miss a lot of invaluable learning. In fact, this student would have been a danger to himself and everyone else if he had been allowed to fly solo at a time when he was technically capable of it. He had made so few mistakes that he wouldn't have had the insight to deal with an unexpected situation if it arose. So I put him through several hours of deliberate 'mistake' situations that I created for him, so he could gain that learning.

One of the 'mistakes' that commonly occurs as a part of the self-discovery process is in trying something new, something that is 'not us'. In the process, we learn more about who we are not, thereby narrowing our definition of who we are. It is an expansion and contraction process which can be shown in Figure 36. The 'who I am not' segment also applies to relationships. Each new relationship is, in some manner, a reflection of you. Often we get into a relationship only to discover that the other person's direction is not ours or that ours is not theirs. Such relationships often complete their purpose early on and end. But we have learned

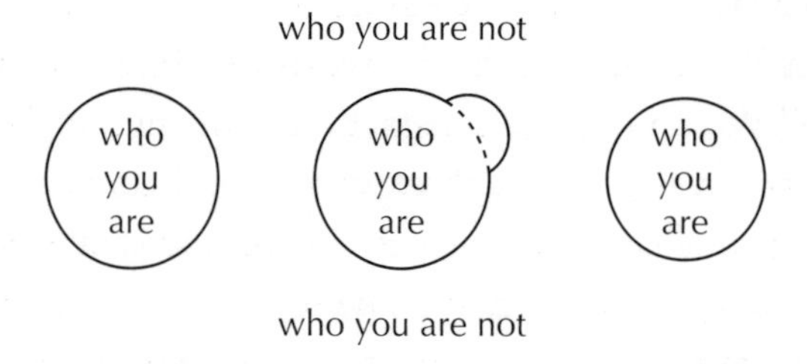

Figure 36: The 'who you are not' expansion/contraction cycle

more about ourselves in the process. Often knowing who or what you are *not* is as important as knowing who or what you *are*.

For some people one relationship over an extended period can provide all the necessary growth opportunities. For others many relationships may be necessary. Neither is right or wrong as long as we are learning and growing.

Although relationships are a primary stimulus to growth it would be erroneous to assume that both partners grow at the same rate, or that they are dealing with the same issues at the same time. One partner may be dealing with feelings of abandonment while the other partner is dealing with feelings of inadequacy. Both can be triggered by the same event. Although there are underlying basic cycles and rhythms to relationships, each person will have their own personal rhythms and cycles. They do not necessarily synchronize. Partners may 'take turns' growing: one partner will provide a stable base while the other partner grows, and *vice versa*.

At some point in each new relationship a realization will dawn: this one is just like the last one! And so, to some degree, each one will be. The patterns of your partner will *always* be a reflection of your own patterns. You can *only* attract a partner whose patterns match yours in some way. Attraction does not happen otherwise.

Unfortunately, in our culture in the West we do not seem to know this about relationships. Numerous studies have been done of marriage: in all the studies happiness peaks in about the first year. By the second year satisfaction begins to drop, reaching rock bottom in the seventh year when divorces are most likely to occur.[3] What does this tell us? Several things. In the first year we are still in the 'honeymoon' stage; the real issues have not yet come up. By the second year those

[3] Gail Sheehy, *Passages* (London: Bantam, 1974), p.129.

issues are arising, and continue to arise until we reach a breaking point in the seventh year. But why do we reach the breaking point? The figures also tell us that people are not dealing with the issues. Otherwise there would be a strengthening and deepening of the relationship by the seventh year. The real tragedy is how unnecessary it all is: if we only understood what is really happening.

Part of the problem in the West, too, is our failure to understand the real purpose of marriage. Marriage is recognition of a spiritual identity. Joseph Campbell reminds us that if we live a proper life, if our minds are on the right qualities in regarding the person of the opposite sex, we will find our proper male or female counterpart. But if we are distracted by certain sensuous interests, we'll marry the wrong person; by marrying the right person, we reconstruct the image of the incarnate God, and that's what marriage is.

Campbell further reminds us that the primary function of marriage is not perpetuating ourselves in children – that's really just the elementary aspect of marriage. And, that there are two completely different stages of marriage: the first is the youthful marriage, following the wonderful impulse that nature has given us in the interplay of the sexes biologically in order to produce children. But there comes a time, when the parents are in their forties or fifties, when the child graduates from the family and the couple is left alone – at which point they often part. They have had a perfectly decent life together with the child, but they interpreted their union in terms of their relationship through the child. They did not interpret it in terms of their own personal relationship to each other.[4]

EARLY DEVELOPMENT PATTERNS

Another pattern that appears in relationships is the pattern of your own early development. Do you start feeling trapped in a new relationship after about six months? This is about the time 'trapped in the womb' feelings begin for many unborn infants. This time between six and nine months is when many of us need to escape the 'confinement' of a serious relationship. Were you 'abandoned' at 18 months of age by a parent leaving or dying? Then 18 months into a new relationship is a danger point when you may subconsciously create a situation where your partner 'abandons' you. All the old feelings from the original event will arise,

[4] Joseph Campbell and Bill Moyers, *The Power of Myth* (London: Doubleday, 1988).

which you will most likely blame on your partner. What has happened is that those feelings have 'come up for healing'. As an 18-month-old child, feelings of that intensity would have been overwhelming or even fatal. So they became buried through the psychological process of repression.

Repressed feelings continue to affect us physically and psychologically even though our conscious memory of them may be virtually inaccessible. Those buried feelings eat away at us, tainting our lives and our relationships. The only way they can be healed is to bring them to the surface where they can finally be felt. We act out the original dilemma: do I limit myself or do I risk annihilation? However, now we can feel as an adult, who can deal with such feelings safely. Thus we create situations in our relationships, with the (often unconscious) cooperation of our partner, which bring up those feelings. It is how love brings up anything unlike itself for healing.

By understanding our own early development, and knowing the patterns that emerge in relationships, we can be aware that what is emerging is old feelings, and rather than blame each other we can then support each other to work through them. A wonderful line quoted by Sondra Ray from the *Course in Miracles* says: 'You are never upset for the reason you think you are.' Through awareness of our own 'danger points' we are able to use relationships constructively for the personal growth of both parties. The reward is a deeper and more fulfilling relationship that gets better with time, rather than the opposite which is much more common where these patterns are not known.

INTIMACY

The dimension of our personality that grows most through this expansion and contraction cycle is our capacity for intimacy. Intimacy is a state of knowing someone else as well as you know yourself and, from that knowing, accepting them. Because our partner is a reflection of ourselves, through this process we also reach a point of self-acceptance. The highest state of humanness, the point of enlightenment (or Christhood, or Buddhahood, or whatever we care to call it), is ultimately a point of total self-acceptance. It is the point to which all cycles of human growth attempt to lead us.

One of the most difficult aspects of self-knowledge is accepting the parts of ourselves we don't want to face – our 'dark side'. This is usually the part of ourselves we keep hidden away, the part of ourselves that we were taught as children was unacceptable. In reality this is not usually the case but our upbringing believes it to be so. Often hidden here are the most vital and alive parts of ourselves, locked away only by our own beliefs. Jung called this the 'Shadow Self', and there was an introduction to it in the Crystal Cave exercise in the previous chapter. Because all things are brought out into the light in the healing process, that part of us will re-emerge too – often at midlife, especially when we are thrown up against our Shadow Self. Nature is full of second chances, and this is the second chance for the personality to fulfil itself as a whole person. All that dwells in the Shadow is still part of us, and there is no way to be a whole person, a real person, until it, too, is integrated into the personality.

In a recent series of films there was an evil villain who had become his Shadow, had embraced the dark side of 'the force'. Yet at the last moment he came to terms with his darkness and became the one to destroy evil. Because he knew evil he was able to defeat it. Only when we know our Shadow can we become its master, rather than pretending it doesn't exist and thus allowing it to master us. This doesn't, by the way, mean that what dwells in our Shadow *is* evil; rather that we treat it as if it is.

When two people are growing together, the question will naturally enough arise: 'What if we grow apart?' It may happen. Life is full of risks, and this is one of them. But equally, it may not. Remember that a strong attraction is an indication of lots of patterns in common, and it may take a lifetime to work through them all. One of the fears many have about relationships breaking up is that they frequently end in pain and recrimination. A growth relationship may end, but it can end with the acknowledgement by both people that they have reached the limits of their growth together and must now go their separate ways. Relationships can end in a loving way as well as a painful one. If your relationship does end, Sondra Ray reminds us that if you have had a growth relationship, the next relationship will always be better than the last. This doesn't mean that the next relationship will necessarily be any easier than the last, but it does mean that all of the growth you experienced in your last relationship does not have to be redone.

Eventually a new pattern emerges, which is in reality the pattern that should have been there all along, until it was side-tracked by our Western, 'civilized' upbringing: growth is a pleasurable experience. It doesn't have to be painful at all. But until our artificial barriers to that experience of growth are brought up for healing, we cannot fully experience the full pleasure of it. In bringing up our barriers to be healed, our partners bring us back to the natural rhythm of life and of growth, the rhythm of the Cosmos, the dance of the galaxies, the harmony that was within us all along. Truly, our partners are our pathway back to the stars.

MIRRORS

We live in a world made of mirrors. Everything that exists in our world serves to mirror ourselves back to ourselves. Love is the natural state of Being. Because the natural cannot long accommodate the unnatural, that which is natural – love – will bring up all that is not love to make it visible, for healing. Because like reflects like, that which is in perfect harmony with the universal Source reflects the perfect balance and harmony of the Source; and is, indeed, a perfect manifestation in matter of the Source itself. We find this state of balance and harmony in the crystal. As mirrors of that which resides within us which is like their own nature, crystals are unsurpassed; they highlight all that is not in perfect balance and harmony for the purpose of healing – real healing, not just the relief of symptoms.

Aside from the personal benefits of real healing, there is a much wider picture to consider. In the Macrocosm we need to realize that because each of us is an integral part of the Universe, our personal growth is part of the growth of the Universal Being. And as the Universal Being grows, so, too, must we. Is it any wonder the pressures for growth are so strong? And, why that which mirrors the most subtle levels of our being back to us, is a powerful tool for self-knowing.

Crystals are such tools, and in the next chapter we put them to use helping us to sort out some of the complex issues raised.

PART FOUR

EXERCISES

CHAPTER 12

EXERCISES

Make it thy business to know thyself,
which is the most difficult lesson in the world.
Cervantes

This book presents you with a variety of techniques from a number of different aspects of self-discovery and self-development, but in no way is it all-inclusive. You will undoubtedly find that you wish to supplement the contents of this book with other sources. The opening of the Self is a multi-faceted operation, and many, many therapies and techniques may ultimately be used. Whether it is through the use of exercises and techniques in this book, through courses you may take or therapies you may undertake, you will find that as shifts begin to take place on the inner plane, your life around you will also begin to change.

The bottom line for much of the work you will be doing with yourself is about facing your own fears. There is only one way, ultimately, to deal with fear – feel it. A fear that is felt, that is confronted, will eventually fade away. During some of the processes in this book, there may be times when you will feel a great deal of personal distress, your body may be distinctly uncomfortable, or you may feel a great deal of confusion. I highly recommend that while you are involved in these processes you seek the guidance of a qualified counsellor or therapist to aid you in

Acknowledgement is due to Walter Bellin, creator of Self-Transformation Seminars, who inspired several of the exercises in this chapter.

your own growth and development. It is important to emphasize that there is no one technique, therapy, or developmental path that is right for everyone.

It is recommended that you keep a detailed notebook with the results of all of the various exercises in this book, and also a record of dreams or other life experiences that occur during the time you are using these techniques. Remember that life is the teacher; and all of the therapies and techniques you do with yourself are merely ways of living your life more fully and completely, and absorbing its lessons more completely.

In noticing the rhythms of your own body, include in your notebook a daily record of your sleep state – how well you slept on any particular night and for how many hours. In doing this over a period of time, you will find certain natural rhythms appear. Also note whether on any particular night you have stayed up beyond your usual time, such as at a party, and notice how over a period of time your sleep rhythms are affected by this.

Read through each exercise and, if possible, put it on tape. You can then play it back to yourself as you do the exercise, leaving yourself enough time between the instructions to complete whatever images or processes are being suggested. In doing these various exercises, I suggest that you do them in a place where it is appropriate to release emotional feelings. And keep a box of tissues at hand! Tears are the natural safety valve of the body, and are likely in all forms of emotional release. Indeed, some of these exercises are intended to invoke strong emotional responses. They may or may not do so, depending on how in touch you already are with your feelings, and whether or not you have done similar processes or exercises in the past. If strong feelings do arise, express them. There are safe ways to do so that are harmless to yourself and others, as you will be shown. Feelings held in are of no value, and these are precisely those blockages to who you really are. But we need to be absolutely clear on one point:

These exercises are in no way intended to stimulate or encourage violence against any actual persons.

If you are doing these exercises in the company of another person, or if you are accompanying someone else who is doing them, it is best that this other person does not interfere in the processes. If you are in the middle of a strong crying release, it will often disrupt the flow of your release if someone presses tissues on you, or attempts to comfort you. It is important to realize that we discharge our unfelt feelings by feeling them, and any attempt to soothe them before they have been fully expressed is robbing you of your experience. As you do these various processes you will discover that your own sense of appropriateness will guide you as to when aid is needed from another person.

Always be aware of your own limits. If you are going into a state where you feel uncertain of your ability to deal with any feelings that arise, then simply come out of the experience. This is not to imply, by the way, that all of the experiences in this book are emotional or traumatic. Many of them will fill you with the joy and excitement of the discovery of who you really are.

Read the book through entirely before beginning any of these exercises. Then you will have an overall picture of what is ahead, and can see the relevance of the various exercises as they occur. Don't be daunted by the task ahead – personal growth and development is a life-long process, and anyone who promises you an 'instant fix' is lying to you – it just doesn't happen that way. Crystals are no more capable of creating instant shifts than any other life process; they are not 'magic pills'. But, as you shall soon discover, they can be vitally important tools in your own self-discovery and self-healing process.

SUPPLEMENTARY TECHNIQUES

The first part of this chapter contains supplementary techniques, which you may find useful at any time during the remaining exercises. These techniques do not directly use crystals. However, as most of the crystal techniques involve working through energy blockages, all of the supplementary techniques can be used to good advantage at any time during the clearing process.

All blockages are a restriction of your own life force. Rage is nothing more than blocked life energy. It is inevitable, therefore, that as deeper and deeper releasings take place you will experience a great deal of rage and anger, often seeming at times unconnected to any surrounding events. Or you will create events in your life that justify the feelings. Recognize that all you are experiencing is your own primal instinct for survival, and that any blockage to the full flow of your own life force will come out as rage or anger. Therefore, the supplementary techniques involve opening the body's energy centres, the chakras, to a rich and full expression of rage. These releases are quite healthy and, if you have had a clean release, you will feel good afterwards. This is the clearest indication that you have actually released blocked energy. If you do not feel good afterwards, you have probably not opened the energy centres fully and should keep repeating the technique you are using until you do.

Another certain indication of a genuine energy release is a feeling of heat radiating from the body. An intense release will produce intense sweating and a feeling that your body temperature has risen. Often, in the moments before a release takes place, the body will feel chilled as it withdraws its energy to protect itself as the fear begins to rise. A feeling of chill, with shivering or shaking, should be taken as a sign that energy is trying to release itself, and you should allow whatever feelings are present in the body at that time to develop further. It is a 'don't stop now' time. The sensations that accompany uncomfortable emotions being released are often in themselves uncomfortable; however, the object is not to make it feel better. In fact, until a clean emotional release takes place, uncomfortable feelings should be made to feel worse! It is only by getting into these feelings that they can finally be released. To attempt to soothe or calm them before they are released only keeps them stuck.

After a powerful emotional release, lie on your left side in the foetal position and allow the new body state to integrate. The integration feeling will be a feeling of energy returning to the body with a sense of calmness and clarity, and a feeling of desire to get on with whatever comes next. It may be necessary to go through several stages of release and integration in order for this feeling to occur. If you are lying in the foetal position and still experiencing uncomfortable feelings there is probably another stage of release to go through. If working with someone else, after a completed emotional release has taken place, there may be a desire to soothe. To do this, the hand should be moved along the spine from the neck downward, 'stroking' the aura 5 to 10 cms from the body.

It is also important to remember that once the releasing process begins, emotional feelings may begin rising to the surface for some period of weeks or months afterwards. And, after an intense emotional release, you may feel tired or sleepy as the muscle tension which held those energies in place relaxes.

A lower level of emotional release – a release which is almost a 'wallowing' in the feeling state – will usually fail to produce a feeling of heat radiating from the body. If you are experiencing this sort of release, you need to go much deeper into your feelings. It is desirable, but not absolutely necessary, to have another person with you while you go through these processes. Your own sense of trust and safety in having another person present while you are in what is often a vulnerable state, will be your guide as to its appropriateness.

Remember though, if you are working with someone with whom you are in a close relationship, as your issues come up, their issues will also be triggered!

Therefore the person who is working with you should be aware of their own feelings that are arising. It may be a necessary agreement of your relationship that you both have personal space and time to work with issues without the necessity to do them with one another. The largest psychological hazard here is to get into blaming each other for the feelings that are arising, and you should both be aware of that tendency if you do work together. Remember: your feelings are yours, and your partner's feelings are theirs.

It is *especially important* to realize that persons or events which bring up feelings of rage in you are merely acting as symbols or triggers for the primal childhood events which created the blockages in the first place. Blaming the person or event in the current time for your feelings is inappropriate, as this person or event has merely served to reflect back to you your own blockage. If you use this person or event as a *symbol while doing the process* and imagine that you are actually venting your anger at that person, remember, *it is NOT OK to do so to the actual person.*

Once you have done a release it is amazing how differently you view the events which brought up the feeling of rage in the first place. You will find in many instances that, in retrospect, the feeling was quite irrational. And yet in the moment before the release the feelings may have felt so intense as to feel life-threatening. When you have cleanly released the feelings through the techniques, you will also find that you will begin to experience an increasing degree of forgiveness for the person who has 'caused' the feeling – with the ultimate goal in mind being to stop blaming other people for your feelings, and just own them as your own.

Supplementary Technique 1

✦ Lie flat on a bed, or a thick pile of mats. You will want a good deal of padding here, as you are going to be kicking with all your strength.

✦ If you have had an opportunity to notice an infant in a crib, when his needs are not being met, he will be kicking furiously away! It is also quite natural for small children to kick out in anger, either at adults or their contemporaries! In raising children, the kicking impulse is inhibited very early on, so much so that it even has an equivalent form of speech:

'How are you feeling John?'

'Oh, I can't kick.' ('I *can't* complain.')

✦ The technique is done lying on your back on the bed, and by raising one leg and the opposite arm as high as possible, kicking down with the heel and striking downward with a clenched fist as hard as possible, putting the full force of your anger or rage into the kick. It also helps if you can verbalize your feelings at this time, either by visualizing and directing a 'comment' to the person who has 'caused' your feelings, or by growling or making some other noise deep in the throat. It is important to make a noise here as it opens the upper chakras and permits a clean flow of energy throughout the body.

✦ Then, raise the other leg and opposite arm, and once again strike and kick downward with all your might. Continue doing this, alternating from leg to leg and arm to arm until you have exhausted yourself and/or the feeling has disappeared.

✦ You may find that you will alternate between periods of deep crying and deep rage in this Supplementary Technique, and the others. There will often be a great deal of grief locked up within the same energy.

✦ When the feeling has passed, roll onto your left side and, covering yourself to keep warm, allow your body to reintegrate. You will either begin feeling good and like getting out of bed, or you may find that additional feelings will arise, and it may be necessary to repeat the exercise several times.

This is a very powerful exercise, and you may even find that it will be difficult for you to do it in the beginning, as you may find it almost impossible to kick! This impulse is so deeply inhibited that you may actually have to fake it in order to get started.

Supplementary Technique 2

✦ Sometimes it is not appropriate or possible to kick hard as in the previous exercise, so I suggest that you do 'kickettes'. These are little short kicks, raising the heels only a few centimetres above the bed and done very rapidly, alternating from leg to leg. These are a great deal less noisy, and will still be very useful for releasing emotions, although the release is not quite as deep as in Technique 1.

Supplementary Technique 3

✦ This is a technique for striking powerfully with the arms, but doing so in a way that is unlikely to cause you physical damage. While the kicking techniques are important for your deep and primal rage, there is also a natural urge to strike out with the arms and hands. The instructions for this technique are a bit more complicated, and it is important to do this correctly, otherwise it can degenerate into wallowing behaviour very quickly, as in a child striking out in a tantrum.

✦ Kneel alongside a bed or a chair with a solid cushion, as in Figure 37a. If you are using a chair, make sure that it has at least 15 cms of cushion and spring, as you will be striking very hard.

Figure 37: Supplementary Technique 3

Pelvis forward/ shoulders back/ chest expanded/ head back/ throat stretched/ body weight supported on thighs

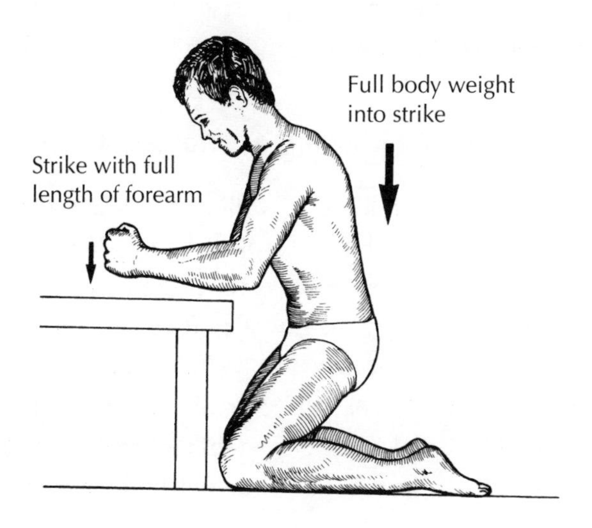

✦ The body is tilted backwards in an arc, as if the body is in the curvature of a bow being drawn. The pelvis is tilted upward, the shoulders are back and the chest is expanded; the head is also tilted back, with the throat stretched and the mouth open wide. This posture opens all of the chakras and permits a clear flow of energy through the body. The weight of the body is supported on the thighs. The fists are clenched, and are held approximately over the shoulders.

✦ The striking motion is done by coming down with the full body weight, and striking the bed or chair *along the full length of the forearm*, rather than using your fists (Figure 37b). *If you strike with your fists only, you may injure your wrists.* Practise this a few times in slow motion before trying it with full force.

✦ It is important to stretch the body fully in the arc before each strike, otherwise this exercise will degenerate into wallowing. You will be able to put enormous force into the blow, so be certain that the chair or bed is quite solid and well padded.

✦ To start the strike, arch your body backwards fully, taking a deep breath through your open mouth and pulling it down into your abdomen as far as possible. As you bend forward to strike, your breath will be forced out naturally. Keep your chin up through the strike, so the breath can exit fully. As the breath exits, bellow as loudly as you can, from as deep in your abdomen as you can. A little squeak in the throat won't do here! The object is to vibrate as many energy centres as possible, and to clear the energy flow as deeply as possible. Primal rage tends to be locked up in the abdomen, and that is what you are trying to reach.

✦ As with the previous exercises, repeat this until the feeling of rage has passed, and/or you have had a deep crying release. Then, roll into the foetal position and allow your feelings to reintegrate,until you feel calm and relaxed.

Supplementary Technique 4 – The Towel Twist

✦ This exercise is done by folding or rolling a towel until your hands fit comfortably around it. The hands should be placed 15 to 25 cms apart, with both hands on top of the twist, and the thumbs towards the body, as in Figure 38. The technique is done by simply twisting the towel, as if you are wringing water out of it. Or, as if you are wringing someone's neck! While you are doing so, making a growling noise deep in the throat will help to break loose the energy block.

✦ This exercise can be done kneeling or standing, and if you practise it a bit you will soon discover that you can put your full body weight into the twist,

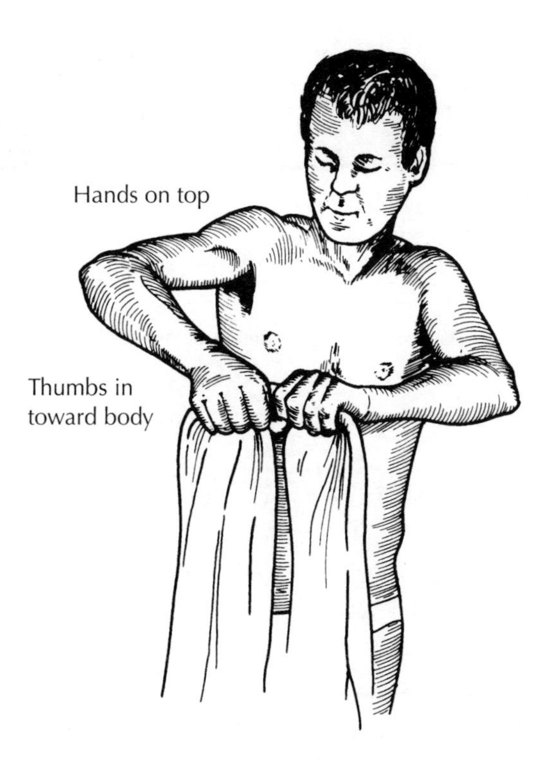

Figure 38: Supplementary Technique 4

especially using the muscles of the shoulders and upper torso. This is a wonderful exercise as it can be done anywhere; you can even slip into the bathroom at someone else's house during a party if necessary. Obviously, the amount of growling you will wish to do is optional!

Supplementary Technique 5

✦ This exercise is useful when you are feeling tightness in the throat or chest, and is designed specifically to release blockages in those two areas. Often, as energy is released from the lower energy centres and moves upward, it will come up against energy blockages in the upper part of the body, creating feelings of tension and pressure. It is the 'feel like crying' feeling. In fact, this is exactly what needs to be done. However, since the crying response is often blocked early on as well (especially in men), we sometime need to give our natural instincts a bit of help.

✦ For this exercise, lie flat on your back with a pillow just supporting the shoulderblades. The pillow should not go under the head, as the head should be

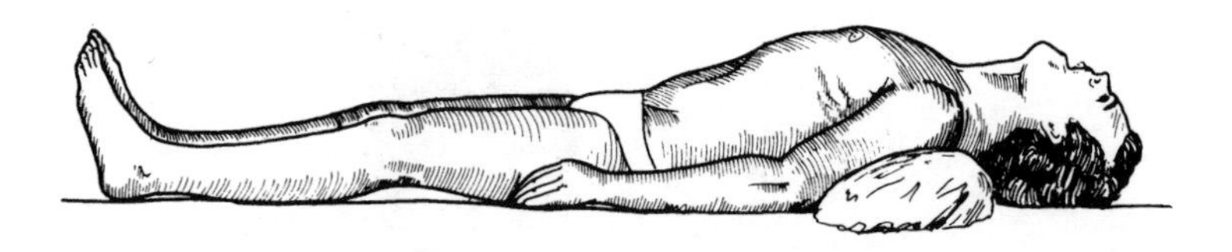

Pillow under shoulders
Head back/ throat stretched/ mouth wide

Figure 39: Supplementary Technique 5

tilted back, with the throat slightly stretched. The mouth should be open wider than normal for breathing.

✦ The exercise can be done in two ways: first, by taking deep breaths through the mouth, breathing deeply into the abdomen; or, by making an 'aaaaaah' sound deep in the throat, vibrating the chest and abdomen. By alternating these two techniques, you will find the one that works best for you at any particular moment.

✦ This technique will often produce a deep crying release, occasionally triggering a deep coughing as if there is something in your lungs that you are desperately trying to get out. This is often exactly the case: when the umbilical cord is cut too quickly, the infant will often be left struggling to breathe and, as panic sets in, a permanent restriction of the breathing will result. What you are actually doing when this deep coughing is triggered is, psychologically, trying to clear your lungs of amniotic fluid. This is a very healthy response and it can be triggered by any number of exercises in this book. You will find that as it occurs, your own capacity for breathing will become deeper and deeper, and a great feeling of aliveness will begin to infuse your body. This may also be accompanied by tingling sensations, especially in the limbs. It is not unlike the feeling of blood returning to your foot when you have had your leg curled up underneath you, restricting your circulation – in this case your circulation is being freed by the removal of an energy block, and it is the feeling of life returning more fully to your body.

Supplementary Technique 6 – Mantras

✦ A useful technique for discovering energy blockages in the chakra energy centres is through a mantra. Many of you will already be doing meditations using a mantra, which is a word or group of words that produce a particular resonance somewhere within you. If you are already using a mantra, then use it in this process; if you do not have a mantra, then you can use the syllable 'OM', or even your own name. The mantra is either sung or chanted, in order to give it a resonant quality. To practise sounding the mantra in each of the chakras, I suggest that you chant your mantra aloud, first being conscious of the vibration at the throat and chest. Then, as you sound the mantra again and again, try sensing its vibration in each of the chakras, starting from the root chakra at the base and working upwards.

✦ After you have chanted your mantra verbally for a while, try closing your eyes in a meditative state, and just sound your mantra internally, without making any audible sounds. In other words, feel it as an internal vibration, rather than a physical one. Again, feel it first in the throat and chest, where you would feel the physical vibrations first; then go once again from chakra to chakra, 'sounding' your mantra in each.

✦ Any energy blockages in any of the chakras will feel as if there is an inhibiting effect on the full vibration of the mantra in that chakra. Often just sounding the mantra in the blocked chakra will cause energy release but, if not, use your crystal over the chakra and move the blocked energy up into the Heart Centre as in the Energy Moving exercise (*see page 196*).

✦ Often an energy blockage in a chakra can be felt as heat radiating from the body. To sense this, move your hand up and down the front of your body (if you are doing the exercise on yourself), or up and down the back, if doing it on someone else. Do this 5 to 10 cms from the body. You will notice temperature changes radiate from the body, and the places where you feel the greatest amount of heat are the places where energy blockages occur. If an energy blockage has been identified by this method, placing a crystal in the warmest area and stroking upwards towards the throat will begin to move the energy block. This type of auric massage is likely to create emotional release.

THE CRYSTAL EXERCISES

This section begins a series of exercises using the reflective power of crystals. All of them have been used with great success in numerous courses. In choosing and programming a crystal for each exercise, you have several options. You can use the same crystal for all of the exercises, you can use a different crystal for each exercise each time you do it, you can use a dedicated crystal for each exercise which is the only one you ever use for it, or you can use a combination of options. How do you know which to use? Decide at that moment. Every time you do an exercise you will be in a somewhat different state within yourself, and/or you will be working with a different aspect of the blockage the exercise addresses. For some a single crystal for all the exercises will be appropriate; for others a different one every time will be best. We are all unique individuals, and the only person who really knows you, is you. But remember, your choice needs to be guided by your feelings and sensitivities, rather than by your intellect. Over-reliance on the intellect is one of the methods by which we feed and sustain our blockages. Be sure to take note of the colour of the crystal you are using and refer back to Chapter 8, where you will find information that will in some way refer to the issues and blockages you are dealing with. Or, you can even choose a crystal based solely on its colour, according to the information in Chapter 8.

You can do the exercises in any order, or skip some of them if you wish. But again, our blockages occur because at some deep inner level we feel they protect us, so the blockages will send us feelings of fear when we start to dismantle them. Quite possibly the exercises you resist the most are the ones that you need the most.

The exercises are arranged in the order they are usually undertaken in courses, in that there is a definite sequence that works best for most people in freeing energy and working through blocks. But it isn't the case for *everyone*, so follow your own instincts. You may wind up doing one or two of the exercises dozens of times, while others only a few times. That is perfectly OK – we all have blockages of different strengths in different places. Remember, too, that the Supplementary Techniques are powerful tools in everyday life, and use them wherever appropriate.

THE HEART EXERCISES

Shifting Energy to the Heart

Purpose

✦ To increase your conscious ability to shift emotional energies from other parts of the body into the heart, where your innate ability to love unconditionally can become increasingly active. Also, to shift your level of awareness of any particular feeling; and to deal with feelings rather than the situations that appear to create them.

Crystal

✦ In practical terms, whatever crystal is at hand when difficult emotional feelings arise. The crystal is placed on whatever part of the body is feeling the greatest distress. Colourless crystals incorporating the benefits of the Brilliance (*see page 116*) are particularly useful.

Programme

✦ To shift the energy from the area of the body in distress into the heart.

Exercise

✦ This exercise is to be used when you are experiencing emotional distress. Lie on the floor or bed and, with your eyes closed, scan through your body to identify where you are feeling the greatest distress. Look for physical sensations in the body – tension, feelings of pain or anxiety, some sort of body feeling. When you have found the area where it feels the worst, place the crystal directly on that part of the body.

✦ Visualize the crystal 'absorbing' that feeling, and when there is a sense of transference to the crystal, move the crystal over your heart. Allow the energy from the distressed area of your body to flow into your heart. As that energy floods through your heart, you may well experience intense emotional release. If there is a feeling of tightness in the heart or in the throat, try Supplementary Technique 5.

✦ It is important during this exercise to be aware of your breathing; there is a tendency in times of emotional stress to stop – *don't*! You may find that your breathing rate will increase dramatically, or you may even experience choking or gagging sensations. Don't try to stop or restrict them. Roll over onto your left side and continue breathing. Allow your body to release whatever it is trying to let go of. A box of tissues at hand is not a bad accompaniment to this exercise.

✦ Several things may happen during this exercise. First, you may feel a pure sense of transmutation of energy in the heart – whatever uncomfortable feelings you had may turn into feelings of joy, of lightness, and you may experience a warm glow or feeling of heat in the heart.

✦ Alternatively, your Inner Being may choose to release these energies from the body through some of the previously described methods – crying, choking, gagging, or coughing.

✦ In either case, when you have completed this exercise and have some sort of release, roll immediately onto your left side, curl up in the foetal position, and allow your breathing to return to normal.

✦ Should images of unpleasant events that created these feelings in the first place arise, take this time of lying on your left side to restructure these events in your own mind, see them as you would have *wished* them to be. In doing so, having released a considerable amount of inharmonious or unbalanced energy, you then feed back into your mind and body positive and loving thoughts to fill the vacuum left by the release of the previous images.

The Lens of the Heart

Purpose

✦ To be able to open and close the heart at will. Open-heartedness in certain hostile situations can be unwise and inappropriate; closed-heartedness in other situations is equally inappropriate. Rather than being an involuntary reflex, opening and closing the heart can be much more under our conscious mastery.

Crystal

✦ Any crystal that you have already been using in connection with your own Heart Centre.

Programme

✦ To reflect back to you the body sensations of open-heartedness and closed-heartedness.

Exercise

✦ This exercise can be done sitting or lying down, with the crystal placed over the heart.

✦ To begin, think of a time when you felt a feeling of overwhelming love for someone, in other words when your heart was very open. As you think this thought, feel the body feelings that are associated with it, especially those in the heart. It is more than likely that you will experience a very expansive feeling in the chest, especially a sensation that the chest muscles have relaxed, and that your shoulders have moved back as a result.

✦ Then, remember a time when someone said something very hurtful to you, particularly a person for whom you felt very open-hearted or had warm feelings for. As you remember this, you will most likely feel a closing sensation in the chest area, as if the chest muscles over the heart have tightened, and you may notice that your shoulders have moved forward. Notice also any other body sensations connected with this.

✦ Go through this cycle a number of times, alternating between open-hearted memories and closed-hearted memories. Each time notice the body response. You can add colour to the visualization as you progress. Visualize red for the opening phase, and blue for the closing.

✦ When you have done this a few times you will begin to notice which muscles are involved, and where and when they tighten up or relax. Then, practise using your body muscles *without* the invoking memories, placing those muscles under conscious control, to reproduce the same body sensations. As you do this, notice how you feel in your heart – open or closed. With practise, you can invoke these sensations at will, and as a consequence of biofeedback you can induce 'mood' changes in your own heart just by invoking the body responses.

✦ The final result of this will be an ability to open or close your Heart Centre at will, and to choose for yourself the state of your own heart as circumstances dictate.

LIFE PURPOSE AND LIFE PATTERN EXERCISES

In later exercises we will address specific blockages, but in these exercises you can begin to get an idea of why you have them. What you will discover is that each and every blockage within you serves a purpose – nothing is by chance. Some blockages will involve unlearned lessons; others may exist solely to strengthen you in some way. Of this last group, it is important to realize that once you have the strength and the block is removed, you still have the strength! Only you are in control of it, instead of *vice versa*. In an earlier chapter we discussed paradox and the spiritual path. Here we find paradox in physical form: that which is your greatest weakness can become your greatest strength, and what you perceive to be your greatest strength may, in fact, be your greatest weakness. Always keep in mind that you and all of those around you, on many planes, planned it this way!

Life Purpose

Purpose

✦ To go back to the moment of your conception, and to see the pattern of your own life.

Crystal

✦ Choose a crystal for this exercise with the intention of reflecting back to you the pattern of your own life. The crystal is held in the hand for this meditation.

Programme

✦ To reflect back to you the pattern of your own life as it will unfold, as seen at the moment of your conception.

Exercise

✦ This exercise is done sitting on the floor, with the crystal held in your hand. You are going to go backwards in your memory in stages, until you are back to the exact instant when your parents' energies connected, and you were conceived.

✦ Begin by going back in your memory to events that took place a year ago, and feel the feelings and the thoughts which were happening to you at that time. Take plenty of time in each of these stages – you will get a better result if you don't rush backwards. Then, go back two years from the present and do the same. Then five years. Then, go backward in five-year stages until you reach the age of 15.

✦ From there, begin going back in one or two-year stages, remembering and feeling how it was to be 14, then 13, and then 12, and so forth. As you begin to reach the earlier years, you will feel your body becoming smaller, and you will begin to remember the perspective of seeing the world from the eyes of a child.

✦ Continue going backward until you reach one year of age, and then continue backwards in two-month intervals, until you reach the age of one month. As you continue to go backwards to the moment of your birth you will find your body becoming even smaller, and then you will feel yourself sliding through a dark tunnel, until you can feel the enclosing walls of the womb around you.

✦ Again, examine your thoughts and feelings – how was it just before I was born? What was I thinking and feeling?

✦ Then continue to go backwards in one-month intervals while you are inside the womb. You will feel your body becoming very tiny now, and you may even have the urge to physically curl up. By all means do so if you feel the desire. As you come closer and closer to the exact moment of conception, you may find yourself floating, awaiting an energetic connection to be made, like a switch being thrown. You may experience this energetic connection as a flash of light – or as a bolt of energy. But, in that moment of energy connection, you will be able to see the pattern and purpose of your life as it will unfold. You will know in that moment the major events and traumas, some of the people you are going to meet, and some of the lessons you will have to learn. And you will also have a knowledge of the purpose of your life.

✦ This may not all occur the first time you do this exercise, but continue to repeat it until you have a clear image of what happened in that first moment. You are likely to find answers to many of the mysteries of your own life here.

✦ When you have found what you wish to find, or at least all that is visible in that moment, allow yourself to return to the womb, and begin to age once again in one-month intervals, noticing at each interval what your thoughts and feelings are, and what your beliefs about life were as they were being formed in the womb. You may make some quite surprising discoveries about some of the ideas and patterns within your life that came from this time. If there are limiting beliefs that formed here, you can use the Tie-Cutting exercise (*see page 203*) to begin releasing them. Then, when you have reached the time of your birth, see yourself sliding down the tunnel, coming out into the world.

✦ As you do this, you may also be aware of any ideas and beliefs that occurred around the time of your birth, and you can begin working with these through the exercises in this book.

✦ Once you are out of the womb, begin progressing in one-year intervals to the age of 15, and then progress in five-year intervals, noticing along the way any life events that have reinforced the life patterns, or any outworkings of the patterns that you discovered at the moment of your conception.

The Pre-Conception State

Purpose

✦ To experience that aspect of your Beingness that existed before you were conceived.

Crystals

✦ For this exercise, use a crystal both for the brow and the heart. Colourless crystals using the Brilliance (*see page 116*) are beneficial.

Programme

✦ To reflect back to you the level of your Being that existed prior to your conception.

Exercise

✦ This exercise is identical to the Life Purpose exercise above, except that this time when you reach back to the moment of conception, you will feel yourself moving rapidly through another dark tunnel. When you emerge from that tunnel, you will find yourself in a place full of light, and you may well find yourself surrounded by other beings, many of whom you will recognize. When you are in this place, you will be able to remember any conversations that were taking place, and any knowledge that you had about your forthcoming lifetime. While you are in this place you will also be able to understand the reason you have taken on the learning that you have in this lifetime, and what greater purpose it all serves.

✦ When you have learned all that you can learn or wish to learn in this place, then feel yourself sliding down that tunnel at the moment of your conception. Then, follow the same procedure to return back to the present time as in the previous exercise.

CUTTING THE TIES THAT BIND

Within the fulfilment of our life purpose and the completion of our lessons, there will be many energetic connections to persons, places, things, ideas and beliefs. Many of these will feed the energies of our blockages and, although appropriate and necessary for our learning, outlive their usefulness as lessons are learned and we are ready to move on. Many of these will be exposed in later exercises, but here are two potent techniques for severing inappropriate ties. Remember that what determines appropriateness or inappropriateness is the function the ties are serving. What is appropriate in a learning phase may be wholly inappropriate later on. How do you know which is which? You don't need to figure it out. As long as your programme is for inappropriate ties, that is all that will appear.

There is a second use for these exercises. You may wish to examine the ties of a current relationship without cutting any of them. If this is the case, simply use the programme Make All Ties in my Current Relationship Visible.

Cutting the Ties that Bind 1

Purpose

✦ This exercise is for cutting inappropriate ties to places, things and ideas that are in any way self-limiting, or which have fulfilled their purpose.

Crystals

✦ A crystal for both the brow and the heart, chosen for their feeling of connection to your own inner clarity.

Programme

✦ To reflect back to you any inappropriate and self-limiting ties to ideas, places and things.

Exercise

✦ As in the Heart Clearing exercise (*see Chapter 11*), you will go into the heart crystal, which is reflecting back to you your own Heart Centre. When you are inside the heart crystal, see it once again as a room, with the faces of the crystal as the walls of the room. Find a comfortable chair inside your crystal room, with its back against one of the walls. Alongside the chair is a toolbox and a pot of healing balm.

✦ In the centre of the room is a pedestal. On this pedestal you will place some object that is symbolic of an idea, belief, or place. Or if you are cutting a tie to an actual thing, such as a car or house, place the object on the pedestal.

✦ This is the place to start cutting ties to the self-limiting beliefs and injunctions that will turn up in the various exercises. For example, if you have a self-limiting belief that says: 'I am always sick', then see yourself sitting on the pedestal in a state of wretched illness. Visualize any attachments that exist to the idea, belief, or object, especially noticing where the attachments connect to your body. These attachments will be seen symbolically – perhaps as cables or cords, or steel bars, or even just as lines of energy. Then, reach into the toolbox alongside your chair, and pull out an appropriate tool for cutting those ties. Move your hands and physically act out the movements of this exercise. When you have finished cutting the ties from yourself, go down your body and pull out the roots of the ties which you have just cut loose. The energetic roots may go entirely through your body, so do whatever is necessary to pull them completely out.

✦ Then, see the ties that have been cut and the roots that have been pulled loose, lying on the floor. Reach into the toolbox and select some appropriate means of disposing of the ties that have been cut loose. You may find a box of matches if the ties are something flammable or, if they are steel bars, you may find a laser to disintegrate them; but whatever method you choose, the bits that have been cut loose and pulled out should be totally destroyed.

✦ After the process of destroying the connections has been completed, reach over to the other side of the chair and pick up the pot of healing balm; smooth it over and into all of the places where the roots of your ties have been pulled from your body, and return the pot to its position alongside the chair.

✦ When all of the ties have been cut, you will see the idea, place or thing fade away and disappear from the top of the pedestal.

✦ When you have completed the exercise, see the crystal beginning to shrink as you begin to get larger, until you pop outside the crystal and you and the crystal both return to your normal respective sizes.

Cutting the Ties 2

Purpose

✦ This exercise is about cutting inappropriate attachments to people in our lives, or who have been in our lives.

Crystals

✦ A crystal on the brow and heart, chosen for a feeling of deep self-reflection.

Programme

✦ To reflect back to you any connections to other people that are not coming from a clear space in the heart, and that are therefore not serving the highest good of you or the other person involved.

Exercise

✦ As in the previous tie-cutting exercise, go into the heart crystal, and once again find yourself seated in a chair with a toolbox on one side of the chair and a pot of healing balm on the other side. Sitting opposite you will be an empty chair, and to the right a doorway entering into the crystal from outside.

✦ Summon into your crystal the person with whom you wish to cut the inappropriate ties or attachments. Have them walk in through the door, and sit in the chair opposite you. Then, visualize any attachments that exist between you and that person, especially noticing where the attachments connect their body to your body. As in the previous exercise, these attachments will be seen symbolically – as cables, cords, steel bars, or again perhaps even just as lines of energy. Then, reach into the toolbox alongside your chair, and pull out an appropriate tool for cutting the ties.

✦ When you have finished cutting them from yourself, offer the cutting tool to the person sitting in the chair opposite. They may or may not wish to take it and cut the ties themselves, but if they do not, it is of no consequence to you, as you are free to cut inappropriate ties any time you choose. If the person has chosen to cut away the ties from their side, then when they are finished, have them hand the tool back to you, and replace it in the toolbox.

✦ Then, go down your own body and pull out the roots of the ties which you have just cut loose. The energetic roots may go entirely through your body, so do whatever is necessary to pull them completely out. The person sitting in the chair opposite you may wish to do the same, if they have chosen to cut the ties themselves.

✦ Then, see the ties that have been cut and the roots that have been pulled loose, lying on the floor between you. As in the previous exercise, reach into the toolbox and select some appropriate means of disposing of the ties that have been cut loose.

✦ After the process of destroying the connections has been completed, reach over to the other side of the chair and pick up the pot of healing balm and smooth it over and into all of the places where the roots of your ties have been pulled from your body. When you have completed that, offer the pot to the other person so that they can complete healing themselves too, if they choose to do so. When they have completed whatever healing they wish, return the pot to its position alongside the chair.

✦ When this healing process has been completed, if you wish to you can now visualize and reinforce any appropriate ties that you have to that person. Or, if this is completing a past relationship and you wish to release this person energetically from your life, then visualize them slowly fading away even as they sit in the chair opposite, until they have completely disappeared.

✦ If this is a person that you do not wish to see again in this lifetime, but do wish to meet in another lifetime, then before you see that person fade away from the chair, attach a thread of gold from your heart to theirs, a thread that will draw you together again in another lifetime.

✦ If it is a relationship that you wish to maintain and continue in this lifetime, then simply see the person get up from the chair, and walk out of the door.

✦ There is no limit to the number of people you can call into your crystal each time you do the exercise, but it is best in all instances to have them come into the crystal one at a time, so there is clarity about the ties that are being cut or reinforced.

✦ When you have completed the exercise, then, as before, see the crystal beginning to shrink as you begin to get larger, until you pop outside the crystal and you and the crystal both return to your normal respective sizes.

THE CHILD, PARENT AND ADULT SELVES

Dr John Harrison makes the point that if illness is to be cured, then some or all of the following need to happen: awareness ('So that's how I make myself ill!'); expression ('Damn you Mom!'); forgiveness ('I accept the burden that raising six kids in the Depression must have been'); and acceptance ('I love me, and I love others'). This will ultimately mean dropping our old system of beliefs and taking full responsibility for who we are. This can only come about through identifying the sources and locations within ourselves of that which limit us. These limits will be found within one of our three 'selves'.

Each of us has essentially three 'selves':

a) the Adult self, which is the grown-up we have become
b) the Child self, which is the child we once were and internally still are
c) the Parent self, the portion of us that is the incorporation of various parts of our parents – their ideas, beliefs, prejudices and, in many cases, their attitudes and beliefs about us.

These are the three 'ego states' that make up every human being. An ego state is a system of feelings accompanied by a related set of behaviour patterns. When you are in your Parent state, you are actually in the same state of mind as one of your parents (or a parent substitute) once was, and you are responding as he or she would, with the same posture, gestures, vocabulary and feelings. The Adult state is the part of you that makes objective appraisals of situations, acts without prejudice, and frequently serves as a mediator between the Parent and Child states. The Child state is where the manner and intent of your reaction is just as it was when you were a little boy or girl.

Everyone, including children and the mentally handicaped, have all three of these states functioning to varying degrees. These three aspects of the personality are often segregated from each other, and are often quite inconsistent, or directly in conflict with each other. Each of these states is useful and necessary, and it is only when they are out of balance with each other that the whole being is out of balance. The conflicts which arise, especially between the Parent and Child ego states, create enormous stresses in the body, and are frequently the source of much illness. Another way of looking at it is that illness is the way our body draws attention to the imbalance in our ego states.

There is an odd notion among many 'spiritual' people that the ego is something to be eliminated or decommissioned. The ego is a perfectly normal and healthy part of the existence of every Being on the earth, and it is the structure through which our learning about living on the earth takes place. Any attempt to decommission the ego is ultimately futile, as you are attempting to decommission the very learning mechanism that you came here for in the first place!

All three of the ego states are necessary, useful and totally desirable. It is only when they are out of balance that problems occur. For example, when the Child received little acknowledgement by recognition of himself as a child, he will often go to extremes to get that recognition when he grows up. In order to defend the wounded part of himself, he will become 'egotistical', seeking to fill in the emptiness. There is nothing 'wrong' with this person – he is merely acting out his need to reharmonize himself, until he can recognize his reflection in the outer world by the responses of others to his imbalanced state. Most energy goes in trying to meet the needs of the inner Child. Any of our needs that were unmet in our own childhood we will continually strive to get met through the remainder of our lives. But, there is a problem.

Because we are reliant on our inner Parent to meet those needs, we are mostly doomed to fail. Our inner Parent has learnt to be a parent from our actual parents, and we parent ourselves as our parents parented us! Where your parents failed to meet your needs, so your inner Parent will fail also. We also attract partners whose Parent selves are exactly like our own parents – they are working through similar patterns to our own, and therefore their parenting backgrounds must, of necessity, be similar. So, our partners aren't able to meet our unfulfilled needs either!

The function of the inner Parent is to create a system of automatic responses so that your Adult self doesn't spend an enormous amount of energy reasoning out trivial or repetitive situations – for example: it is your inner Parent who says 'look both ways before you cross the street'. It is therefore unnecessary for your Adult self to reason out the necessity for doing so each time; all that your Adult self has to do is compute the cars that are on the street, and compute your probability of safely reaching the other side.

All people have a complete, well-structured Adult self that only needs to be activated or uncovered. People who are 'immature' are only people in whom the Child takes over inappropriately. Likewise, 'mature' people are those in whom the Adult self is in control, often inappropriately, and in whom the Child will take over on occasion (such as when large amounts of alcohol have been consumed), often with unproductive results.

There is much pleasure to be obtained from the Adult state, and it usually comes in the form of activities where computation is successful, such as planning the outcome of a business activity, budgeting your income successfully, card games where skill with reasoning is essential, flying, sailing, and other types of mobile sports, and so forth. Another major task of the Adult self is to regulate the activities of the Parent and Child states and mediate between them when conflicts arise. If the Adult has not been uncovered or fully activated, the internal battle that can take place between the Parent and Child can consume enormous amounts of energy, and severely limit the productivity of the life of the person involved. Clearly, sorting our Parent–Child conflicts must be a major concern in the growing process.

In many ways the Child can be the most valuable part of the personality: the

Child contributes charm, pleasure and creativity. If the Child is confused and unhealthy, constantly seeking what was unfulfilled in its own childhood, then the balance of the entire individual is upset. The reflection in the world of this state is the need to fulfil the unmet needs of the inner Child.

There is the natural Child within us, the state of innocence and openness in which we were born, and there is the adapted Child, who has had to modify his behaviour under Parental influence. His behaviour is as his parents wanted him to behave: behaviour often dictated by the imbalances in the parents' own lives. The result of this is that the child closes off part of his being, his heart, in order to survive in an environment that is not natural to his own state of Being. Thus, working with healing the Heart Centre of necessity involves seeking out the imbalances in the inner Parent/Child relationship.

To emphasize once again: all three aspects of the personality have important and necessary survival and living values, and it is only when one or the other of them disturbs the healthy balance that there is a necessity for inner corrections to be made. The good news about all of this is that it is possible to make these corrections. All of the behaviour of the Parent and the adapted Child is learned behaviour and it ultimately becomes a matter of re-educating both aspects of the Self. This is where the power of the Adult comes into play. Because our inner Parent fails to meet the needs of our inner Child (as our parents failed to meet these needs), that role can be taken over for a time by our own Adult. And, as our Adult is meeting the needs of our inner Child, so can we also begin re-educating our inner Parent so that we can begin parenting ourselves as we had always wanted our parents to parent us. Our Child self knows what it wants and needs, and for some reason our parents were unable to fulfil those needs. As we discover the inadequacies in our internal Parents, we can also gain deeper understanding of our natural parents, thus opening the door to forgiveness.

The reason all of this exists in the first place, is that these are the lessons that you have chosen to work through in this particular lifetime. You have chosen the parents that you did, in order that they would fail you in appropriate ways, to make certain you learned the lessons you are learning. All parents fail. If they didn't, you would have nothing to learn.

The initial stage of the healing process involves identifying the three different parts of the Self, and then beginning to work constructively with those parts, to first meet the needs of the inner Child, and secondly to re-educate the Parent self, so that you can begin fully meeting your own needs.

✧

As stated above, one of the main reasons we create relationships is to meet the needs of our inner Child. But, because you always attract partners who have Parent selves like your own Parent self, they are never able to meet those needs either. Your partners are there as mirrors, so that you can begin to see, understand and forgive your own parents. In the following exercises, you will use the reflective powers of crystals to reflect back to you these aspects of yourself, and for you to begin working constructively with them for self-healing.

Discovering the Child Self

Purpose

✦ The purpose of this exercise is to identify the Child self, and to begin a dialogue between the Child self and the Adult self, leading to the fulfilment of the needs of the Child.

Crystals

✦ Two crystals are used for this exercise: a crystal to reflect back to you the Child self, and a crystal to reflect back to you the Adult self. The crystals are placed as described in the exercise.

Programme

✦ One crystal is programmed to reflect back your Child self and the second to reflect back your Adult self.

Exercise

✦ This exercise takes no note of the Parent self, as it is purely to identify the Adult and the Child selves and begin a dialogue between them, allowing your Adult self to fulfil the needs of your Child that the Parent self is unable to do. And, through discovering what needs went unmet, to get an insight into how your learning experiences were set up.

✦ The exercise is done using two chairs, and two crystals. The two chairs should be placed side by side, so it is easy to move from one chair to the other with your eyes closed. The Adult crystal should be placed on one chair, and the Child crystal should be placed on the second chair.

✦ To begin the exercise, sit in the Adult chair, holding the Adult crystal in your hand. Close your eyes, and allow the feeling to come over you that you have when you *know* that you are in a fully Adult state. That is, totally clear, totally non-judgmental, totally non-emotional. It doesn't matter whether or not you have spent any amount of time in this state; just allow it to be reflected back to you, whether it is well-developed or not. Then, imagine that you are going to leave that Adult person sitting in that chair, and physically move your body to the second chair, leaving the Adult crystal on the first chair. Do this with your eyes closed, as it helps to sustain the visualization. When you are in the Child chair, hold the Child crystal in your hand, and go back to a time in your childhood when you felt very upset by something one or both your parents had done. If there are many such occasions, choose the one which brings up the worst feelings in the body as you sit in the chair.

✦ The deeper you go into these feelings, the more you will be in a childlike state. If someone were to speak to you at this time, you would answer with child-like phrases and possibly even in a childlike voice. You may not accomplish this fully on the first attempt, but the more you practise this exercise, the more you will *become* a child in the exercise.

✦ When you are in your Child state, become aware of the Adult sitting next to you. Know that your Adult self is capable of fulfilling whatever need you have at that moment as a child. If you are in pain or distress, what action could that Adult take to help you feel better, to make the pain go away? A cuddle? Words of reassurance? Whatever you need in that moment that would make you feel better, simply allow your Adult self to fulfil it. If the need is for a cuddle for example, then just visualize and feel that Adult in the chair next to you putting their arms around you, and holding you in whatever way you would like to be held. If the need is for reassurance, then let your Adult self speak the words to you that you would most like to hear. And so on.

✦ If you are working with a partner in this exercise, then the partner can ask you the questions about what you are feeling, and what you would like your Adult self to do to relieve that feeling. But, it is **not recommended** that your partner act out the role of Adult. The object of this exercise is to fulfil your *own* needs, without the need to resort to external sources. In doing so, you will energetically clean up your own inner relationships, which will be reflected outwardly in more fulfilling outer relationships.

✦ When your Child self has had its needs met by your Adult self, then physically move back into the Adult chair, and allow the Adult part of you to be reabsorbed by your body. When you feel integrated, then do some deep breathing and open your eyes. The more times you do this exercise, the more insight you will gain into how your life-lessons were created by your situation. You may, at some point, even go back into your infant state. That is perfectly OK, but you will need to communicate with your Adult self non-verbally.

Discovering the Parent Self

Whether you were raised by them or not, your biological parents set up for you your major life-lessons. Your genetic inheritance, your womb and birth experiences, all came from them. Thus who and what they were is the foundation upon which your entire life is built. Even if you never knew them, or, for that matter, don't even know who they were, their imprint is still within you, and is still knowable.

The Parent self is that part of you that directly incorporates aspects of your parents. Which specific aspects those are, and how they relate to your life, can be revealed through this exercise. Any links to them that are inhibiting the full development of your life today can be cut using the Cutting the Ties process (see above).

In the following exercises you will be able to make contact with the part of yourself that is part of them. Using the information from the previous exercises on life purpose and pattern, these exercises should help to clarify why you chose that particular set of parents.

Purpose

✦ To identify the Parent self, and begin a dialogue between the Parent and the Child selves in order to identify areas of inner conflict.

Crystals

✦ You need three crystals for this exercise, one for the Parent self, one for the Adult self and one for the Child self, placed as per the directions.

Programme

✦ Each of the three crystals is programmed to reflect back to you that particular part of yourself – the Parent, the Adult and the Child.

Exercise

✦ This exercise is done using three chairs, one for the Parent self, one for the Adult self, and one for the Child self, with the appropriate crystal placed on each chair; the Adult chair in the middle, and the Child chair in the same position as the Child chair in the previous exercise.

✦ Begin this exercise sitting in the Child chair, identify the Child self, then move to the Adult chair, leaving the Child crystal in the Child chair; as in the previous exercise make this physical movement with your eyes closed.

✦ When you are in the Adult chair, identify the Adult feelings; then, with your eyes still closed, and leaving the Adult crystal on the Adult chair, move into the Parent chair, and pick up and hold in your hand the Parent crystal.

✦ Take a couple of minutes to visualize seeing the Adult you sitting in the middle chair, and the Child you sitting in the Child chair. See the Child you as you actually looked as a child. As you sit in the Parent chair, you may begin to notice different body feelings and sensations, feelings and sensations that are distinctly different from those you experienced in the other two chairs.

✦ When you feel some sort of identity with your Parent self, see if there is anything you would like to say to your Child self, and do so. Do this out loud if possible, verbalizing to the Child any feelings, thoughts, or anything else that comes to mind that you would like to say to the Child.

✦ If your Child self is particularly angry, you may well experience the Child saying something back to you in return. Should any sense of conflict begin to develop between your Parent self and your Child self, leave your Parent sitting in the Parent chair, and physically move back into the Adult chair. Then, in your Adult state, you can become the mediator of the conflict and, in this state, you may need to offer explanations to both the Parent and the Child selves for their point of view of each other.

✦ For example, if your Parent self should say to your Child self: 'I am sorry I don't give you more time,' your Child might come back with something like, 'You don't really love me.'

✦ The Adult, as mediator, might then explain to the Child that sometimes parents have other responsibilities, such as earning a living, and are not always able to give the child what it wants at that moment, and that this does not mean that the child is unloved; in fact, it may mean just the opposite – that the parent's way of expressing love to the child was to work hard in order to provide the child with adequate food and shelter. This may not be the kind of love that the child *wanted*, but none the less it *was* love. Children are remarkably open to reason, and you will probably find this sort of an explanation is readily accepted by your Child self, or at least a new state of realization will dawn for the Child. In the real-life situation, this was probably true; the parents didn't give the child enough time, but they were, in their own way, giving the child love, although they never bothered to explain it to the child (or even recognized a need to do so).

✦ The next stage for the Adult self would be to turn to the Parent and explain that although he or she is giving the Child love in his or her own way, the Child is unable to see it that way, and that the child's *real* need is for more time.

✦ There is nothing wrong whatsoever with acting out these activities in your own life; when you have finished the exercise, let your Parent self take your Child self out for an ice cream! In fact, wherever possible, I encourage acting out (in a healthy way of course) any of these activities which fulfil the Child part of yourself. You will find that in your own life, you have actually denied yourself the very things which your parents denied you.

✦ There are an infinite number of variations on the Parent/Child conflict, but all of them will revolve around the Child self not getting some real or perceived need met. Often the Parent self will feel unjustly accused, and it is in the Adult's capacity for dispassionately seeing the situation as it really is that the Parent can be re-educated to see that the needs of the Child self are met, and the Child can be re-educated to see that his *realistic* needs are met, and likewise to see when his needs are unrealistic.

✦ When you have completed this exercise, draw all three of the selves back together, take a few deep breaths, and come back fully into your body.

Many of the patterns passed on to you by your parents were those passed on to them in turn by their parents. Part of understanding our Parent self is to understand where their patterns came from.

Understanding your Parents

Purpose

✦ To identify the Mother and Father aspects of your Parent self in enough depth to be able to see and understand their own problems and limitations, especially those that deeply affected you as a child.

Crystals

✦ A crystal for the Mother self, the Father self and your Adult self.

Programme

✦ Each crystal is programmed to reflect back to you the appropriate aspect of the Parent self – the Mother self and the Father self – and your Adult self.

Exercise

✦ This exercise is done with three chairs and three crystals, as in the previous exercise. The Father chair should be placed to the right of the Adult chair, which you are sitting in, with the Mother chair to the left of the Adult chair. This positioning identifies with the male and female sides of the body, and provides less body confusion when you are switching roles.

✦ Begin the exercise by sitting in the Adult chair and remembering some particularly painful incident, or series of incidents, for which you 'blamed' your parents. Try to find one incident each for your father and mother.

✦ Since this is done in the Adult state, you will be discussing these events with your parents on an adult-to-adult basis, and therefore having identified by now the Child self, you as an Adult should request your inner Child to remain quiet and not get involved. You can do this by visualizing the small child inside you, and speaking directly to that child as if the child were actually present within your body.

✦ Leave your Adult self sitting in the centre chair, and move into the chair of the Parent with whom you had the first identified difficulty. Pick up and hold the parent crystal, and visualize your own body transforming into the physical body of that particular parent. When you have done this exercise a few times you will actually feel yourself *becoming* that parent. Then, visualize your Adult self asking you as your parent whatever questions you would always have liked to have asked that parent about that incident. You might also have your Adult self ask that parent why they behaved as they did in that situation, and what were their own fears and perceived limitations in dealing with it. Eventually, you will find yourself answering as if you actually *were* that parent.

✦ When you have completed the exercise with the first parent, return that crystal to that chair, move back into the Adult chair, pick up the Adult crystal and re-identify yourself with that Adult state. Then, placing the crystal back on the chair, move into the second parent chair, repeating the procedures as with the first one.

✦ If you have issues with one parent much more than the other, this exercise can be done with only that parent with whom you have a need to deal with at the moment, although it is a good idea to use the third chair and third crystal to separate out the parent that is not involved from the one that is.

✦ At the end of this exercise move back into the Adult chair, and reintegrate as in the previous exercise.

When you have done these exercises a number of times, you can dispense with the chairs entirely, and do the exercise sitting on the edge of a bed, or perhaps on a couch – anywhere where it is possible to make a physical movement of your body. As you become more and more proficient with these roles, you will eventually find it unnecessary to move the body at all, as you will be able to identify from certain body feelings which part of you is your Child self and which part of you is the Adult self. Both of these states will have different body sensations, and as you do this exercise in the chairs you will eventually begin to notice that you feel different physically when you are in each of these ego state.

INJUNCTIONS

Many of the self-limiting beliefs and activities of the Parent self take the form of *injunctions*. An injunction is essentially a command to do or cease doing something. 'Be a good girl/boy!' is a double injunction. It requires you to do something – be good – and cease doing something else – being bad. It is one of the most powerful and potentially destructive of all injunctions, as what is defined as 'bad' is often something normal and natural that is, for varying reasons, unacceptable for your parents.

In the following exercises, you can begin to search your own experience for those injunctions which have limited your life. The first exercise is concerned with looking at some of the clichés and sayings that were common in your family. As children, we often take these very literally (i.e., take them to heart). You will want your notebook and pen close at hand, and you may find it necessary to write some of these down with your eyes closed, so that you don't miss any of them – some of them may flash past very quickly. In the exercise, look for any stereotypical situations, and the stereotypical remarks that either of your parents would have made. Alternatively, look for any sort of sayings that your parents continually repeated: for example, 'money is the root of all evil'. Such a saying, taken literally, would certainly cause us to limit our ability to make money, for who, after all, wants to be evil! Most of the limiting injunctions you discover will be located in your Child self.

In the following exercises you will begin to discover what some of your self-limiting beliefs are and where they came from, and will move towards the deeper understanding that is forgiveness – your final release from them.

Injunctions 1

Purpose

✦ To uncover family sayings and beliefs that may have shaped your beliefs about yourself as a child.

Crystals

✦ For this exercise, use crystals on both the brow and the heart. This exercise involves the memory of those sayings that you have 'taken to heart'.

Programme

✦ To reflect back to you ideas and beliefs, especially clichés, that have shaped your self-image.

Exercise

✦ Allow yourself to remember a pleasant time as a child, to remember how it felt to be that child. As you feel being the child, feel the presence of your parents around you. Go first to whatever age you intuitively sense you picked up the strongest injunctions. It is possible that there are others that are even deeper and stronger, and as you repeat this exercise at later times, others may come to the surface. For now, though, go to a particular age when one of these sayings stuck.

✦ If you are not able to go to a particular age, then you may well remember these injunctions by completing the following sentences: 'Daddy/Mummy [use whatever terms here that you actually called them by as a child] always used to say "..."' Or you might remember particular situations when Daddy/Mummy could always be counted on to say '...' As you recall these sayings, be particularly aware of your body sensations, and if you experience any sort of body distress, move the energy into the heart using the Shifting Energy to the Heart exercise (*see page 196*).

✦ When you have completed the exercise, make a list in your notebook of the various injunctions, and note for each injunction that you remember, what your experience of it was – what was your understanding of its meaning as a child, and how that has affected the way you see your life now.

Injunctions 2

Purpose

✦ The purpose of this exercise is to uncover the more subtle injunctions, some of which may have been unspoken. You will probably wish to do this exercise a number of times, as you are likely to uncover quite a large number of them.

Crystals

✦ A crystal on the brow and on the heart, chosen for their sense of subtle reflection.

Programme

✦ To reflect back to you the subtle injunctions that have been self-limiting.

Exercise

✦ This exercise can be done sitting or lying down, although you may find it more powerful sitting, with the feet firmly on the ground and the spine vertical. There are an enormous number of early life situations that can be examined here, and you will probably wish to repeat this exercise a number of times.

✦ In this exercise we will be looking for the life-limiting injunctions that are subtle or implied. For example, what did it mean in your home when you were told 'be a good boy/girl'? Almost always this answer will involve a list of things that you *did* do, and a possibly longer list of things that you *didn't* do. As you remember each of these things, try to feel in your heart the subtle nuances of them. For example, as you began to exhibit more and more independence, did your parents assert strong pressures to control you? A subtle message from this could be 'stay a dependent child'. Or, perhaps you overheard a remark your mother or father made to a friend: 'He/she is such a sickly child.' The injunction from this would be: 'be sick!'

The physical body is our vehicle for learning. As stated, it is the perfect reflection in flesh of the state of our Oneness with our Source. But in the Western world in particular, we tend to live in our minds much more than in our bodies. Re-establishing body connection is a valuable part of the healing process, because our body sends us the vital messages through its feelings and sensations that connect us to life around us. Life is not meant to be analysed in the mind; it is meant to be sensed by the body. The first exercise of this section is to help put you in touch with your body, and focus on it in a way you have perhaps not done before.

Meeting Your Body

Purpose

✦ To be in touch with the various parts and aspects of our physical body, and to make the energetic connection with those parts necessary for experiencing full aliveness.

Crystal

✦ A crystal that gives you a sensation of 'groundedness'. In this exercise, the crystal is placed on each body part in turn, as that body part is being experienced.

Programme

✦ To make subtle energetic connections throughout the body, and to re-integrate any separations that have taken place energetically through the body.

Exercise

✦ For this exercise, lie on the floor or on the bed, with or without clothes as you wish. To do the exercise, the crystal is placed on each portion of the body in turn, and time is taken to experience through the crystal the reflection of the function of that particular part of the body in your life. For example, place the crystal on your right foot (you'll have to do this one with the knees bent), and then the 'consciousness' of your foot will be reflected back to you from the crystal. In other words, experience the 'footness' of whichever foot the crystal is on. Take a moment to remember pleasurable times in your life where your foot has played a major part – a walk through a favourite place, climbing a hill, stepping out of a train, or bus, or plane, to meet a loved one, etc. Then, take a moment to thank your foot for the good service it is giving you, all the places it has taken you, and all of the good things in your life that have related to being able to stand, walk, and so forth.

✦ Then move the crystal to the ankle, experience your own 'ankleness' and likewise go through various times in your life when your ankle has given you support and pleasure. And so on up the body.

✦ Where the arms and legs are concerned, do them separately, and see if there is any difference in the experience of the left- and the right-hand side of the body. The right side of the body tends to be associated with masculinity, and tensions and pressures on the right side tend to deal with father issues; and the reverse on the left side. The knees are particularly important, as they are one of the main areas of energetic blockage to do with parent issues.

✦ You may wish to draw a diagram of your body in your notebook, making a note of your body responses as you do the exercise.

As revealed earlier, physical illness is a way in which our body demonstrates to us our need to re-examine our inner beliefs. The body is closely identified with the Child state, and therefore any unresolved issues or any unmet needs involving the Child self will be reflected in the body. This can take the form of physical illness, or it can take the form of injury to the body. In this exercise we will examine the body in more detail to see what we can learn about the ideas and beliefs that underlie our illnesses.

Roots of Illness

Purpose

✦ To identify specific ideas and beliefs that are associated with any specific illness or injury that you have.

Crystal

✦ A crystal to reflect back to you any specific imbalance in your body energies and to connect that imbalance to a specific idea or belief.

Programme

✦ To reflect back to you the idea of belief that is at the root of a specific ailment.

Exercise

✦ Lie on your back for this exercise. The crystal will be placed on the specific body area where a symptom is occurring; if you have had an injury to a specific body part, place the crystal on that area. If you have an illness that involves a particular area of the body, place the crystal on that location. Allow your full awareness to flow into the crystal, and, as you do so, you will find certain body feelings and sensations in that particular place.

✦ Allow yourself to go into your Child ego state, setting aside the Parent and Adult selves. As you are in the Child state, allow the feelings that are associated with the crystal to associate themselves with a specific childhood or infancy event. There are several questions to ask your Child self at this stage, and these questions can be asked by your Adult self who is sitting alongside, observing the proceedings. The questions are: 'When did I first experience these feelings or sensations?' 'What event was associated with them?' 'What belief do I have about myself as a result of this experience?' And finally, 'Why have I given myself this illness/injury?'

✦ When you have discovered answers to these questions, your Adult self can ask your Child self: 'What actions can I take to relieve the underlying feelings that are creating this illness?' and, 'What part of my beliefs about myself or the state of the world need to be changed to release this illness/injury?'

✦ When you have answers to these questions, you can use other techniques in this book to release those beliefs and feelings, and fulfil the unfulfilled needs that underlie the illness. Use the Tie-cutting Technique (*pages 203–4*) for releasing beliefs and ideas about yourself, and the Adult/Child Technique (*page 210*) for meeting your own unfulfilled needs.

✦ While you are in the Child state, you may become aware that some of the illnesses you have are directly connected to illness and beliefs that your parents had. You may also be aware that your parents made certain statements about their health, or about your health, that are energetically affecting your body. Some of these may have turned up in the Injunctions exercise (*page 217*), but some of them may also appear in this exercise. Again, use the Tie-cutting exercise to begin releasing your attachment to these beliefs.

That which we fail to forgive, binds us. Forgiveness, real forgiveness, comes from a deep realization that those with whom we have issues have been our teachers, just as we asked them to be in the pre-conception state. The closer we can come to that realization, the more we can recognize that, in the end, there is nothing to forgive. This stage seldom comes all at once, but the following exercise can help set that energy in motion.

Forgiveness

Purpose

✦ To consciously and deliberately complete the act of forgiveness with any person who has 'caused' you pain and suffering.

Crystal

✦ A crystal to go over the heart, chosen for a feeling of freshness and newness.

Programme

✦ To reflect back to you the deepest levels of your own forgiveness, and to reflect back to you your own sense of completion with people from your past and present.

Exercise

✦ This exercise is done sitting, with a crystal over the heart. Go into the crystal as in the previous exercises, experiencing your crystal as a crystal room. You will find a chair against one 'wall' of your crystal, for you to sit in. Opposite that chair will be another chair, for the person with whom you wish to have completion.

✦ There is a door to the right-hand side of the chair sitting opposite, and a door to the left-hand side. The person with whom you wish to complete through forgiveness will enter through the right-hand door, and exit through the left.

✦ Invite each person in turn to come through the door and sit in the chair, and say to each person in turn: 'I understand that what you did was to teach me more about myself, to help me return to my full Humanity. In expressing my forgiveness to you, I release any anger, hatred, resentment, or any other feeling other than love, that I have felt for you as a result of our experience together. And I ask your understanding and forgiveness that I did not understand at the time what you were trying to do.'

✦ You may find other words to use that are equally appropriate for you.

✦ If the person in the opposite chair is someone you have never seen, such as the doctor who delivered you or someone who caused you pain at birth, or is an even more abstract Being, such as God, then visualize a person who has an appropriate symbolic form – your perfect image of the word 'doctor', or whatever personification God might take on.

✦ Be aware of your own feelings and responses as you do this exercise. Even if you have feelings for the other person or Being that are not purely love at this point, complete the exercise anyway. The act of intention to forgive will set in motion other events and experiences in your life that will lead you to that completion. Don't forget to put yourself in the opposite chair. The one person you almost always forget to forgive is yourself. Forgive yourself for all of your mistakes, all of your blunders, all of the trouble and pain you have got yourself into. For, from the very deepest level of your Being, these are the lessons that you have given yourself. And forgive your body for all of its aches and pains and ills and hurt. Once again, it is only doing these things as part of the teaching you have chosen for yourself.

✦ You may become aware of energetic connections created by your experiences with others – 'ties that bind'. Should you do use the Tie-cutting exercise on pages 203–4. When you have completed the experience, allow the crystal to shrink back to its normal size and for you to return back to yours.

Many of us carry a deep subconscious guilt about wanting to be alive and wanting to have a body, as we believe that in so doing we have separated ourselves from our own Source. For many of us, perhaps for all of us, our experience of having our first body was as if we cut ourselves off from God in order to get it. And, when we began to experience the body's malfunctions that were designed to teach us specific lessons, we blamed God for punishing us, believing that He was doing so because we had taken on a body in the first place. This next exercise is to put you in touch with the feelings and experiences of the first body. Remember that the universal principle of *movement into density* was fulfilled in that body, and whatever happened as a consequence was part of what was *meant* to happen.

Purpose

✦ To experience directly the extreme density of the first body, and to put you into closer connection with the material world around you.

Crystal

✦ A crystal that feels as if it embodies the words 'The Earth'.

Programme

✦ To reflect back to you the energy connections of your lower two chakras and their connection to the energies of the Earth.

Exercise

✦ Sit in a chair with your feet firmly on the ground, or in the lotus position. The crystal should be placed as near as possible to the base chakra (*see Figure 32, page 110*). Begin breathing very deeply, pulling the breath as low into the abdomen as possible. As you breathe more and more into the abdomen, begin to feel as if the intake of breath is swelling the genital area. As you become more and more in touch with the sensations in the lower portion of your body, allow your consciousness to sink downward through your body, until your full awareness is in the lower two energy centres. As you do this, you may become aware of an intense heaviness in the rest of the body, and while you are in this state, try to lift your arm. You may well find that it is difficult or almost impossible to move.

✦ In this leaden state, you may well become aware of the level of consciousness of the crystal; extremely slow, extremely deliberate but none the less at a very subtle level, still conscious. As you are aware of that level of consciousness of the crystal, you are also aware that your own physical body is part of that same level of consciousness. Because our body is made from minerals, we are and have always been involved with the mineral level of being, although because its rate of life pulse is very low, we have tended not to notice it.

✦ Give yourself plenty of time to get out of this meditation: begin to move your energy back upwards through your chakras until you are fully aligned within your body again. It may feel that it is taking a great deal of time to get out of the dense feeling, and if it does appear so to you, don't panic. What you are re-experiencing to a large degree is how your very first body felt – dense, leaden, and so difficult to move around that you may well have felt trapped inside it. This is the root of the 'trapped in the body' feelings that many people have.

BEYOND THE BODY

Having worked with the body in these exercises, it is now time to go to a higher level of energy – the energies connected with the upper energy centres. While doing the next exercise, you will be meeting a wise Being, and it is important to remember that the person you are meeting is yourself. This is not some disincarnate entity, nor a spirit guide, nor a person outside yourself. It is, in a sense, a projection of the Being at the deepest level of your own heart, but that Being projected into human form. It is the person that you have the potential to become, a person in full manifestation of their own Humanity.

Having gone to a very high level of your own Beingness in this exercise, you can begin to become aware of the difference between the highest and most subtle levels of your Being, and the part of your Being that is directly connected to the matter of this planet. It is intended to show you how far you have travelled to be able to wear a physical body and, as a result of that great distance travelled, why a certain amount of inner connection was lost at some point in your life. You may find further information about this in the last exercise.

The Pyramid of the Self

Purpose

✦ To be in contact with your Higher Self.

Crystal

✦ This is a crystal to go on the brow chakra, so choose a crystal that will reflect back to you your own highest level of clarity.

Programme

✦ The programme is to reflect back to you the highest levels of your own consciousness, and to enable you to communicate constructively with those levels.

Exercise

✦ To begin the exercise, visualize yourself out of doors, in some location where you will find a pyramid. This could be in the sacred precinct of an ancient city, it could be an Atlantean temple, or this pyramid may just exist in the middle of grassy fields – whatever image gives you a feeling of comfort and safety, together with a feeling of the sacred, as you will be meeting a very ancient and wise being on the top of this pyramid – one who has the answers to the mysteries of your own life.

✦ Approach the pyramid in whatever manner seems appropriate to you. You may find yourself dressed in robes, or you may find yourself in ordinary attire. Once again, choose whatever lends itself to your sense of impending connection with something important in your own life. As you approach the pyramid you will see that it has a lengthy staircase leading to the top. At various levels of the pyramid there will be places where you can stop and rest and catch your breath if necessary.

✦ Set the scene for the day in some detail – the amount of sunshine, the location of the sun in the sky, the scent of the air, the surrounding sounds. Allow yourself plenty of time for the climb – this is a meeting you have been waiting for for a very long time, so a few minutes more to be totally focused on the event will not go amiss. As you begin to climb, allow yourself the physical sensation of feeling your legs move as you climb from one step to the next. Hear the sound of your shoes or sandals or feel your bare feet on the steps, and be aware that as you climb, your vista of the location surrounding the pyramid will become larger.

✦ You will find that there are seven levels to the pyramid and, as you reach each level, you will probably want to stop and catch your breath. At each level, you may see that there are boxes full of flowers, and each level will have flowers of a different colour. If colour aids you in visualization, you will find that the flowers in the first level are red, proceeding upwards in the rainbow colours through each level.

✦ As you reach the top level, you will see that the top of the pyramid is a broad platform upon which is a gateway – a gateway made entirely of crystal. You will know that this gateway is the door to another dimension: another dimension of yourself. And, waiting on the other side of the gateway, will be a wise and ancient person, a person who is your Higher Self.

✦ So, approach the gateway and, when you are ready, step through. It is as if you are stepping inside a crystal – experience a feeling of total balance, total harmony, and total crystal clarity. On the other side of the gateway, you will find that the platform of the pyramid, being in a different dimension, appears to extend endlessly in all directions. At the same time the sky is above you, the air is crisp and clear and the sun is shining brightly. And, in the distance, stands a figure.

✦ This figure will walk towards you. Greet this person in whatever way feels appropriate. You will find that you can converse quite clearly with this person, and you will find answers here that you have been seeking about your own life.

✦ When you have finished your conversation, walk back out through the crystal gateway, and you will find yourself back in the same dimension as the pyramid, back at the material level of reality, although still on a high plane. Gently begin climbing down, until you reach the bottom of the pyramid and plant your feet firmly on the earth once again.

✦ As soon as your eyes are open, record at once any details of the conversation you had with your wise Being.

The purpose of the previous exercises has been to put you in touch with various levels of your own Being to give you a greater awareness of the multitude of life forces that are at work within you. In the next couple of exercises, you will discover how those life forces relate to the flow of Life in the world around you, and some ways to help you attune to that flow. As your own life is ultimately linked with the rhythms of the Earth itself, true healing cannot take place without once again becoming part of that rhythm.

The Pulse of the Earth

Purpose

✦ To attune yourself to the natural pulse and rhythm of the Earth Being.

Crystal

✦ The crystal for this meditation is placed on the heart. Choose a crystal that feels like it embodies the words 'The Earth'.

Programme

✦ To reflect back to you the pulse of your own life that is in harmony with the natural pulse of the Earth itself.

Exercise

✦ This meditation is done out of doors, and although it is desirable to have your body in contact with the earth, you will probably find that a blanket, especially one made of a natural material such as cotton, will not affect the intensity of the experience.

✦ Lie with your head to the north and the crystal resting over your heart. Take in several deep breaths and let them out slowly, and then let your breathing go into whatever pattern is natural for you at that moment.

✦ As you breathe, feel as if you are breathing the soil beneath you into your lungs and exhaling it. You will soon find your breathing falling into a natural rhythm which may well be different from the one you began with.

✦ Feel as if your body is melting into the Earth, and that you and the Earth are one Being. As you do this, you will find that there is a very natural rhythm which seems to come from the Earth itself, but which penetrates and permeates your own Being.

The Pulse of Plants

Purpose

✦ This exercise is designed to help you feel the natural pulse and rhythm connected to the Plant Kingdom, through its highest expression, the tree.

Crystal

✦ A crystal selected to reflect back to you the natural pulse and rhythm in the Plant Kingdom.

Programme

✦ To reflect back to you the pulse of life expressed through the living essence of a tree.

Exercise

✦ Any tree will do for this exercise, although you need one where you can sit with your back to the trunk, with your spine as fully in contact with the trunk as possible. The crystal is placed over the heart. As you sit with your back to the tree, close your eyes and let your breathing fall into your own personal relaxed pattern.

Plate 1 left: Apatite. From Wolley farm, near Bovey Tracy, Devon, England. © The Natural History Museum, London

Plate 2 below: Garnet group. A collection of crystals and cut stones. © The Natural History Museum, London

Plate 3 above: Topaz and tourmaline group. A collection of rough specimens, crystals and cut stones. Tourmaline to the right, topaz to the left. © The Natural History Museum, London

Plate 4 left: Feldspar, variety microcline. Fine crystal of green feldspar, variety microcline (amazonstone) on matrix from Pikes Peak, Colorado, USA. © The Natural History Museum, London

Plate 5 top right: Fluorite, Calcite and Pyrite. A group containing fluorite (right), pyrite crystals (left) and cleaved rhombohedra of calcite, variety Iceland Spar (centre). © The Natural History Museum, London

Plate 6 right: Corundum group, rubies and sapphires. A collection of rough specimens, crystals and cut stones. © The Natural History Museum, London

Plate 7 left: Beryl crystals. Beautifully formed crystals of aquamarine, heliodor, morganite and emerald. © The Natural History Museum, London

Plate 8 below left: Diamond crystals. Clockwise from top left (yellow matrix): in beach conglomerate from Namaqualand; in kimberlite from South Africa; and in matrix from Siberia. © The Natural History Museum, London

Plate 9 below: Octahedral crystals of spinel. © The Natural History Museum, London

Plate 10 right: Group of crystals. From top to bottom: idocrase, gypsum, barite, axinite and beryl. © The Natural History Museum, London

Plate 11 below: Beryl, variety emerald. Crystals and gem. © The Natural History Museum, London

Plate 12 below right: Pegmatite. Specimen of a pegmatite with tourmaline crystals from Cornwall, England. © The Natural History Museum, London

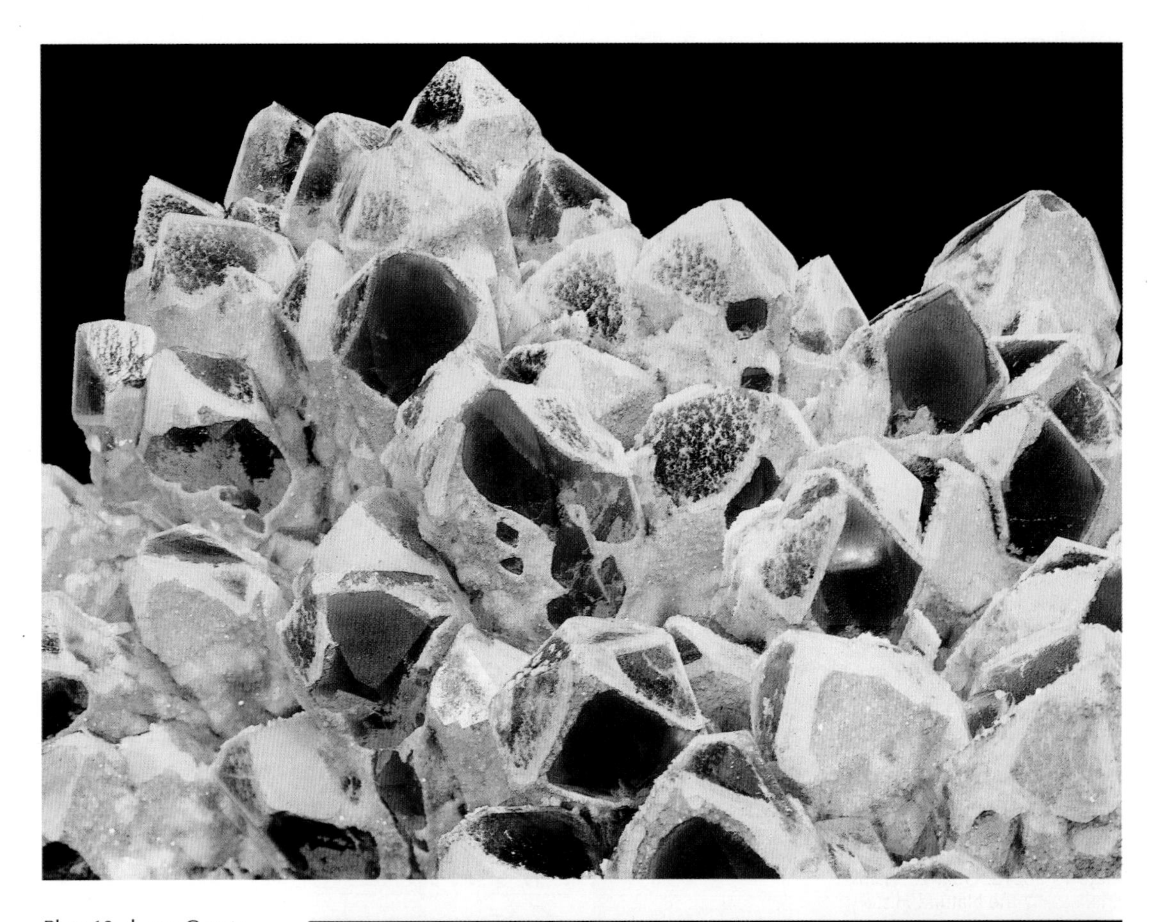

Plate 13 above: Quartz, variety amethyst. Amethyst crystals coated with small quartz crystals, from Brazil. © The Natural History Museum, London

Plate 14 right: Quartz, variety citrine. A cluster of dark brown crystals from Madagascar. © The Natural History Museum, London

Plate 15 above: Quartz. Prismatic crystals of white quartz in association with iridescent chalcopyrite from Cornwall, England. © The Natural History Museum, London

Plate 16 below: Zircon group. A collection of crystals and cut stones. © The Natural History Museum, London

Plate 17 above: Peridot, Sinhalite, Spinel and Chrysoberyl. A collection of crystals and cut stones. © The Natural History Museum, London

Plate 18 left: Tourmaline. Bi-coloured hexagonal crystal of tourmaline with quartz from Mesa Grande, San Diego, California, USA. © The Natural History Museum, London

Plate 19 right: Blue topaz crystals. Natural blue crystals from Virgem de Lapa, Brazil. Specimen from the Collection of the City of Strasbourg. © The Natural History Museum, London

✦ Then visualize yourself melting into the trunk of the tree, with the crystal staying 'outside' the tree. As you feel an increasing sense of oneness with the tree, you will begin to feel another pulse, another breath. This will be the pulse of the tree itself, and through that pulse you can begin to experience 'treeness'. The first time I did this exercise, I was suddenly aware of the sunlight on my leaves!

✦ To complete the experience, visualize the crystal (which has stayed outside the tree), feel your own connection to that crystal, and let it feel as if it is 'pulling' you out of the tree.

AND FINALLY . . .

The final exercise in this chapter, and the next-to-last in the course, deals with past lives, and it is the last exercise for that very reason. Past-life regression is of a certain usefulness in self-discovery, but it only supplements the other techniques of self-discovery that you have been using throughout the book. Its *only* value is as it relates to the life you are living *now*. If you are not comfortable with the idea of past lives, then you can finish this chapter here. If you wish to explore the matter further, then the final exercise is good for exploring lives you may have lived at any time, or in any place. An understanding of past lives does permit one important step forward in growth: as you become more and more aware of your own aspect of choice in coming into life, you will become increasingly aware that all that has happened to you in this life has been your creation and your choosing.

Some readers may have already experienced, or will experience, memories of past lives. For those who have not, and for those for whom the idea of past lives is not acceptable, be assured that there is nothing in this text that requires such a belief. Further, the fundamental point of past-life work is *not* about remembering past lives – it is about remembering the unfinished *lessons* of past lives. Life is about learning, whether in this life or others. The biggest single pitfall is to *identify* with any of your past lives. Forget it. You may well have been the Queen of Sheba or whoever, *but you are not her now*. You are whoever you are now, with *this* personality, in *this* lifetime. What you have now is what you are meant to be dealing with, and past lives are valuable only in the context of what is happening in your life now. What was the *lesson* of being that person in that life, the lesson that was incomplete then, and which you are still working on in this lifetime?

The River of Time

Purpose

✦ This exercise can be used for exploring any past life, to discover the unfinished lesson or lessons that are still being worked through in your current lifetime.

Crystal

✦ In choosing a crystal for this exercise, let your intuition guide you to one that 'feels' as if it is connected to an unfinished lesson. It is unnecessary for you to have had any previous memories of this time – just go with the feeling.

Programme

✦ The specific programme for this crystal is to reflect back to you lessons that originated in another lifetime, and have generated events in this lifetime. You can use a 'searching' programme, in which you would be looking for *any* reflection from a past lifetime that is relevant to the working out of your life at the moment.

Exercise

✦ To begin this exercise visualize going somewhere out of doors, a place you would be happy and comfortable to return to. You will find yourself on the brow of a hill, with a gentle slope running down to a river below you. Fill in the details of the day – the smell of the flowers, the wind in the trees, the sound of birds. When the image is clear in your mind, walk down the gentle slope to the river, and hear the gurgle of the water, smell the scent of the river itself, and feel whatever other details about the river you wish to add. This is a gentle and peaceful river, and along the bank you will find a boat tied up.

✦ This is a unique river, for it is a river of time, and you will find that it flows backwards. When you are ready, climb into the boat, cast off from the bank, and allow yourself to drift gently down the river. In the beginning, you may see yourself standing on the bank as a young adult, and then later as a child, and then even further as an infant sitting on the bank watching you float past. You will come to a place where trees have spread out over the river to make a tunnel. After you pass through this tunnel, you will see people standing along the bank at various intervals, people that you have been in other times.

✦ As you float further back on the river you will begin to see other people along the bank, people in other costumes, and perhaps even of a different sex than you are now. These are all people that you have been in other lifetimes, and you can float back down this river any time you wish to explore any of those lifetimes. But for the moment, we are going to a lifetime connected to current life-patterns and events, reflected by the crystal you have chosen.

✦ As you float further down the river, you will begin to notice a certain feeling coming from the crystal that you are holding for this meditation. It is a feeling that will somehow correspond to a feeling you had in the lifetime it is reflecting and, as the feeling from the crystal begins to match the feelings that surround you in the river, you will see a person standing on the riverbank. This is the person who you were at that time, and that person will serve as your guide to explore the relevant portions of that lifetime. When you see that person, bring your boat to the bank, step out and join your guide.

✦ Your guide will then lead you along a pathway up the riverbank, a riverbank just high enough that you will not be able to see over it as you step from the boat. You will then climb to the top of the bank, and you will see unfold in front of you a time and place that was important to you then, a place connected to whatever lessons and events are being created in this lifetime. Your guide will show you through that time and place – its buildings, costumes, and important places to you at that time. As you walk along the pathway, you may see and meet people who were important to you then, and you may recognize some of them as being important to you now in this lifetime.

✦ Your guide will then take you to a certain place, a very specific place where the events happened which generated the patterns that you are working through in this life. Your guide will then leave you standing or sitting in a safe place, where you can watch him or her act out the events as an observer.

✦ Your guide may be joined by others, and they will then act out for you those events. Give yourself a few minutes for all of this to take place. You may see it as one event, or it may be a whole series of events. You may feel the feelings that your guide was feeling, experience those experiences, and feel the deep inner connection of those events to this lifetime.

✦ When your guide has finished acting out those events, should your guide have died in the process, or his or her body become injured or damaged, then take a moment from your place of observation to reach out and heal your guide. If life has departed from that body, then see the life return; if the body has been injured, see those injuries heal over, and see that body come back into wholeness and wellness.

✦ Your guide will then rejoin you, and will lead you along the pathway back to the river. If there is anything you don't understand about how those events which your guide has acted out have influenced you in this lifetime, your gentle stroll back to the river is the time to have a chat, and your guide can explain things to you as is necessary.

✦ As you come back over the hill and down to the river, you will notice that it is now flowing forward in time, even though your boat is where you left it. Bid goodbye to your guide, climb into the boat, and cast off from the bank once again. As you drift along forward in time, you may wish to see standing along the bank other people that you have been in other lifetimes – other lifetimes where you have been working through the lessons still incomplete from the lifetime you have just visited.

✦ Make a note of who these people were for the moment, and you can come back and explore those lifetimes with those people as your guide at any time. Eventually you will return to the tunnel of trees, and after passing through back into this lifetime, you will again see yourself as an infant, as a child, as a teenager, and as an adult, all standing on the river bank as you float past. As you pass each, you may see an event or events at some or all stages of your life that have helped to bring the unfinished lesson or lessons you have just discovered into your current lifetime. Eventually and unhurriedly you return to your starting place and, when you come out of your meditation, pick up your notebook and pen and record as many details as you can remember.

CHAPTER 13

REFLECTING THE HERO WITHIN

✧

> The brave man is not he who feels no fear, for that were stupid and irrational; but he whose noble soul subdues its fear, and bravely dares the danger nature shrinks from.
>
> Joanna Baillie

It is often said that we are our own worst enemies. The side of ourselves that we must confront when we make the choice for personal growth is – apparently, at least – the most formidable. That is why it is hidden away deep inside us. There are genuine risks in opening up – truly, there is no way for you to fully anticipate who you might become through the awakening process. You can only discover it by becoming it. To open our hearts and confront and re-confront ourselves takes courage, a heroic approach to life. It is the quest to discover yourself.

To 'look for the hero inside ourselves' is an essential truism of human development, reflected in the basic pattern of life. There is a universal formula of the mythological hero journey, which Joseph Campbell calls:

a) separation,
b) initiation, and
c) return.

The hero ventures forth from the commonplace world into a region of supernatural wonder: fabulous forces are encountered there and a decisive victory is won. The hero comes back from this mysterious adventure with the power to bestow benefits on his fellow human beings.

A child is compelled to give up its childhood and become an adult – to separate from its infantile personality and psyche, undergo the initiation of growth, and come back as a responsible adult. It is the fundamental transformation that everyone has to undergo: to let die this position of psychological immaturity and to be reborn into the courage of self-responsibility and assurance. Death and resurrection is the basic pattern of the universal hero's journey – leaving one condition and finding the Source of life to bring you forth into a richer or mature condition. It is the birth–life–death–rebirth cycle within our own lives. Every time we take a new step in the direction of growth, we repeat this cycle.

The ultimate aim of the hero's quest must not solely be for oneself, but for the wisdom and power to serve others. When the quest leads to the real inner truth, the truth of who we really are, it is one of the things that that truth automatically requires us to do. One of the most important ways a hero does this is that, as mature, responsible adults, we serve society through the very virtue of our being.

Within the hero's journey are the trials, tests and ordeals of life. Life is a school and, as in any school, the most important lessons are often the hardest. The tests of the hero are designed to see to it that he or she is really a match for their task. Does he or she have the courage, the knowledge, the capacity, to enable him or her to serve? Bill Moyers notes:

> In this culture of easy religion, cheaply achieved, it seems to me we've forgotten that all three of the great religions teach that the trials of the hero journey are a significant part of life, that there's no reward without renunciation, without paying the price.[1]

Growing up in our 'fast-everything' culture, many of us have been led to believe that by finding the right guru, by joining the right group, by chanting the right mantra, by getting the right crystal, it follows that we will somehow achieve effortless enlightenment. When we are disappointed and disillusioned when we fail to find satisfaction, is it really a mystery why? The Koran says, 'Do you think that you shall enter the Garden of Bliss without such trials as came to those who

[1] Josephy Campbell and Bill Moyers, *The Power of Myth* (London: Doubleday, 1988).

passed before you?' In the Gospel of Matthew, Jesus said, 'Great is the gate and narrow is the way which leadeth to life, and few there be who find it.' Consciousness is transformed either by the trials themselves or by illuminating revelations; it is these trials and revelations that are the real goals of the Quest.

As we expand our Self-awareness, new worlds open up and new dimensions of old worlds unfold. The world becomes a more complex place than we could have imagined. Yet paradoxically, as complexity unfolds, the truth behind it becomes simpler and simpler, until we at last comprehend that All is One.

Our own development, whether we call it self-actualization, personal growth, psychological development, or spiritual awakening, comes to exactly the same thing in the end. Abraham Maslow studied a large number of self-actualized people, and he saw parallels between the actual characteristics of the self-actualized and the ideals urged by religion: the transcendence of the ego self; the fusion of the good, the true and the beautiful; wisdom, honesty and naturalness; the transcendence of selfish and personal motivations; increased friendliness and kindness; the easy differentiation between ends (like tranquillity and peace) and means (money, power, status); the decrease of hostility, cruelty, destructiveness, etc, and an increase in decisiveness, self-affirmation, and justified anger and indignation.[2]

So, residing deep within each of us is our eternal dimension – sometimes referred to as the Soul, sometimes the Inner Being, sometimes the Higher Self, or sometimes just the 'Self'.

The Self is described as:

> . . . the most elementary and distinctive part of our being – in other words, its core. This core is of an entirely different nature from all the elements (physical sensations, feelings, thoughts, and so on) that make up our personality. As a consequence, it can act as a unifying centre, directing those elements, and bringing them into the unity of an organic wholeness.[3]
>
> At the heart of the Self there is both an active and a passive element, an agent and a spectator. In this sense the Self is not a dynamic in itself; it is a point of witness, a spectator, an observer who watches the flow. But there is another part of the Self –

[2] Abraham Maslow, *Motivation and* Personality (New York: Harper and Row, 1987), p.158.

[3] Molly Young Brown, *The Unfolding Self* (Los Angeles: Psychosynthesis Press, 1983), p.11.

> the will-er, or the directing agent – that actively intervenes to orchestrate the various functions and energies of the personality, to make commitments and to instigate action in the external world.[4]

The Self is therefore seen as an integrating centre of that which *is* the essential person – their underlying behaviours, feelings, roles, thoughts, physical manifestations and even gender. But the Self is also the point of ultimate Oneness with the Source of all being – the life of the Universe, its stars, planets, atoms, molecules, energies, thoughts, feelings and all else. It is the ultimate goal of all hero journeys, and it is only by taking the path of the hero that it can be found.

Where do we find this Self, our own Being of being? In our own hearts.

It is written: 'In the beginning was the Word.' You are your own Word; but the Word must come from the Heart.

FINAL EXERCISE

Finding the Hero Inside Yourself

The greatest heroic act is the willingness to undertake the process of personal growth, to be willing to face ancient and deep fears and to take down the barriers between who you have become and who you really are.

Purpose

✦ To discover and be in touch with the hero inside yourself, the part of yourself where you can draw courage when necessary to complete the inner tasks your life has chosen.

Crystal

✦ A crystal that reflects the courageous part of yourself.

Programme

✦ To reflect back to you the part of yourself that heroically picks up and carries on, despite fear and setbacks.

[4] *Ibid.*, p. 13.

Exercise

✦ In this exercise, you will meet a wise and strong Being. This is not a disincarnate entity, nor a spirit guide, nor a person outside yourself. The person you are meeting is *you*. When we are beset with worry and fear, we often forget this part of ourselves exists, but it is there in all of us. By being firmly in touch with yourself through this exercise, you can more easily visualize, and then embody, that dimension of yourself when needed.

✦ With the crystal in place over your heart, take in a few deep breaths and let them out slowly. As in the Heart Cleansing exercise (*see page 196*), become aware of your own heartbeat. Focus initially on the heartbeat, rather than the crystal. As you become more and more focused on your heartbeat, feel that heartbeat as the centre of your being, as if everything that you are is focused in that beat. And as you become more and more focused on the heart, then extend your awareness to include the crystal resting on it.

✦ As you become more and more focused on the crystal, visualize the crystal becoming larger and larger, and your body becoming smaller and smaller. Eventually the crystal will become larger than your body, and you can then allow yourself to slip inside the crystal. Experience being in your crystal as if being inside a room – the facets of the crystal are the walls of the room. Find a chair along one wall of the crystal room, and be seated.

✦ When you are ready, a shimmering light will gradually appear along the wall opposite you. As the light brightens, a human form will appear within it. Dressed as a warrior, or in some other appropriate costume, this figure embodies the deepest strengths within you – the hero within. Strength radiates from this figure, a tangible strength you can feel. Know that this strength is yours, and you can draw on it at any time you wish. You can converse with this figure, and can receive guidance and direction from it.

✦ When you have received any messages this figure may impart, stand. When you are standing, this figure will approach you and merge into you. Feel yourself *become* that figure. If your figure is a warrior wearing armour, feel the weight of the armour. If he or she is carrying a sword, feel the grip of the sword and its weight and sharpness. If your figure is dressed in some other costume, feel yourself dressed like that. This figure is you, in full possession of all the strength and courage within you.

✦ Know that you can become this person at any time. When you are afraid or need extra strength in everyday life, feel yourself become this figure. It is the real you.

✦ When you feel complete with the experience, allow both yourself and the crystal to return to their right sizes. Take a few deep breaths, and become aware of your surroundings again. When you are ready, your eyes will open naturally.

CONCLUSION

Many scientists are now beginning to accept what is known as the 'Gaia principle'; that is, that the whole of the Earth is itself a living organism. And, that the nature of that organism is Nature. Is it so far a step beyond to realize that the Universe itself is also a living organism? The Universe, too, is a creature of cycle and pattern and rhythm – and consciousness. The name we have given to that consciousness is God, in the many forms that name takes.

We have seen that man is part of an increasingly complex series of relationships, and we have also seen that those relationships follow a set of natural patterns which are, ultimately, the patterns of the Universe.

Man is a reflection of the Universe, through its patterns. A microcosm of the Universe.

We know too that evolution is a universal pattern. Stars evolve, planets evolve, and, in the end, the Universe itself evolves. The five universal patterns are the footprints of its evolutionary process. Like all else in the Universe, so we too must evolve. Desmond Morris, author of *The Naked Ape*, reminds us that many exciting species have come and gone. So, finally, must we. It is the nature of things. The question is, do we evolve into something even better, to express further movement into complexity and a higher embodiment of Universal consciousness, or do we fail to evolve and ultimately become extinct?

Perhaps we are evolving to become a more conscious part of that process. Indeed, perhaps we were created *specifically* to become a part of that process. For better or for worse, we are now a part of the evolution of most creatures of the Earth, mostly through unconsciousness of our own animal nature and its connectedness with all other life.

As a species we have attempted to grow beyond the apparent 'limitations' of our biology. At the moment we do this by ignoring these limitations, pretending that they don't exist. The result has been catastrophic both for ourselves and for the planet. But we are not here to ignore our animal nature, manifested as the physical body. We are here to discover that full Oneness with the Universal Source *is* the physical body; *is* the spirit made flesh; *is* love made matter. Only when we once again begin to live the life that nature has evolved us for can we truly begin to heal the rift from our Source, mirrored by our separation from our own bodies and from each other.

But what of the life of the Universe? Can there be any doubt that the Universe itself is a living being – that it is the manifest body of God? And that the life force embodied throughout the Universe in all its multitude of forms is itself the life of God? As we have discovered, the Universe is moving into ever more complex patterns and relationships. As it does so, it develops its own need to rediscover and reintegrate its new embodiment of Self – just as we do.

To more fully understand our role in the life of the Universe, it is helpful to understand at what point the Universe is in its own life. How can we know? One answer comes from the amount of hydrogen it has converted into heavy, denser matter. If it is in the Universe's plan for itself to convert all of the hydrogen, the process could run for another ten thousand times the current age of the Universe. If we understand man as a microcosm of the Universe, we can get a sense of how far along in its lifetime it is by converting its age to human terms.

The Universe is about three days old.

The Universe is a young place – its move into density and complexity is just beginning. The physical body of God is still being created, and there is a lot of creating to do yet. If God and Man are One through our mutual patterns, then God must have a need for growth too – growth beyond just the physical; growth in Beingness. Growth that is the result of self-experience and self-discovery.

If God is a learning being, then what better way to learn about both creation and that which you have created than to have parts of yourself that also create. If the Earth is populated by four thousand million creators, then each day there are four thousand million new experiences of Creation.

Some may find this idea of God as an unfinished, learning being unsettling.

Many wish to see God as rigid, fixed, unchanging. And, paradoxically, so He is. The love that *is* God *never* changes; it is its *embodiment* that is always changing, ever seeking fuller ways to express itself.

The spiral path of the Universe is the same as ours: an expanding capacity for relationship, for experience, for self-knowing, for the Self-expression of love.

If we are part of God's own self-discovery and learning as a result of our mutual patterns, then what does this tell us about God?

Paradoxically, if you are all that exists, what else is there?

God is, above all, most profoundly alone.

Perhaps this is the most basic universal pattern of all. If you think about it, God, in taking on a body, has also created a sense of separateness. Stars are separate from planets, are separate from men. How does God resolve His own separateness?

Perhaps He seeks the answer through us.

God, Man and Minerals, all reaching for Unity.

The spiral goes on.

REFERENCES

Bohr, Niels, *Atomic Physics and Human Knowledge* (New York: John Wiley & Sons, 1958).

Brown, Molly Young, *The Unfolding Self* (Los Angeles: Psychosynthesis Press, 1983).

Campbell, Joseph, *Myths to Live By* (London: Bantam, 1972).

Campbell, Joseph and Moyers, Bill, *The Power of Myth* (London: Doubleday, 1988).

Crichton, Michael, *Jurassic Park* (New York: Ballantine, 1990).

Harrison, John MD, *Love Your Disease* (London: Angus and Robertson, 1984).

Heisenberg, W., *Physics and Philosophy* (New York: Harper Torchbooks, 1958).

Liedloff, Jean, *The Continuum Concept* (London: Penguin, 1986).

Lowen, Alexander, *Bioenergetics* (London: Penguin, 1975).

Maslow, Abraham, *Toward a Psychology of Being* (New York: Van Norstrand Reinhold, 1968).

—, *Motivation and Personality* (New York: Harper and Row, 1987).

Moss, Richard MD, *The I That is We* (Berkeley: Celestial Arts, 1981).

Palmer, John D., *An Introduction to Biological Rhythms* (New York: Academic Press, 1976).

Ray, Sondra, *Loving Relationships* (Berkeley: Celestial Arts, 1980).

Rodegast, Pat and Stanton, Judith, *Emmanuel's Book* (New York: Bantam, 1985).

Rosenzweig, Mark and Leiman, Arnold, *Physiological Psychology* (New York: Random House, 1989).

Sheehy, Gail, *Passages* (London: Bantam, 1974).

Thomas, Lewis, *The Lives of a Cell* (New York: Bantam, 1974).

Books by Ronald (RA) Bonewitz

Cosmic Crystals
The Cosmic Crystal Spiral
The Pulse of Life
The Crystal Heart
The Timeless Wisdom of the Egyptians
The Maya Prophecies
The Wisdom of the Maya/A Maya Oracle
The Beginner's Guide to Pyramids
The Timeless Wisdom of the Maya

Books by Lilian Verner-Bonds

The Complete Book of Colour Healing
Colour Healing
A Practical Guide to Colour Healing
Principles of Palmistry

with Joseph Corvo

The Healing Power of Colour Zone Therapy

Audio Cassette

'The Healing Rainbow – A guided journey to the inner self', with colour and crystal guidance – narrative and music.

For all enquiries regarding books, cassettes, private tuition, readings or courses, please send an S.A.E. to:
The Colour Bonds Association
137 Hendon Lane
London N3 3PR
UK

INDEX